Resonant Dissonance

Resonant Dissonance

THE RUSSIAN JOKE IN CULTURAL CONTEXT

Seth Graham

NORTHWESTERN UNIVERSITY PRESS / EVANSTON, ILLINOIS

Northwestern University Press
www.nupress.northwestern.edu

This book has been published with the support of the Andrew W. Mellon
Foundation.

Printed in the United States of America

10 9 8 7 6 5 4 3 2 1

Library of Congress Cataloging-in-Publication Data
Graham, Seth.
    Resonant dissonance : the Russian joke in cultural context / Seth Graham.
      p. cm. — (Northwestern University Press Studies in Russian literature and
theory)
    Includes bibliographical references and index.
    ISBN 978-0-8101-2623-7 (cloth : alk. paper)
    1. Russian wit and humor—Social aspects. 2. Russian wit and humor—History
and criticism. 3. Political satire, Russian—History and criticism. I. Title.
II. Series: Studies in Russian literature and theory.
PG3099.W5G73 2009
891.78402—dc22

                                             2009019635

For Paloma

Contents

Acknowledgments

Research for this book was carried out primarily between 1998 and 2004 and was supported in part by a grant from the International Research and Exchanges Board (IREX), with funds provided by the National Endowment for the Humanities, the U.S. Department of State, and the U.S. Information Agency. Support was also provided in the form of a grant from the Fulbright-Hays Doctoral Dissertation Research Abroad Program of the U.S. Department of Education, and fellowships from the Center for Russian and East European Studies and the Graduate Program for Cultural Studies at the University of Pittsburgh, and the Andrew W. Mellon Foundation. None of these organizations is responsible for any of the irresponsible views expressed by the author.

I must also thank many people for their sage advice and generous help. Nancy Condee was an ideal *Doktormutter* and valued friend throughout the process of writing, and I am eternally grateful to her for teaching me the value of being ruthlessly pragmatic about studying theory and also the pleasure of frequently theorizing one's personal life. I will always be in debt to my other teachers at the University of Pittsburgh—Vladimir Padunov, Helena Goscilo, David Birnbaum, Jane Harris, Mark Altshuller, Elena Dryzhakova, and Mark Lipovetsky—for their unflagging professional and personal encouragement. My mentors and colleagues at the University of Washington, Stanford University, and the School of Slavonic and East European Studies at University College London have provided me with a series of stimulating and welcoming settings in which to work on this book. Parts of the book have also benefited from careful readings by Colin McCabe, Moya Luckett, Valery Belyanin, Emil Draitser, Donald Barton Johnson, Jesse Labov, and Seth Lerer. For their support and advice on joking and other matters over the years, I am grateful to Petre Petrov, José Alaniz, Sasha Prokhorov, Lena Prokhorova, Jerry McCausland, Lisa Di Bartolomeo, Sarah Slevinski, John Kachur, Julia Houkom, Mike Brewer, Ben Sutcliffe, Olga Karpushina, Irina Makoveeva, Maria Jett, Nadia Kirkov, Dawn Seckler, Sara Schwartz, Yasia

Semikolenova, Ilya Goldin, and Daniel Wild. Many friends and colleagues in Russia have contributed immeasurably to my understanding of humor, literature, and Russia, including Sasha Arkhipova, Misha Lur'e, Katia Efimova, Vadim Lur'e, Ol'ga Lebed', Katia Belousova, Volodia Supik, Irina Shilova, Zoia Khotkina, and Zara Abdullaeva. I'm grateful to Sergei Iur'evich Nekliudov and Aleksandr Fedorovich Belousov for valuable guidance and professional generosity and for organizing a two-day roundtable on the *anekdot* at the Russian State Humanities University in Moscow in 1999, at which I was able to present some of my preliminary ideas. I'm similarly obliged to Lesley Milne for organizing a conference on Russian humor at the University of Nottingham in 2000, and Bob Donnorummo at Pitt for hosting an incomparable series of research-sharing gatherings over the years.

My parents, Don and Betty Graham, instilled in me an intellectual curiosity and sense of humor that have served me well in my work and in my life in general. My wife, Paloma García Paredes, has supported me in every way during this long project, and for that and much more I'll always be grateful. This book is dedicated to her.

Resonant Dissonance

Introduction

> Laughter is an awesome force, a mark of
> optimism, a symptom of mental health.
> —Leonid Brezhnev

> When people throw excrement at one another
> whenever they meet, either verbally or actually,
> can this be interpreted as a case of wit, or merely
> written down as a case of throwing excrement?
> This is the central problem of all interpretation.
> —Mary Douglas

THE RUSSIANS borrowed the word *"anekdot"* from the French (*l'anecdote*) in the mid-eighteenth century and never gave it back. Since the early twentieth century, the Russian word has had a primary connotation similar to that of the word "joke" in the Anglophone West: an exceptionally productive form of oral culture consisting of a brief, terminally humorous narrative and/or dialogue.[1] The *anekdot* (plural *anekdoty*) is fictional, formulaic, and of anonymous provenance; it violates taboos; and it shares with its Western cousin compositional features such as the punch line and an affinity for tripartite constructions:

Stalin is giving a speech. Suddenly someone in the audience sneezes. "Who sneezed?" demands Stalin. (Silence.) "First row, stand up. Take them out and shoot them all!" (Thunderous applause.) "Who sneezed?" (Silence.) "Second row, stand up. Take them out and shoot them all!" (A long ovation.) "Who sneezed?" (Silence.) "Third row, stand up. To the firing squads!" (Thunderous applause, the whole audience is on its feet, shouts of "Glory to the Great Stalin!") "Now, who sneezed?" At the back of the audience, a man says "I did! I did!" and collapses in tears. Stalin looks at him and says: "Gesundheit, comrade!"[2]

An American, a Frenchman, and a Russian are marooned on a desert island. They have no food, so they start to fish. Suddenly they catch a golden fish. "Let me go, kind sirs, and I'll grant each of you a wish," says the fish. So the castaways line up and make their wishes. The American says, "I want to be back in America with a luxury home and a million bucks in my pocket." He disappears immediately. The Frenchman says, "I want to be in Paris with a beautiful woman." He, too, disappears as soon as he's made his wish. The Russian says, "A house?! A woman?! Ah, what a great bunch of guys we had! I want a case of vodka and everyone back here right now!"

Although the *anekdot* and the joke clearly share many attributes, the dissimilarity of their cultural environments makes the terms less synonymous than one might expect, even in the post-Soviet era (to say nothing of the geopolitically bipolar period that preceded it). In addition to expected differences in thematics and political significance, the *anekdot* and the joke diverge in subtler ways that have to do with the relationships of their respective cultures to language, to narrative, and—of course—to humor.

I mention the Western joke here at the outset solely as a point of reference; my approach is not comparative. This study does not cover Russian humor's place in international jokelore or how Russian *anekdoty* about Ukrainians differ from American jokes about Poles. The focus here is a different spectrum of parallelism and contrast: the essential links and productive contradictions between the *anekdot* and other constituent forms of Russian and Soviet culture. My take on the significance and specificity of the *anekdot* departs from previous analyses by locating the generic essence of the *anekdot* in the nature of its relationships with its fellow texts and genres. The particular ways in which *anekdoty* articulate the changing values, moods, and conflicts of the society—as jokes everywhere do—are inseparable from those relationships. Accordingly, the materials relevant here include not only a corpus of *anekdoty* representing the genre's major thematic cycles and compositional models,[3] but also sources from the Soviet era and beyond (in both directions) with which the *anekdot* has had truck of one sort or another or with which the genre has been mutually referential. I will have occasion to reference oral narratives and written memoirs, journalism, prose fiction, poetry, song lyrics, slogans, proverbs, tales, films, television programs, encyclopedia and dictionary entries, arrest information, legal statutes, Party programs and resolutions, statements by government officials, and state-published (i.e., non-oral) *anekdoty*. Anthropologist Mary Douglas wrote in 1975: "Joking as one mode of expression has yet to be interpreted in its total relation to other modes of expression."[4] Her statement is still largely valid more than three decades later. This book does not pretend to fill the lacuna (studying anything in its "total relation" to other things is more a life's work than a monograph project), but it is an attempt to take up Douglas's implicit challenge in the limited context of a particular culture and its jokes. Quite arguably the jokes told in that culture—twentieth-century urban Russia—had a rhetorical potency unmatched outside of those temporal and geographical boundaries. The evidence for that potency includes the many thousands of Soviet citizens imprisoned for telling, writing down, or laughing at *anekdoty;* the flood of published collections of *anekdoty* that followed the end of Soviet censorship; and the many examples of *anekdoty* that themselves comment on the importance of the genre.

While my central argument is framed by discussions of the pre–Joseph Stalin (including pre-Soviet) and post–Mikhail Gorbachev incarnations of the *anekdot,* most of the texts I analyze date from the period between the rigidification of Soviet cultural policy in the early 1930s and the end of Soviet censorship in the late 1980s. The emphasis, moreover, is on the period from the early 1960s to 1986, incorporating all of what is known as the Stagnation period of Soviet culture (the apogee of the popularity of the *anekdot*), plus additional years on each end that are significant to the development of the genre.[5] That span of history in the USSR saw not only the coagulation of a highly standardized way of life that provided ample fodder (and ample situational contexts and free time) for oral satire, but also the appearance of a series of texts that provided source material for the topical cycles that to this day constitute a large portion of the *anekdot* corpus. Mass culture itself—a brimming reservoir of texts, tropes, and types at the disposal of the urban educated Soviet "folk"—became a prolific source of raw material for popular oral cultural production.

Visual narrative texts were an especially rich fount. For example, El'dar Riazanov's 1962 film *Gusarskaia ballada* (Hussar's Ballad) and Sergei Bondarchuk's 1965–67 adaptation of *Voina i mir* (War and Peace) together spawned a cycle about a fictional nineteenth-century Russian ballroom lothario, Lieutenant Rzhevskii.[6] Vitalii Mel'nikov's 1966 film *Nachal'nik Chukotki* (Head of Chukotka) helped to inspire a cycle about the Chukchi, an ethnic group related to Eskimos, who live in the arctic northeasternmost province of Russia.[7] Max Otto von Shtirlits, a fictional Red Army mole in Nazi Germany, the protagonist of Tat'iana Lioznova's 1973 television miniseries *Semnadtsat' mgnovenii vesny* (Seventeen Moments of Spring), became the subject of an enormous cycle.[8] Two animated series from the late 1960s and early 1970s—one, directed by Fedor Khitruk, featuring Vinni-Pukh and Piatachok (the Russian names of A. A. Milne's Winnie-the-Pooh and Piglet) and the other, directed by Roman Kachanov, featuring Gena the Crocodile and his furry, big-eared sidekick, Cheburashka—generated large cycles still popular today.[9] The last Soviet visual text to inspire a significant cycle was Igor' Maslennikov's 1979–86 series of television films based on Arthur Conan Doyle's Sherlock Holmes stories. The most famous cycle to come out of the golden age of the *anekdot* developed around Vasilii Ivanovych Chapaev, famed peasant-general of the Russian Civil War and martyred protagonist of *Chapaev,* the 1934 film by Georgii Vasil'ev and Sergei Vasil'ev, which was released during the Stalin period but enjoyed a renewed surge of popularity beginning with the celebration of its thirtieth anniversary in 1964, after which the film was frequently shown on television and in children's matinees.

The prominence of cycles based on films and television programs testifies to a crucial point that has not been sufficiently emphasized in studies of the genre: a great many of the Soviet Union's best-known *anekdoty* are most directly based not on unmediated, abstract sociopolitical and historical concepts, or on real-life personalities or groups, or even on current events, but rather on the representations of these things in the mass media and especially in the output of the Soviet culture industry. The intertextuality of the *anekdot* is not limited to cycles grounded in cultural texts, however. Many explicitly political *anekdoty* play off mass-media representations and specific examples of discourse in much the same way as the previously mentioned aesthetic cycles. The jokes of the early 1970s about Vladimir Il'ich Lenin, for example, typically target not Lenin's political activities or policies but the state's ambitious, hagiographic packaging of the 1970 Lenin centennial. One of the best-known Lenin jokes, for example, is a list of commemorative souvenirs produced for the jubilee, including the following:

[T]alcum powder ("Lenin's ashes"), cologne ("Spirit of Lenin"), a triple-wide bed especially for newlyweds ("Lenin is always with us"), and condoms in the shape of the heads of Lenin himself ("Lenin in you") and his wife, Nadezhda Krupskaia ("Naden'-ka," a pun on a Russian diminutive for the name Nadezhda and a colloquial way to say "put it on!").

Brezhnev jokes, too, were inspired as often by the various composed mythologizations of the general secretary's persona as by the policies and actions of his administration. One canonical example of the Brezhnev joke, for example, takes its cue from the frequently televised ceremonies at which he was decorated for his ongoing service to the country:

What would happen if Brezhnev were eaten by a crocodile? The crocodile would be shitting medals for two weeks.

The cumulative model of Russo-Soviet history, society, and identity represented in state-generated or state-sanctioned texts of all varieties provoked the growth of parallel models in response.[10] The *anekdot* corpus was one of the most comprehensive of those models and certainly the most (implicitly and explicitly) allusive. The use of neomythological strategies of image construction by the state was a frequent point of departure for the *anekdot,* which, as folklore, is itself a generic descendant of cultural myth and therefore is predisposed to engagement with other such descendants on multiple levels. The tendency toward allusion (implicit or explicit) across the various categories of an *anekdot* cycle (cultural, political, ethnic, sexual) is evidence of the genre's role as a medium for popular commentary. In content, of course, the *anekdot* was almost invariably irreverent toward, or simply indifferent to, the prevailing ideology (and morality). The genre's alternative representations, however, were not merely rebuttals of the progressively less compelling semantic premises of the Party line, but also ironic, stylized rehearsals and exposés of the signifying practices used to communicate those premises. It was a vehicle for critical commentary not only on Soviet state socialism, but also on the ham-handed proprietary attitude toward discourse exhibited by the state as a producer and controller of texts. The implicit assertion of *anekdot* culture was that mainstream discursive practice not only was generating a huge body of defective utterances and images, but it also was contaminating the very act of symbolic (especially verbal) expression itself as a category of human behavior.

Although folklorists and other scholars have addressed the question of the formal properties, thematic taxonomy, and structural evolution of the *anekdot,* the genre has not been properly contextualized synchronically, that is, within the overall generic taxonomy of Russo-Soviet culture.[11] Ol'ga Smolitskaia was on the mark when she wrote in 1996 that study of the *anekdot* was still in its "romantic stage" and that compilers and analysts alike were still enamored of its "independent spirit."[12] While subsequent years have seen considerable improvement in the scholarly rigor of "*anekdot*-ology," a wealth of material remains for critical analysis.

Discussions of the genre, particularly by Western (including émigré) commentators, have frequently emphasized how political *anekdoty* heroically—if symbolically—challenged official Soviet ideology. In such views, *anekdoty* are considered significant insofar as their clandestine exchange enabled Soviet citizens to experience the psychological and moral pleasure of what George Orwell famously called "tiny revolutions."[13] Some have given the *anekdot* a more direct political significance. Humor theorist Arthur Asa Berger wrote of its agitational function in the defeat of Eastern-bloc Communism: "[Political jokes] destroy[ed] [people's] sense of obligation to the regime that [was] controlling them, so that when an opportunity [came] to overthrow the regime, there [was] a common desire to do so."[14] Zara Abdullaeva granted Soviet-era joke tellers an even higher degree of political agency:

We can marvel at the extraordinary social role that the anecdote [*sic*] played [. . .] as it whittled away at the tragic and at the same time comic foundations of official ideology/mythology and bred in ironic Soviet man the pride of slaves who feel victorious when they recount their anecdotes [. . .]. That man's fate could depend on his right to anecdote is the discovery of Soviet civilization.[15]

The arguable excess of such panegyrics aside, there is no question that the *anekdot* had a high ideological valence during the Soviet period. The history of persecution for *anekdot* telling is a sufficient demonstration of this fact. Historian Roy Medvedev recently claimed (without presenting any specific evidence) that "about 200,000 people" served time in the gulag for *anekdot* telling during the Stalin years. The statute in the Stalinist penal code under which oral or written reproduction of *anekdoty* was punishable was Article 58, which criminalized "anti-Soviet agitation and propaganda." The statutorily enforced taboo applied not only to overtly political *anekdoty* (e.g., leader jokes), but also to any that appeared to interpret satirically or irreverently the model of reality presented in state media and socialist-realist texts. The taboo applied even to so-called *bytovye anekdoty* (*anekdoty* about everyday life), a fact that testifies not only to the strong current of moralism in the ideology (most *bytovye anekdoty* are sexually themed), but also to official awareness of the disruptive potential of the *anekdot* as a category of expression, regardless of the content of individual instantiations of the form. Like a typewriter and a sheet of carbon paper or a shortwave radio, the *anekdot* was a suspect apparatus to possess. As Iurii Sokolov has put it: "The logic involved [in prosecutions for joke telling] was itself anecdotal: today you tell a dirty joke about Emma, tomorrow it'll be a satirical one about the System."[16]

While the vast majority of *anekdot*-related arrests date from the Stalin period, there are isolated accounts of official persecution (and sometimes prosecution) during the subsequent decades of Soviet power. In 1957, for example, there was a small wave of arrests for *anekdot* telling (Aleksandr Belousov, personal communication). Article 190 of the Brezhnev-era penal code allowed for up to three years of imprisonment for "propagation of known falsehoods denigrating the Soviet system."[17] Smolitskaia relates an apocryphal account of a conference in the 1960s or 1970s at which a scholar damaged his own career, as well as those of the conference organizers, by daring to present a paper on the *anekdot,* complete with the following joke about the first Soviet cosmonaut, Iurii Gagarin:

> Gagarin's young daughter answers the phone: "Daddy's flying around the Earth and will be back today at 7:00 P.M., and Mommy went out to buy food, so there's no telling when she'll be home."[18]

In 1983, just two years before Gorbachev came to power, a twenty-three-year-old Leningrad woman named Irina Tsurkova was sentenced to three years in prison for "systematic propagation in oral form of [. . .] *anekdoty* lampooning the activities of the Communist Party of the Soviet Union."[19]

While it is clear why so many *anekdoty* were illegal under Soviet power, the *anekdot* represents a special case among the outlaw texts of Soviet culture; for much of Soviet history the state treated the entire genre as inherently anti-Soviet. The official culture industry readily co-opted other folklore genres such as the folktale, the proverb,[20] and even the *chastushka* (a two- or four-line humorous ditty), encouraging the composition of socialist-oriented "fakelore" and scholarly emphasis on politically progressive pre-Revolutionary folk texts. The *anekdot*, however, did not yield so easily to ideological colonization and integration into the Soviet *ars poetica.* The state tried, of course. Collections of eighteenth- and nineteenth-century literary and transcribed oral *anekdoty,*[21] as well as translations of *anekdoty* from other traditions (especially those of Central Asia and the Caucasus[22]), saw publication during the Soviet years, though in relatively small numbers. "Official" jokes were compositionally similar, only with state-approved content. Such establishment *anekdoty* appeared in periodicals such as *Krokodil* as well as in joke books (usually translations into Russian of jokes by and/or about non-Russian nationalities), repertory guides for *estrada* (variety-stage) comedy, prose fiction, films, and so on. Unlike other genres, the aboveground variety of the *anekdot* was, predictably, no competition for the popular form. Even though short comic narratives and dialogues were published in official periodicals and books throughout the Soviet period—and after the death of Stalin were performed on the variety stage, at *kapustniki* (amateur, roastlike student talent shows), and in frequently televised humor competitions known as *KVN* [*Klub veselykh i nakhodchivykh,* "the club of the jolly and witty"][23]—they were almost never called *anekdoty.* Instead, they were labeled *shutki* (jests), *miniatiury* (miniatures), *khokhmy* (gags), *reprizy dlia klounov* (quips for clowns),[24] and so on. So, when popular cynicism began to peak under Brezhnev, it found potent expression in a satirical genre whose very name was anathema to official culture. A taboo-breaking act could be initiated by the mere announcement of the genre one was about to perform: "*Anekdot!* . . ."

One reason for the generic embargo, of course, was the state's awareness that the diminutive size and oral nature of the *anekdot* made it an ideal medium for rapid and clandestine propagation of unvetted ideas and sentiments. The genre's portability and its status as taboo were reflected in the typically private and/or marginal settings in which *anekdoty* were told: the holiday or party table; the apartment kitchen; stairwells, bathrooms, and other locations used as smoking or rest areas in workplaces and institutions of higher learning; train compartments; queues for goods or services;[25] lunchrooms or recess areas in primary and secondary schools; the *bania* (bathhouse); and drinking spots such as *pivnye bary* (beer bars) or outdoor areas where men would gather *na troikh* (in threes) to share a bottle.

The association of the *anekdot* with such settings not only reflects its illicitness but also testifies to another distinctive feature of the genre. Unlike the *chastushka*, which shares the brevity and satirical potential[26] of the *anekdot* but is rhymed and usually sung, the *anekdot* blends easily into conversation; it is both an aesthetic composition and a form of speech. Its "centauric" nature, like its orality and brevity, added to its ideological potential: it was an ironic, organic example of the art-life link to which Soviet cultural engineers aspired.

The *anekdot* was ambiguous in other ways, too. Because of its traditional role as a medium for popular irreverence toward elites, its class origins were simultaneously impeccable and suspect; although its pre-Revolutionary value in mocking priests and landowners was clear, its utility as a contemporary, productive genre was problematic, considering the current ruling "class." One humor theorist has described popular satire as a natural by-product of a social situation in which "the intelligentsia has long recognized the inherent emptiness, absurdity, and cultural abnormality of the ruling class, and considers that class's claims on the power to lead society to be inherently unjustified and therefore ridiculous." Although this reads like a post-Soviet or émigré description of the premise behind the Stagnation-era underground *anekdot*, it is in fact Soviet Commissar of Enlightenment Anatolii Lunacharskii's characterization of the Revolutionary proletariat's satirical impulse and was published in the early 1930s at the very end of a period of active debate over the place of satire in the Revolution.[27]

The *anekdot* represented a combination of medium and mode that proved particularly tricky to conscript into the army of cultural forms mobilized in the service of the Revolution. As popular oral satire, the *anekdot* was difficult to reconcile with the official view of contemporary folklore as the organic expression of the Soviet People's gratitude for and contentment in the new world (Maksim Gor'kii himself wrote that "pessimism is entirely alien to folklore"[28]). Beginning with the consolidation of Stalinist cultural policy in the 1930s, humor and satire as modes of expression were increasingly assigned to the realm of professional and not explicitly folkloric art forms (film, literature, theater). Moreover, professional comic texts were dominated by examples of nonsatirical humor ("recreational drollery," to use Mikhail Bakhtin's term[29]). Especially (though far from exclusively) during the ascendancy of Stalinism, the state encouraged or tolerated the use of satire only with a very narrow aim—for example, when a common enemy was officially identified (NEPmen, Trotskyites, Hitler, capitalism, Ronald Reagan, corrupt bureaucrats, and so on). When it was allowed, satire of domestic phenomena and personalities was severely limited. A Soviet émigré wrote in

1932 that that the "arrows" of official Soviet satire did not reach higher than "the secretary of a factory Party cell," that above that level there was a strict taboo on satirizing officials.[30] The satirical newspaper *Krokodil* (founded in 1922) initially published domestically directed barbs (at stupid bureaucrats, for example), but by the 1930s it was completely under the aegis of *Pravda* and its satire was directed almost exclusively toward the capitalist West.[31]

The anonymous nature of *anekdot* genesis proved a particular irritation to the state. A 1982 article in the newspaper *Komsomol'skaia Pravda* (Communist-Youth-League Truth) speculated about the personality of the faceless, nameless composers of *anekdoty* (specifically, of Chapaev jokes):

> We will not speculate as to what motivates those who compose vulgar *anekdoty* about the Civil War hero whom we have loved since childhood. Their author is always anonymous. But his interior aspect shows through [. . .] rather clearly: a pathetic, rotten little soul who is aware of his own damaged nature and his own lack of any sense of responsibility and who is bent on destroying, or at least debasing, eroding, and defiling, that sense in others [. . .]. Civic infantilism, mental immaturity, and political naïveté: those are the sources of nourishment for the weeds that grow like thistles in our verbal culture [. . .]. Often a mental collapse begins with just such a seemingly insignificant departure from one's principles [. . .]. Today, anti-Soviet centers in the West are putting out collections of *anekdoty* gathered from the gutter or, more commonly, scribbled by them. These *anekdoty* are slanderous to our country and its heroes. It is obvious that they don't like it in the West when our boys play Chapaev or Matrosov [heroic World War II fighter pilot— SG]. They would very much like to deprive the Soviet youth of its heroic ideals [. . .]. The war of ideas finds resonance not only in the pages of newspapers or in the debates of philosophers. The front of that war runs through the heart of every person.[32]

Given the ideology's affinity both for folkloric patterns of representation and militarism (literal and metaphorical: note the "war of ideas" referred to at the end of the article), it should come as no surprise that there was official interest in humor from early in the state's history. Soviet cultural leaders sought to harness humor (like all other modes of discourse) to the interests of the Revolution. In the 1920s, when Moscow was inundated by *anekdoty,* there was even a proposal to designate the genre an official form of self-criticism in Bolshevik culture.[33] The Bolsheviks admired the agitational potential of the *anekdot* and especially its capacity to spread rapidly. In a 1927 article in *Novyi lef* (New Left), V. Pertsov referred to the *anekdot* in botanical terms: "A gust of wind, the seeds are spread like dandelion fluff, and the *anekdot* is instantly planted in tens of thousands of heads at once."[34]

In the late 1920s, Lunacharskii conceived a book to be titled *A Social History of Laughter* (which he never wrote) and formed a "committee for the study of satirical genres" under the auspices of the Soviet Academy of Sciences. Lunacharskii's writings on humor characterize it as a "weapon"—a metaphor that would be more or less institutionalized.[35] Dmitrii Moldavskii, author of the memorable 1981 study *Tovarishch Smekh* (Comrade Laughter), explained: "The hero of Soviet satire is Comrade Laughter, [. . .] who takes on the world of greed, bourgeois vulgarity, idiocy, ignorance, and bureaucratism, and says to readers and viewers: 'Those are our enemies!'"[36] As a weapon, humor was something not only to deploy in defense of the Revolution, but also something to which to limit access, to control, to keep out of the hands of the irresponsible.

The *anekdot* came to represent a threat and an affront to authoritative models of discourse in part because it frequently embodied those models more deftly and convincingly than state cultural production did. Even the genre's characteristic patterns of propagation and consumption reproduced mass-media fantasies of popular culture and its role in Soviet society. In a scene near the end of Grigorii Aleksandrov's 1938 film musical *Volga-Volga*, for example, the title of peasant-heroine Strelka's "Song of the Volga" becomes literalized when a storm blows the sheet music (which is apparently written on waterproof paper) off a ship and into the Volga River. By the next day, the song is on the lips (or instruments) of everyone Strelka meets downstream in various individual performances that nevertheless retain the spirit of the original, thus demonstrating the universal appeal of true folk creativity and the people's unanimous and unambiguous receptivity to it. That the *anekdot* moved through the culture in essentially the same way, only in reality,[37] indicates that it was not only an efficient medium for parody, but also its very existence exposed state cultural products themselves as naive self-parodies. Moreover, the *anekdot* blends easily into conversation; it is both an aesthetic composition and a form of speech and thus an "organic" example of the seamless art-life continuum to which Soviet cultural engineers aspired. (Recall the famous first line of the 1931 mass song "Ever Higher": "We were born to make the fairy tale come true" or the definition of socialist-realist art as a depiction of "life in its revolutionary development.") Every *anekdot* teller was a momentary Mozart to a faceless army of mass-media Salieris.

The difficulties that ideologically aggressive authorities have had maintaining such control have cultural roots that predate the USSR. The official Russian attitude toward laughter, writes Sergei Averintsev, has been traditionally ambivalent, owing to the tension between *smekh i grekh* (laughter and sin), between the sacred and the profane, the ecclesiastical and secular.[38] The dichotomy between the two categories of thought and expression—

Mikhail Bakhtin calls them simply "the serious" and "the comic"—became as important to the Soviet state as it had been to premodern religious authorities (in Russia and, earlier, in Western Europe). The institutionalization of a discursive "two-world condition" relegates popular comic forms to the unofficial realm, where—as the history of the *anekdot* illustrates—such forms can thrive and become the bases of complex parallel cultures in their own right.[39]

THE IRONY PAGEANT

The shibboleth of anti-Soviet thought—that the official interpretation of reality was inhumane nonsense—was by the time of Stagnation a foregone conclusion, common knowledge in the cultural tradition of which the *anekdot* was a part. For this reason, there was something unaesthetic (and depressingly unfunny) about simply stating that knowledge in those terms. The following exchange from the notebooks of Sergei Dovlatov implies as much, in a form akin to the *anekdot* itself:

> I call [Anatolii] Naiman and say, "Tolia, let's go visit Leva Druskin." "No way," he says, "that guy is so Soviet." "What do you mean, Soviet? You're making a mistake." "Anti-Soviet, then. What's the difference?"[40]

Anekdoty, especially political ones, expressed the foregone conclusion in a concise, aesthetically compelling manner and foregrounded the nonsensical as often as the inhumane spasms of the ideology. After a certain point, Soviet social life was so rife with absurdities and incongruities that official representations of that life as rational, unified, and congruous were, for a wide swath of the citizenry, impossible to consume without irony:

> On a visit to a collective farm, Khrushchev is chatting paternally with the farmers. "So, how's life?" Nikita Sergeevich jokes. "Life's great!" the farmers joke back.[41]

This *anekdot* explicitly references, in fact, an incongruity that was central to Soviet culture: the distance between the jocular, "targetless" laughter encouraged by the post-Stalinist culture industry as the desirable form of humor, and the cynical, mocking laughter that was increasingly characteristic of the irony-saturated popular collective.[42]

The parodic impulse that found expression in *anekdoty* was in contrast to impulses informing other unofficial forms, including many of the writings of prominent dissidents, who sought to bear witness, to explicate the ideology's criminal illegitimacy. But the iconoclasm of such inscribed anti-Soviet sentiments was rarely effected on the level of textual form, and such writers did not eschew the uncritical use of models (the novel, the slogan, the newspaper editorial) that the official ideology itself championed as the most appropriate for the expression of essential truths. The *anekdot* (as the previous Dovlatov quotation suggests) was not a frontline strategic weapon in the dissident arsenal.[43]

As Mikhail Bakhtin helpfully tells us, every utterance is by definition responsive to previous utterances.[44] What is significant about the *anekdot* as a speech genre was its tendency to display its responsive nature, to draw attention to its position vis-à-vis other discourse. *Anekdot* telling was not merely a response, but a performance of response, just as dance—as Richard Bauman points out—is both movement and a performance of movement.[45] The performed engagement of the *anekdot* with other forms encompassed a spectrum of abstraction from concrete texts, to the more inchoate "master narrative" of Soviet ideology that engendered myriad tropes and icons, and finally to the level of form: representational conventions, styles, and distinctive features of other extant genres, modes, and media. In other words, the *anekdot* was a vehicle not only for rebuttal of the progressively less compelling semantic premises of the ideology, but also for parodic rehearsals of the signifying practices employed to communicate those premises.

During the Soviet period, this feature distinguished the *anekdot* both from other popular genres and from the various forms of official discourse: censor-approved cultural production, media texts, political decrees and speeches, slogans—that is, all utterances produced and/or vetted by the state, which represented itself as a "speaking subject." I do not mean to imply that official attempts to imbue all texts with appropriate ideological content resulted in an integrated and coherent expression of the ideology, only that knowledge of those attempts on the part of the "listeners"—and not simply the content of official utterances—affected the nature of the popular response. That response implicitly and explicitly challenged the state's credibility and competence as a producer of texts, not merely its legitimacy as a political entity.

As a medium for participation in Soviet society's network of verbal communication (albeit in small, trusted collectives), the *anekdot* articulated a premise about discourse itself that was a threat to the necessary discursive solipsism of official speech. The blind spots of the prevailing worldview, along with the state's aggressive delineation of acceptable and unacceptable models of discourse, created a great potential for transgressive acts on formal levels. A critical mass of the popular collective came to perceive official utterances as disingenuous and mechanistic performances, as moribund speech. As such, state discourse embodied what Henri Bergson considered a fundamental comic stimulus: "something mechanical encrusted on the living."[46] Mass-media texts were simultaneously legible as political and comedic.[47] That built-in, self-contradictory modal duality invited a very deep irony indeed, and the collective ironic reflex—which threatened authoritative models of discourse by "removing the semantic security of 'one signifier:one signified'"[48]—was manifested with increasing frequency over the course of the Soviet period via the performance of *anekdoty*.

PREDECESSORS AND PREMISES

Humor theories—explanations of why people laugh at the things that they laugh at—are commonly divided into three broad categories.[49] *Superiority* theories examine the phenomenon of humor from the premise that its main function is to give people the pleasure of feeling superior to others by laughing at their weaknesses or misfortunes. This idea has its origins in Plato ("Philebus") and Aristotle (*Poetics*) and was subsequently elaborated by others, most notably Thomas Hobbes (*Leviathan*). *Relief* or *release* theories hold that humor's function is to provide a psychic and emotional safety valve via which people can purge themselves of otherwise dangerous anxieties, fears, and hostilities. Sigmund Freud is the most prominent proponent of this theory, though Herbert Spencer articulated a similar idea decades earlier. *Incongruity* theories argue that laughter is a response triggered by the juxtaposition of two incompatible images or ideas, though there is a schism between those who consider the mere perception of incongruity to be the key stimulus (incongruity-perceived theories) and those who believe that it is the resolution of incongruity in a surprising way that triggers the laughter reflex (incongruity-resolved theories). Henri Bergson (whose interpretation of humor also incorporates elements of superiority theory) and Arthur Koestler are the most oft-cited thinkers to espouse this premise, though it can be traced back to René Descartes, Arthur Schopenhauer, and Immanuel Kant.[50] All of these theoretical premises can be supported by "*anekdot*-al" evidence, and I will refer back to all of them as necessary in what follows.

Humor was a topic of theoretical interest in Russia before and after 1917. Nikolai Chernyshevskii wrote in an 1863 article that laughter allows people to acknowledge "ugliness" or other unpleasant qualities in others and thereby to take pleasure in their own contrastively positive qualities (a variant of the superiority theory).[51] Chernyshevskii also distinguished the comic—the essence of which he identified as "predominance of form over idea"—from the sublime, in which ideas take precedence over form.[52] His attention to the role of form in a potentially comic stimulus anticipates Bergson's belief that the primary source of humor is behavior or gestures that show an excess reliance on form (or formality), to the risible detriment of "naturalness." Varieties of the incongruity theory have taken root in Russia. In 1922, for example, Viktor Shklovskii published a short article using *anekdoty* to demonstrate his conclusion that the comic derives from "double semantic comprehension of one phonetic sign," an idea that privileges the pun but would also find resonance in a cultural atmosphere in which double-talk was an assumed attribute of all mass-media communication.[53]

Subsequent Soviet works on humor typically espoused the "humor as a weapon" thesis or played it safe by supporting their theoretical observations with examples from pre-Soviet culture (for example, Vladimir Propp's *Problemy komizma i smekha* [Problems of Laughter and the Comic] and Dmitrii Likhachev's "Smekh kak mirovozzrenie" [Laughter as a Worldview]). Iurii Borev's "Komicheskoe, ili o tom, kak smekh kaznit nesovershenstvo mira, ochishchaet i obnovliaet cheloveka i utverzhdaet radost' bytiia" (The Comic, or How Laughter Punishes the World's Imperfection, Purges and Renews a Person, and Affirms the Joy of Existence) combines (in its very title) two views that correspond to two general types of acceptable humor in the USSR: as a means of liquidating undesirable aspects of social life and as an expression of one's expansive, joyous reaction to life itself.

A Soviet-era interpretation of humor that has particular relevance to the study of the *anekdot* is Mikhail Bakhtin's elaboration of carnival as a "special idiom of forms and symbols."[54] Like Bergson's notion of laughter as a means for the exposure and correction of "inelasticity" in human behavior and speech,[55] and Barbara Babcock's observation that a crucial function of the comic is to "remark on the indignity of any closed system,"[56] Bakhtin's treatment of the popular carnival impulse focused on its "hostil[ity] to all that [is] immortalized and completed."[57] His description of medieval carnival culture as "a second world and a second life outside officialdom [. . .] in which all [. . .] people participated more or less"[58] read as a virtual allegory for Soviet unofficial culture.[59] The crucial current of "grotesque realism" is another element shared by Bakhtin's characterization of carnivalesque expression and the Soviet-era *anekdot*.[60]

The history of humor studies in Russia is itself an instructive narrative, as it also illuminates the evolution of the *anekdot*. The first edition of the *Bol'shaia sovetskaia entsiklopediia* (Great Soviet Encyclopedia, 1926) noted two attributes that would soon number among the most prominent constituent features of the *anekdot* and ensure its taboo status: its contemporary topicality and its utility as a form of sociopolitical satire. The *Encyclopedia* thematically classifies *anekdoty*

into two large groups: *anekdoty* of a general nature, about everyday life, ethnic groups, etc.; and *anekdoty* that correspond to specific contemporary events. Of particular note among the latter is the political *anekdot*, which acquires great agitational significance during social crises as a special kind of weapon for political struggle [. . .].[61]

This entry is among the last published Soviet acknowledgments of the genre's modern urban connotation.[62] For most of the Soviet period—especially after the explosion in popularity of the underground *anekdot* in the 1960s and right up until the end of state censorship in the late 1980s—Soviet reference and scholarly works dealt almost exclusively with the older (and by then secondary) meanings of the *anekdot:* (1) a written genre popular in the eighteenth and nineteenth centuries that narrated a trivial but factual (and not necessarily humorous) event in the life of a historical figure; (2) a short and witty account of an unusual and often fictional event or situation that was shared orally or read aloud and was sometimes used as the seed for a full-fledged literary work; (3) a traditional (i.e., rural) form of short oral narrative closely related to, or a subcategory of, the folktale.

As the encyclopedia definition acknowledges, by the 1920s the genre in its most widespread form had evolved into something different from historical, literary, and traditional folk *anekdoty.* The latter-day *anekdot* is in fact a combination of certain features of the older instantiations, and it was already in the process of overtaking them in popularity and productivity by the end of the nineteenth century.[63] Nevertheless, its status as the most productive genre of Russian urban folklore was officially ignored for decades. Although Soviet philologists published studies of the older politically inert incarnations of the *anekdot,*[64] including the traditional folk *anekdot,* such scholarship was exceedingly rare in contrast to the frequent treatments of other oral genres such as the folktale, the *bylina* (heroic ballad), and the *chastushka.*[65]

Through the prism of humor theory, Stagnation society appears to have been a perfect storm for the rise of the *anekdot.* Superiority-theory partisans can point to the affront felt by a disenfranchised intelligentsia living in a society ruled by presumed cultureless bumpkins. Relief theorists can make the case that popular oral satire provided a safe outlet for the anger, frustration, and fear produced by living in an authoritarian state. Note also how Bakhtin's notion of carnival as symbolic authorized transgression[66] is a sort of relief theory on the level of the cultural collective rather than the individual psyche. Those who consider incongruity the crucial factor in humor find evidence in the many *anekdoty* that play on the baffling logic of the prevailing ideology, the rampant gaps between ideology and practice, and the increasing artificiality and automatism of the words, actions, and policies of official structures and leaders.[67]

Douglas helpfully pointed out a "common denominator" shared by Bergson's and Freud's approaches, both of which in one way or another viewed the joke "as an attack on control."[68] The types of control against which the *anekdot* has been mobilized are many, and include not only the obvious excesses of the Soviet security apparatus, censorship organs, and political system, but also the ostentatious contortions necessitated by the state's own approach to verbal and other forms of representation.

A productive understanding of the *anekdot* privileges neither its anti-Communist credentials nor its emotional value to its consumers. It is also desirable to avoid, however, neglecting the genre's constitutive extrinsic associations in favor of overly formalist description. Thus my list of the defining generic features of the *anekdot* (see chapters 3 and 4) not only draws on established methods of isolating and describing folkloric forms but also takes a cue from the notion of speech genres and the so-called "practice theory" understanding of discursive forms as "historically specific elements of social practice, whose defining features link them to situated communicative acts."[69]

Although the *anekdot* rapidly acquired new, historically specific features in the transformed sociopolitical atmosphere following the October Revolution, it is a mistake simply to draw a thick red boundary at 1917 on the time line of its generic evolution. In some respects, the *anekdot* is just as susceptible to continuity arguments as other cultural forms whose historical development straddled the tsarist and Communist periods. The intact traditional status of the *anekdot* as taboo, in particular, contributed to the organic nature of its evolution, consumption, and propagation during the Soviet period; it did not make the transition from oral to written culture (as the folktale had in the nineteenth century[70]) because for almost sixty years it could not be publicly inscribed.[71]

Despite the legendary independence of the Soviet *anekdot*, its development was closely linked to that of state textual production. Always a register for popular sociopolitical sentiment, the *anekdot* was thematically occupied as never before with official policies, actions, and discourse as they reflected more and more clearly the state's goal of horizontal and vertical monopolies on all forms of human activity. As that goal was pursued on an increasingly symbolic discursive level from the 1960s on, the function of the *anekdot* as meta-discourse (i.e., verbal commentary on verbal culture) became primary. The genre's formal and semantic flexibility (one scholar of the nineteenth-century *anekdot* called it a "loosely regulated narrative of potential"[72]) made it a natural medium for spontaneous performed rejoinder. Furthermore, as a genre capable of effortless parody, owing in part to the fact that the *anekdot* borders on so many other genres, the corpus of *anekdoty* burgeoned during the Soviet period and displayed new formal varieties based on the many new genres and texts to emerge from the prolific founts of mass-media discourse.

The functionality of the *anekdot*, like that of other representational forms, evolved along with the society, and with the obtaining views of textual representation within that society. The genre accrued new stylistic and thematic attributes in each major stage of Russo-Soviet cultural history: during the decades of urbanization and modernization that culminated in the Revolution; in the tumultuous early years of Bolshevik rule; after the decisive ascendancy of Stalinism and Socialist Realism in the early 1930s; again during the relatively liberal Thaw period following Stalin's death; yet again after the onset of the so-called era of Stagnation under Brezhnev and his ephemeral epigones, Iurii Andropov and Konstantin Chernenko; during perestroika; in the "postideological" discursive free-for-all that began with the end of the USSR in 1991; and finally in the as yet poorly defined environment of Putinism. Each of these periods engendered characteristic texts and tropes with which the profoundly intertextual *anekdot* has engaged on multiple levels. I want to begin, however, with a bit of philological archeology: the prehistory of the genre's Soviet instantiation.

Chapter One

Generic Provenance

> *Anekdoty* are the daily sustenance for our
> conversations. If there were no such thing as
> *anekdoty,* we would be forced to die in the
> flower of youth from apathy and hemorrhoids,
> just to spite the author of the book *No More
> Hemorrhoids.*
> —Nikolai Nekrasov, 1846

THIS CHAPTER TRACES the historical arc of the word
"anekdot" through its various associations in European (and eventually Russian) culture, up to the emergence of its twentieth-century meaning. A variety of text types (humorous, rhetorical, historiographic, didactic) contributed generic DNA to the bloodline of the future Soviet *anekdot.* Although jokes are among the most ancient of still-extant verbal forms,[1] the story of that bloodline begins in earnest in the sixth century A.D., which saw the composition of the first titularly "anecdotal" text. The genealogical approach here will illuminate a subsequent analysis of the distinctive presence of the *anekdot* in Soviet popular culture, a dynamic context in which the genre itself would continue to evolve and—especially in the Brezhnev period—thrive as never before. Beginning a historical survey with the first text to bear the name "anecdote" is appropriate, since that text was, like its eventual namesake in Soviet culture, a clandestine and mischievous redaction of the official history of an empire.

ETYMOLOGY

Although the word *"anekdot"* entered Russian as a cognate of the French during the time of Voltaire,[2] its etymological ancestry begins much earlier, with the Greek *anekdotos* (plural: *anekdota*), literally "unpublished."[3] The first recorded use of the word was in reference to historian Procopius of Caesaria's scathing account of private lives and personalities in the court of the sixth-century Byzantine emperor Justinian I.[4] Procopius himself did not give his book a title; four centuries after his death, the lexicographer Suidas listed the work as *Anekdota* (Unpublished Things) in a tenth-century bibliography to indicate that *The Secret History* (as it is known in English and Russian) had not been published during its author's lifetime. Suidas's entry was the only available information about the work for hundreds of years, as the text itself was discovered only in the seventeenth century by the director of the Vatican library. Upon its discovery, *The Secret History* provoked vehement debates among scholars of Byzantine history and of Procopius's historiography in particular. Its unadorned and often vulgar depictions of the abuses of power, character flaws, and even the physical repulsiveness of Justinian, Empress Theodora, and the empire's greatest general, Belisarius,[5] stand in sharp contrast to the reverent, patriotic tone of Procopius's other, published, histories of the emperor's reign.[6]

The dramatic contradiction between Procopius's *Anekdota* and other historical writings of the time (including his own) foreshadowed the eventual association of the Russian *anekdot* with illicit, irreverent discourse. Procopius's authorial duplicity brings to mind the ideologically schizoid nature of *anekdot* culture in the Soviet Union, where, for example, the most prolific secret compiler of political *anekdoty*, Iurii Borev, was also the author of a seminal textbook of Marxist-Leninist aesthetics,[7] and where Soviet president Mikhail Gorbachev declared in a 1989 television appearance that, in the pre-perestroika period, "*anekdoty* were always our salvation."[8] Procopius himself was keenly aware of the possible impact of his book *The Secret History* on future readers. In his foreword, subtitled "The Purpose of This Book," he anticipates both the oppositional and palliative functions of the twentieth-century *anekdot*: "Those who in the future, if so it happens, are similarly ill-used by the ruling powers will not find this record altogether useless; for it is always comforting for those in distress to know that they are not the only ones on whom these blows have fallen."[9]

Another element the sixth-century text has in common with its latter-day Russian namesake is a foundation in oral discourse. Much of the scandalous information Procopius recorded had previously circulated in the form of rumors and legends.[10] This is not to claim that there is a generic identity between Procopius's *Anekdota* and Soviet-era *anekdoty*, of course; between the tenth and twentieth centuries the term (in its various renderings in the European languages) acquired and shed a variety of inscribed definitions and cultural connotations. It will, however, prove useful to keep in mind the first composition to bear the label (a private, critical, historical narrative composed parallel to official public histories) when examining the cultural orientation of the *anekdot* in the Soviet Union—an empire that laid claim, after all, to being a descendant of the Byzantine empire of which Procopius wrote.

THE FOLK *ANEKDOT*

From the time that Russian folklorists began analyzing and cataloguing native folk texts in earnest in the mid-nineteenth century,[11] consensus has classified the *narodnyi* or *fol'klornyi* (traditional folk) *anekdot* as a subcategory or offshoot of the *skazka* (folktale).[12] More specifically, scholars have documented its generic proximity to (or near-identity with) the *bytovaia skazka* (tale of everyday life), one of the three recognized major categories of Russian tales, in addition to the *volshebnaia skazka* (wonder tale, sometimes referred to as the magic tale or fairy tale) and the *skazka o zhivotnykh* (animal tale). This is not to say that *anekdoty* never employ motifs or devices associated with the other categories; they began to do so with particular frequency when children's television programs became a chief source for *anekdoty*. But the *anekdot* and the tale of everyday life share several compositional and linguistic features, a preponderance of comic imagery and devices (though they are much stronger in the *anekdot*),[13] and a narrative emphasis on human interaction and behavior in mundane situations. The two genres' shared concern with social themes is reflected in the demographic range of protagonists they have in common: "fools, clever thieves, priests, masters and laborers, spouses, etc."[14] Local color and social relations play central roles, especially in the *anekdot*. One list of typical *anekdot* protagonists and situations includes "dunces and picaros, the peasant in the big city, bazaar scenes, the Great Russian and the Little Russian [i.e., Ukrainian—SG], Jews, Tatars, Gypsies, shepherds, wanderers, and monks, each with his own peculiarities, humor, and original style of speech."[15] This rather specific and varied collection of dramatis personae indicates the temporal distance between such narratives and their ancient textual prototypes, which are also the prototypes of narrative fiction in general: mythological stories about "picaros/tricksters."[16] Yet, at the same time, the *anekdot* reflects the entire tradition of characterological types. Folktales (and, by extension, *anekdoty*) are part of a tradition of profane texts that arose parallel to sacred narrative tradition, with its creation and initiation myths. Jack Zipes saw the emergence of parodic doppelgängers of mythological narratives as evidence that "from the beginning, individual imaginations were countering the codified myths of a tribe or society that celebrated the power of god with other 'non-authoritative' tales of their own."[17] He further suggested that such responses to sacred, authoritative discourse afforded the "individual imaginations" a measure of stolen, if symbolic, power by "transform[ing] the supernatural into magical and mysterious forces which could change their lives."[18]

The shift from supernatural to magical and eventually to realistic plots is traceable in the evolution of narrative genres. The myths to which Meletinskii and Zipes referred begat a lineage that includes all three categories of folktale, fables, and even the picaresque novel.[19] As folk narrative evolved from a form of symbolic apprehension of an inscrutable reality into a medium for creativity and entertainment, it preserved certain features that appeared fantastic or magical once the "primitive" belief patterns that had engendered the features had become obsolete.[20] This is the trajectory that presumably led to the wonder tale. The tale of everyday life, the last of the folktale categories to emerge, is concerned with worldly phenomena and social relations rather than timeless, supernatural origins (the metaphysical genealogy of the culture) and thus is the farthest removed from mythological narrative.[21]

The most common motif in everyday tales and *anekdoty* is stupidity, often in juxtaposition and conflict with its opposite; Meletinskii wrote that *anekdoty* in particular "are created around the 'stupidity-intelligence' [*glupost'-um*] axis," and that the presence of the two extremes gives the genre its characteristic "absurd paradoxicality."[22] The descendant of the trickster-myth hero is most commonly a *durak* (fool) but may also be a *khitrets* (latter-day trickster figure, from *khitryi*, which can mean devious, clever, and/or resourceful). Often the fool's naïveté and uncritical acceptance of illogical explanations for phenomena leave him open to deception and exploitation by the *khitrets*. Sometimes the fool himself is a trickster in fool's guise and achieves a goal (food, money, a wife) thanks to others' underestimation of fools or simply through dumb luck; the standard index of folktale motifs includes a subsection called *anekdoty o schast'i po sluchaiu* (*anekdoty* about accidental good fortune).[23] This character type is sometimes referred to as a *shut* (buffoon) and is considered by scholars a hybrid of or link between the *durak* and the *khitrets*.[24] The motif of "strategic idiocy," as we shall see, is highly relevant to the Soviet *anekdot*.

Sometimes the fool's simpleminded behavior is a manifestation of his stubborn belief in magic or miracles, a motif that lends support to readings of the *anekdot* as a "comic reaction to the mythological notions of primitive folklore."[25] Everyday tales and *anekdoty* are not only evolutionarily distant from the ancient worldview that originally engendered narrative; they are also challenges to purely supernatural (mythological, magical, or Christian) explanation for events and human behavior. Some eighteenth-century collectors and compilers of folklore explicitly emphasized this point.[26]

Everyday tales like the so-called democratic satirical novella, the everyday tales' counterpart in the nascent secular literature of seventeenth- and eighteenth-century Russia, are cultural expressions of structural changes in Russian society effected mainly by the Petrine reforms. Those reforms involved several impulses that influenced the evolution of both folk and literary narrative in Russia: reduction of the authority of the Orthodox Church in favor of the monarchy;[27] establishment of a structured hierarchy of urban professions and social classes; and an influx of Western literature (initially from Poland) that resulted in part from Peter the Great's aggressive Westernization of Russian culture. These reforms thrust social and secular themes to the forefront of cultural consciousness. Jack Haney wrote that the everyday tales that flourished during this period "reflect social conditions and mores that simply did not pertain to Russia before the eighteenth century [. . .]. The themes of infidelity, greed, laziness, dishonesty, drunkenness, and just plain bad luck are played out in the stratified society that Russia had become by the end of [that] century."[28]

Eventually, everyday tales and *anekdoty* came to dominate the folktale corpus. N. P. Andreev organizes the material in his 1929 *Ukazatel' skazoch-nykh siuzhetov* (Index of Folktale Motifs)[29] as follows:

I. Animal folktales
II. Folktales proper
   A. Wonder tales
   B. Legendary tales
   C. Novelistic tales
   D. Tales about foolish devils (giants, etc.)
III. *Anekdoty*[30]

Anekdoty comprise almost 40 percent of the motifs catalogued by Andreev, and everyday tales (which he includes under his "novelistic tales" rubric) comprise another 20 percent. Furthermore, those two categories have the lowest percentage of motifs in common with or known in the Western European oral tradition; more than 66 percent are original Russian motifs.[31] The prevalence of native material testifies to the status of *anekdoty* and everyday tales as vehicles for sociocultural introspection and the portrayal of local and national phenomena, events, and issues.

The content of the older two categories of folktale remained stable—animal tales still embraced anthropomorphism, and magical objects and creatures remained central in wonder tales—but these two categories, too, lost their explicitly mythological function and became primarily entertainment genres. This process was most visible in children's culture (fairy tales), but also in "high" culture; in the late eighteenth century, when Russian writers had begun to appreciate the folktale and to compose literary tales of their own, the genre was just as popular as the novel and the novella.[32] Oral literature in general in Russia had long been less exclusively associated with the lower classes than in Western Europe. Roman Jakobson contended that oral culture was "at the service of all levels of the social hierarchy."[33]

Compilers and authors of folktales were not ethnographers; they chose texts for their amusement and entertainment value and explicitly referred to that criterion in titles. M. D. Chulkov, for example, gave his four-part collection *Peresmeshnik, ili Slavenskie skazki* (The Mocking Bird, or Slavic Folktales, 1766–68) a subtitle suggesting why and when the tales might be read: *dlia preprovozhdeniia skuchnogo vremeni* (To Get Through Dull Times).[34] This function of the folktale, wrote Kurganov, is a product of its primeval origins in agricultural peasant society, where the genre's slow pace and deliberate "retardation" of the narrative, as well as its elaborate beginning and ending formulas, made it a useful means to while away the hours during "long, rural winter evenings" or while traveling. (This, suggested Kurganov, is why those in sedentary professions such as carriage drivers [or, today, cabdrivers] tend to make good storytellers.)[35]

Even in an environment of renewed appreciation for the aesthetic functions of literature, however, the folktale had by no means migrated completely into the realm of entertainment. Many eighteenth- and nineteenth-century writers—Nikolai Karamzin, for example—emphasized (O. K. Gerlovan used the term "rehabilitated") the instructive potential of the genre as an engaging illustration of virtue triumphing over vice.[36] The term *"bytovaia skazka"* has even been rendered in English as "moral tale."[37]

As Pel'ttser and Harkins have observed, the essential divergence of the *anekdot* from the tale is its lack of a message.[38] The didactic function of the folktale, and not only the portrayal of supernatural participation in and influence on human affairs, was what the folk *anekdot* implicitly rejected, and it is what represents the crucial difference between the *anekdot* and folktales of all three categories. In this respect, the folktale and the folk *anekdot* parted company under circumstances similar to those surrounding the divergence of the historical and literary *anekdoty* (see the following discussion); in both cases, the latter genre eschewed the moralism characteristic of the former.[39]

In addition to its novel discursive functions, the folk *anekdot* has compositional and other features that confirm its status as an independent genre. The mono-episodic narrative structure of the *anekdot* represents a dismantling of the series of linked narrative episodes characteristic of the folktale.[40] In this regard, Kurganov attributed the emergence of the *anekdot* as a genre separate from the tale to an extratextual influence: the city.[41] The atomistic, serialized nature of the *anekdot* corpus likewise reflected the accelerated urban tempo. It also represented a further separation of "profane" folk genres such as the *anekdot* from the sacred myths that had engendered the practice of narrative in the first place and that were "overtly and covertly interconnected" as part of a comprehensive and transcendent worldview.[42]

The *anekdot* rapidly became a genre of choice not only for contemporary mundane themes with no "message," but also for vulgar and taboo topics. Within the thematic and stylistic range of the folktale tradition from which it came, the *anekdot* is particularly close to the erotic tale.[43] Both tend toward a shorter, simpler narrative style than the mainstream folktale. Both forego wordy and/or rhyming openings such as "V nekotorom tsarstve, v nekotorom gosudarstve" (In a certain kingdom, in a certain land) or "Zhil da byl" (literally "There lived and there was," the Russian equivalent of "Once upon a time") in favor of plain narrative prose that immediately establishes the protagonist(s) and/or the setting: "One day an old woman went . . ." or "A peasant man said to his wife. . . ."[44] Moreover, what was not among the most prominent features of the folktale genre—the sexual explicitness of the erotic tales—became central in the breakaway genre of the *anekdot*.

An especially important departure from the folktale is the fact that a folk *anekdot* was frequently told as if it were an actual occurrence, even when it was obviously fictional.[45] The teller of a folk *anekdot* would often claim a firsthand connection to the protagonist(s) or at least report the immediate source of the *anekdot*. Aside from the obvious written/oral distinction between literary/historical *anekdoty* and folk *anekdoty*, they are distinguished by the fact that the written *anekdot* almost exclusively depicts important and famous people—monarchs, politicians, writers, artists— while its folkloric counterpart is populated by fictional characters, though of recognizable types.[46] It is significant that the profession of the truthfulness of an *anekdot* was not to be taken as a literal claim that the narrated event actually happened. In contrast to its historiographic counterpart, wrote Kurganov, the folk *anekdot* states a "truth" on a more abstract psychological or philosophical level.[47] Moreover, preemptive claims of veracity forestall any connection to the supernatural world and therefore any implication of higher moral authority on the part of the text or its teller. At the same time, the fictionality of the text precludes links with real-life figures, that is, with secular sources of authority. In this sense, the declaration of the veracity of an *anekdot* might even have been an ironic, implicit reference to the historical *anekdot*.

Ethnographic truth was also important, though again through the filter of the entertainment mode; the "fact" presented in the *anekdot* "was interesting insofar as it was a fact taken from folk life . . . and . . . presented in a playful form."[48] A speaker might enhance claims of the text's veracity by using specific toponyms[49] and personal names, a device that distinguishes the *anekdot* from the folktale with its "certain kingdoms" and nameless peasants, priests, shepherds, and so on.[50] The use of such details is a feature that the *anekdot* shares with other types of nonfolktale prose such as fabulates (a narrative related as a real-life event that happened to a third party), rumors, and legends.[51]

The folk *anekdoty* included in the best-known collection of Russian tales, Aleksandr Afanas'ev's *Narodnye russkie skazki,* have much in common with contemporary *anekdoty* (and with Western jokes, for that matter). Again, the motif of stupidity is rampant. Blatant idiocy, lapses in logic, and touches of black humor are common. Note the comic lack of self-awareness implicit in the following *anekdot* (a mother calling her son a "whoreson"):

> An elderly mother was scolding her son not to go swimming in the river: "And if you drown, you whoreson, don't bother to come home!"[52]

Self-defeating logical misfires are also frequent:

> One winter's day a carriage was traveling on the ice of the Volga River. One of the horses suddenly reared up and tore off toward the bank; the driver jumped down and ran after it, and was about to give it a swat with the whip when the horse fell through the ice, dragging the entire load with it. "You should thank God you went off under that ice," cried the peasant; "otherwise I'd have thrashed you good!"[53]

Anekdoty could also express cynicism and antisentimentalism, often in the person of a mean, callous, or otherwise undutiful wife:

> A young peasant was leaving on a hunting trip and his wife was seeing him off. After walking a mile she started to cry. "Don't cry, wife, I'll come home soon." "You think that's why I'm crying? My feet are frozen!"[54]

Some of the *anekdoty* in the collection are simple wordplay based on the linguistic ignorance of foreigners:

> A German goes into a Russian church. The deacon starts reading the gospel: "and Salafiil begat Zorobabel . . ." The German spits and says: "Phooey! What nonsense! A bird as small as a nightingale [*solovei*] giving birth to a big bird like the crane [*zhuravl'*]!"[55]

Other categories of *anekdot,* especially those published in *zavetnye* (forbidden) collections, indicate the genre's relationship to the tradition of so-called *potaënnaia literatura* (hidden literature) in Russian culture, which satirized figures of authority such as priests or even monarchs.[56] The satirical and politically or religiously heretical strain in the *anekdot* is also in part the legacy of groups that served as the performers and preservers of short oral (and many other cultural) forms in Russia for centuries: minstrels and buffoons.

MINSTRELS AND BUFFOONS

By the time humorous narratives began to appear in print in Russia in the eighteenth century, cultural forms about or inspired by popular entertainers—traditionally referred to as *veselye liudi* (jolly people)—had been part of Russian folklore for centuries, testifying to a strong native tradition of popular performing arts. There are references to *skomorokhi*[57] (minstrels) and *shuty* (buffoons[58]) in the oldest East Slavic written texts dating from the eleventh century. Orthodox ecclesiastical authorities began to frown on such performers within a few decades of the Christianization of Kievan Rus' in 988 and never relented. Although the church was suspicious of all native traditional culture,[59] since that culture predated the arrival of Christianity, the church reserved particular scorn for the *skomorokhi,* purportedly because they had evolved from a class of pagan priests. The church considered the *skomorokhi* "virtually the embodiment of paganism, and, with their close ties to the people, a very real threat to the new religion."[60] Thus the minstrels' image in written texts—the overwhelming majority of which were religious until the seventeenth century—was almost exclusively negative. In an entry in the *Primary Chronicle* for the year 1068, the monk Nestor warned that "the devil deceives us, with all manner of enticements he draws us away from God, with horns and *skomorokhi.*"[61] The *Pchela* (Bee), a twelfth-century Slavic translation of classical aphorisms, lumped the minstrels as a class together with prostitutes and accused them of "singing villainous songs." The sixteenth-century *Domostroi,* Muscovite Russia's most prominent guide to proper behavior, called the laughter and merrymaking inspired by the *skomorokhi* "devilish."[62] Compare these characterizations with that of the hypothetical *anekdot* teller in the *Komsomol'skaia Pravda* article I cited previously.

Beginning in the twelfth century, the *skomorokhi*—initially known mostly for instrumental music, dancing, and what today are called circus arts such as juggling, acrobatics, and trained bear acts—gradually became professional performers (and thus preservers) of native oral literature. The minstrels performed the heroic ballads known as *byliny* and also became associated with other oral genres, such as the historical song, the folktale, seasonal and wedding songs, and various incantations and proverbs.[63] When the fall of the Kievan dynasty and continued scorn from the church forced most *skomorokhi* to migrate north toward Novgorod in the thirteenth and fourteenth centuries, their audience profile changed significantly. The repertoire with which some of the *skomorokhi* had entertained (and glorified) the Kievan princes was, predictably, not suited to village audiences. So, in a process analogous to the later emergence of "purely" humorous and entertaining narratives out of the tradition of the didactic historical *anekdot,* the *skomorokhi* modified texts by, for example, adding "humorous or fantastic" elements to *byliny* to give them broader appeal.[64] Again, Soviet popular culture would see its own comic revisions of epic texts.

The frequency and stridency of the church's denunciations indicate that it was aware of the reputation and influence the minstrels enjoyed among the folk, who "not only rushed willingly to see the spectacles but would commit [*skomorokhi*] repertoires to memory."[65] The *skomorokhi* and their audiences influenced each other's oral literature. The minstrels would incorporate traditional folk forms and motifs into their acts and spread them from village to village as they traveled. The original compositions and forms of the *skomorokhi,* in turn, influenced the development of folk culture.

One folkloric genre from the Novgorodian tradition that shows the influence of the *skomorokhi* is the short comic dialogue, which Vlasova calls "a special type of folk *anekdot*":[66]

"Simon Polikarpovich, how old are you?"
"Seventy, grandma, seventy!"[67]

"Why the long face, Fedul?"
"I accidentally burned my caftan."
"Is there a big hole in it?"
"All that's left is the collar."[68]

"I caught a bear!"
"Bring it here!"
"He won't budge!"
"Then come here yourself!"
"He won't let me!"[69]

Such texts were preserved in their original form or embedded in folk songs, folktales, and plays depicting visits by the *skomorokhi,* an element of peasant life that itself found vivid and approving reflection in folklore. Positive images of the minstrels in folklore also probably indicate their own attempts to counter their negative portrayal in church writings by composing texts in which minstrels exhibit heroism or even possess magical powers.

Under Ivan the Terrible in the second half of the sixteenth century, the *skomorokhi* enjoyed something of a reprieve, at least from the secular authorities, and were invited to perform at court.[70] Their most requested genre during this period was the historical song, especially songs that glorified the tsar's latest military campaign. Later, after the persecution resumed, these songs were reworked, and Ivan was transformed from a heroic protagonist into a villainous or comic figure. A famous song about Ivan's capture of the Tatar capital of Kazan, for example, was reduced from a near-eulogy "to a mere anecdote."[71] The reworkings of texts by the *skomorokhi* subjected other rulers to similarly irreverent treatment, including even the Christianizer of Rus' himself, Vladimir, "the Sun of Kiev," who had traditionally figured in heroic ballads as a King Arthur–type figure.[72]

The minstrels' long struggle for survival in the face of church and, increasingly, government persecution found reflection in the sharp, socially oriented wit and anticlerical tone of the songs, tales, dialogues, and other texts they performed. One Soviet commentator, appropriately emphatic about the antireligious and politically irreverent elements of *skomorokh* art, overstated the minstrels' cultural place only somewhat when she called them "the persecuted representatives of the folk [*narodnaia*] artistic intelligentsia."[73] Zguta was slightly less dramatic and anachronistic, describing the *skomorokhi* not as the "intelligentsia" of the common folk but as "the cultural spokesmen of a basically oral, peasant society."[74]

Popular regard for the *skomorokhi* was probably enhanced by their irreverence toward institutions of authority. Like the cult-priests from whom their profession descended, the minstrels displayed special knowledge of, and a willingness to speak frankly about, forces that controlled life and death. The role of the *skomorokhi* indicates the ritualistic and mythological roots of cultural performance, the palpable power of the storyteller, the trickster, a figure who mediates between the supernatural and the mundane.[75] The minstrel, like the trickster, the jester, and the fool, is both a character in and a transmitter of vestigially mythological narrative.

Tsar Aleksei Mikhailovich officially outlawed minstrelsy in 1648, and nine years later the church excommunicated the *skomorokhi* en masse. Most members of the now-illegal profession found other means of livelihood or slipped into poverty, but some continued to perform, wandering among the villages and towns of the Russian countryside. The rise of written culture and the beginning of professional theater in Russia effectively snuffed out the remnants of the minstrel class within a century and a half of the tsar's decree. The final firsthand references to them date from the late eighteenth century; a visitor to Siberia in 1768 wrote of performances by "intelligent fools who sing aloud about past history."[76]

The legacy of their seven-century presence in Russian popular culture, however, is apparent in a wide variety of forms and texts from the realms of folklore, music, theater, and dance. Just as the minstrels had inherited a corpus of oral literature from the obsolete Kievan court poets, the tales and ballads brought to the north by the *skomorokhi* were passed along to the peasant *skaziteli* (storytellers) who would become the primary preservers of Russian oral literature in the eighteenth, nineteenth, and twentieth centuries.[77] This historical connection between the *skomorokhi* and the subsequent traditions of which the folk *anekdot* was a part, as well as the strong element of irreverence and parody the minstrels fomented in Russian folk culture, make their contribution to the development of the *anekdot* an important one.

With the lasting secularization of the tsarist state and the subordination of the church under Peter in the early eighteenth century, popular performers appeared again at the imperial court. Like other Petrine innovations, the *pridvornyi shut* (court jester) had Western European origins, as did literary portrayals of jesters, which began in earnest in 1519 with the publication of *Ein Kurtzweitiglesen von Eulen Spiegeln,* the anecdotal exploits of the German Til Eulenspiegel.[78] Eulenspiegel appealed most to common folk, since he was typically depicted doing "battle with the upper classes."[79] The German jester spawned similar literary figures in other countries, including Poland, whose "national jester" was a character named Sowizdrzał.[80]

By the time books about Sowizdrzał were translated into Russian, stories about the most famous such figure in Russian history and literature, Ivan Balakirev, court jester to Peter the Great, were already part of the native oral culture. Peter, the chief innovator in Russian imperial history, in the *anekdoty* is continually impressed by Balakirev's creative solutions to problems:

One time his Majesty the Tsar [Peter] became so angry that he ordered Balakirev out of his sight and told him not to dare show his face again. "Remove yourself from my land! I don't want to see hide nor hair of you!" shouted the enraged tsar. Balakirev vanished from Petersburg and there was no news about him for a long time. But one day Peter was sitting at the window and suddenly saw Balakirev and his wife pass by casually in a carriage. Infuriated by this impudence, the tsar ran outside and yelled to him: "Who gave you permission to violate my decree by showing your face on my land, you scoundrel?" Balakirev stopped the carriage and said: "Your Majesty! My horses are indeed on your land, I will not dispute that, but you did not banish *them* from the fatherland. As for my wife and me, we are on our own land." "What do you mean?" "It's very simple and normal: allow me to show you documentation of a land purchase." Balakirev handed the tsar a piece of paper. The sovereign burst out laughing when he looked and saw that there was a layer of dirt on the floor of the carriage. He read the proof of purchase of the Swedish land and forgave Balakirev.[81]

Like other historical figures who enjoy textual immortality as folk heroes, the anecdotal Balakirev is almost certainly a composite of other, less famous jokers and typical folkloric characters.[82] In the introduction to an 1899 collection of *anekdoty* about Balakirev, he is identified as a man of simple stock who was eventually made a nobleman for his services to the emperor.[83] He is credited with relieving the occasional painful spasms that Peter suffered as a long-term result of being poisoned as a child (reportedly, by his half sister and rival, Sofia). By amusing the anger-prone and unpredictable ruler, Balakirev is said to have saved many a life.[84] The imperial-era introduction also predictably locates the cultural significance of the jester's jokes and behavior in their "instructive . . . depiction of the mind of the Russian and his zeal for his monarch."[85] Another *anekdot* collection from the same decade, however, credited Balakirev with serving Russia's national interest in a more concrete way by "constantly telling the tsar the truth to his face . . . and thereby enlightening Peter to many things of which he otherwise would not have been aware."[86]

SHORT HUMOROUS GENRES

The Romantic-era renovation of the historical *anekdot* (see following discussion) was an alchemic blending of that form with other types of texts: humorous short narratives known by other names and the folk *anekdot*. Interest in the former grew out of the writers' aesthetic playfulness, while their interest in the latter reflected their commitment to a conscientious representation of their native culture. Similar impulses would inform the Soviet intelligentsia's embrace of the *anekdot* a century later.

Storytelling as a form of amusement in Russia certainly predated the association of the word *"anekdot"* with short narrative humor. Adam Olearius, a Dutch scholar who wrote a detailed account of his visit to Muscovy in the 1630s, was struck by Russians' penchant for telling vulgar stories for entertainment. He noted:

> [They] speak of debauchery, of vile depravity, of lasciviousness, and of immoral conduct committed by themselves and by others. They tell all sorts of shameless fables, and he who can relate the coarsest obscenities and indecencies, accompanied by the most wanton mimicry, is accounted the best companion and is the most sought after.[87]

Although the phenomenon of short written humorous texts—like that of the historical anecdote—was a foreign import, such texts quickly took root in Russia, in large part owing to the native tradition of oral humor of which

Olearius wrote.[88] The first collections of humorous material to appear in Russia, like the first anthologies of didactic texts, were translations of works published in Poland in the seventeenth century, an age of pronounced Polish influence on Russian culture.

In Poland such texts were called *żarty* or *facecje*, the latter term derived from the Latin *facetiae*, anthologies of which had first appeared in Italy in the fifteenth century. Longer humorous narratives were already well known in Europe by that time, most famously the fourteenth-century classics *The Decameron* and *The Canterbury Tales*. Like those works, *facetiae* drew on the age-old oral traditions of Europe and the East, and the development of both the literary novella and the *facetia* was marked by continuous mutual influence.[89] One scholar wrote that the *facetia* emerged because the type of humor and thematics characteristic of it were such strong currents in earlier narratives that, soon after the appearance of the novella and other secular forms of literature, "the jocular texts among them became more and more preponderant, and ultimately collections began to contain quite obscene anecdotes intended not to instruct and admonish the reader, as before, but only to amuse him."[90] "Natural selection" (Jakobson and Bogatyrev called it "prophylactic censorship") by the cultural consumer isolated and privileged certain types of texts.

Like the historical anecdote, the *facetia* and related humorous written texts came relatively late to Russia. The Petrine era saw a flowering of such literature in both published and manuscript form.[91] Such material was initially accessible only by readers who knew Latin or Polish, but translations soon appeared. Anthologies typically included narratives of various lengths and types. A 1680 collection entitled *Smekhotvornye povesti* (Laughable Tales), for instance, contained *facetiae*, longer stories, and a chapter from *The Decameron*. Humorous narratives in Russia were associated with such anthologies well into the nineteenth century. The translated works were popular mostly among the educated classes—scholars, students, officers, and so on—until the early nineteenth century, when the upper crust began to abandon such "low" forms in favor of the emerging culture of high literature (the process that inspired Aleksandr Pushkin, Petr Viazemskii, and others to take measures to preserve the salon *anekdot* and other such forms). Short humorous genres thus were left to lower classes such as petty bureaucrats, merchants, and peasants.[92] Anthologies began to appear mostly in the simplistic chapbook format known as *lubochnaia literatura*, illustrated with woodcut prints.[93] The most popular collection was *Starichok-vesel'chak* (The Jolly Old Man), first published in 1789 and reprinted repeatedly and almost unaltered for more than a century.[94] As a type of literature intended for and consumed (though not produced) by the folk, *anekdoty* and other texts in the *lubok* form came into contact with the folkloric corpus. There they supplemented and merged with existing oral forms,[95] including the folk *anekdot* and the folktale. The exile of the *anekdot* from high culture also isolated it from the scrutiny of censors, official and unofficial alike, fomenting its rise as an expedient medium for clandestine discourse.[96] The folk *anekdot,* as a descendant of the profane forms that coexisted in Russian culture with mythological and, later, Christian narratives, had long functioned as just such a medium. Its intermingling in the nineteenth century with the previously examined forms contributed to its subsequent emergence as the most productive Russian oral genre of the twentieth century.

THE HISTORICAL ANECDOTE

Centuries before the word *"anekdot"* appeared in Russian, its etymological ancestors (initially only the Latin *anecdota,* but soon its cognates in the modern European languages, as well) were in common use in Western European letters. In Johannes Gutenberg's day, the term was still being used as Suidas had used it five hundred years earlier: in the titles of books containing previously unpublished classical texts (*Anecdota graeca, Anecdota graeco-byzantina,* and so on). Its semantic field soon expanded, however, to include not only newly published ancient writings but also newly inscribed, previously uncited historical occurrences. In this form, the anecdote became a prominent genre of Renaissance historiography. Like the first work to bear the name, these anecdotes were accounts of small but memorable and characteristic events in the lives of elites, usually royalty or military leaders. They were presented and received as depictions of actual events, a form of miniature historiography that complemented histories of more momentous happenings and also lent a tone of humanity and immediacy to the biographies of important figures. The novelty of the information in historical anecdotes was the most significant defining feature of the genre at this stage in its development, when it had tactical value in the professional competition among historians, who would report (and sometimes invent) new information for the sake of originality.[97]

As *The Secret History* demonstrates, the latter-day association of the anecdote with nonconformist thought has ancient origins. Unlike Procopius's unambiguously antiestablishment book, however, later historical anecdotes typically echo the lionizing tone of larger historiographic works. The political conformism of the genre persisted for some time and is certainly present in most of the texts published in Russia under the rubric *"anekdoty"* in the eighteenth and early nineteenth centuries. In Western Europe and, later, Russia, historical anecdotes were often published together with examples of other short genres, such as the parable and the apothegm (a terse, instructive saying or maxim) in anthologies intended to encourage the reader to behave virtuously by emulating great personages. Such collections were widely known in Europe beginning in the sixteenth century, and they entered Russia via Poland in the late seventeenth or early eighteenth century, several decades before the word *"anekdot"* became part of the Russian language. One of the first was the Polish collection *Apothegmata*, which was published in Poland at the end of the sixteenth century and appeared in Russian translation in 1711 during the reign of Peter the Great, with the following subtitle: *Three Volumes of Short, Rhetorical, Edifying Tales. Included Therein Are Various Questions and Answers, Lives, and Deeds, Words, and Conversations of Various Ancient Philosophers. Translated from the Polish by Order of His Majesty, the Tsar.*[98]

While the secularly homiletic tone of the historical anecdote was a Renaissance-era development, its mechanics and many of its compositional elements are traceable to classical antiquity, when short genres such as the legend, the apothegm, the fable, and the tale served rhetorical purposes similar to that of the contemporary *anekdot:* to express an idea in a captivating, distilled utterance uncluttered by abstraction or extended explication.[99] The frequent presence of surprise endings in these genres, as well as their brevity, made them modally flexible, that is, adaptable to both comic and serious subjects. Indeed, the earliest Russian compilers of translated apothegms emphasized the co-presence in the texts of *dulce* and *utile.* In 1764, a St. Petersburg teacher named Petr Semenov published an anthology of translated texts with a lengthy title:

A Reasonable and Complex Companion, or A Collection of Good Words, Reasoned Ideas, Quick Retorts, Well-Considered Jests and Pleasant Adventures of Renowned Men of Antiquity and the Current Age, Translated from French and Supplemented with Similar Material by Latin Writers for Both the Benefit and the Amusement of Society.[100]

Native Russian historical *anekdoty* began to appear a few decades after the first translations of Polish collections. Peter the Great himself, whose reforms had introduced a plethora of sociopolitical and cultural ideas unprecedented in Russia, was, naturally, among the first native subjects of the genre of choice for communicating previously unknown information. Despite their association with the reforms, however, early (and many later) Russian historical *anekdoty,* like the genre's older, European counterpart, affirmed the status quo in no uncertain terms. One 1809 collection, for instance, has another concise title:

Russian Anecdotes, or Great Memorable Actions and Virtuous Examples of
Glorious Men of Russia, Renowned Monarchs, Military Commanders, Civil
Servants, Merchants and Other Individuals of All Callings, Distinguished by
Their Heroic Firmness, Intrepid Spirit, Zeal, Philanthropy, the True Right-
ness of Their Affairs and Many Other Examples of the Unwavering Devotion
to Faith, the Monarch and Love for the Fatherland.[101]

Compilers of these *anekdoty* obtained (or claimed to obtain) their
material from interviews with firsthand witnesses to the actions of the historical personages depicted (or their descendants). They also found material
in letters and other documents, but the firsthand sources were considered a
hallmark of the genre. Even though the very use of the word "*anekdot*" implied the veracity of the information presented, publishers sometimes emphasized that veracity more explicitly by highlighting the method of collection in a title: for example, the 1788 book *Anecdotes about Emperor Peter the
Great, Heard from Various Individuals and Collected by Iakov Shtelin.*[102]

Russian historical *anekdoty* depict their VIP protagonists displaying
those qualities most emblematic of occupants of their positions. In *anekdoty*
about monarchs, for example, the ruler typically demonstrates his or her
wisdom, magnanimity, and/or good humor with a comment or action that
fulfills a textual function similar to that of a punch line:

After his victory [against the Swedes] at the battle of Poltava, Peter I [the
Great] invited some captured officers to his table. He proposed a toast: "I
drink to the health of my military teachers!" The Swedish field marshal,
Reinschild, asked Peter whom he favored to call by such a name. "You, sirs,"
was Peter's reply. "In that case, Your Majesty has shown his teachers terrible
ingratitude [on the battlefield]." The ruler was so pleased by Reinschild's re-
tort that he immediately ordered that the field marshal's saber be returned
to him.[103]

His Majesty [Peter the Great], attending a session of the Senate one day, became incensed upon hearing of various thefts that had recently occurred. He
angrily vowed to put the thievery to an end, saying to his prosecutor general,
Pavel Ivanovich Iaguzhinskii: "Draft this very minute a decree in my name
to the whole country, stating that anyone who steals an amount sufficient
to buy a rope shall be summarily hanged." The prosecutor general, pen in
hand, listened to the stern order, but hesitated. He replied to the monarch:
"Your Highness, have you considered the probable consequences of such
a decree?" "Write what I ordered you to write," the sovereign interrupted
him. Still, Iaguzhinskii did not start writing, and finally smiled and said to the
monarch: "Most Gracious Sovereign! Do you really want to be an emperor

without servants or subjects? We all steal, only some steal more than others, and more obviously." His Majesty, who had been deep in thought, heard this amusing answer, burst out laughing, and fell silent.[104]

These two *anekdoty* show Peter reacting not only with restraint but also with a sense of humor to retorts that might provoke rage and punishment from a less enlightened leader.[105] In other *anekdoty* the sovereign herself, Catherine the Great, is the source of a witty remark:

> Countess Branitskaia, noticing that Catherine II [the Great] took snuff with her left hand rather than her right, as was the custom, asked the reason. Catherine replied: "As a woman tsar [*tsar'-baba*], I must frequently offer my hand to be kissed, and I consider it unseemly to suffocate everyone with the odor of tobacco."[106]

In Russia, anthologies of short anecdotal texts were widely read, both in printed and manuscript copies, and heard in church (though not the three cited above, most likely), where clergy would recite them aloud as illustrations of religious concepts. They were also recommended for recitation by military officers to their soldiers and by landowners to their serfs.[107]

Categorizing this apparently unscholarly text type as a form of historiography is not unusual, considering the accepted nature and purpose of that field at the time. Recorded history was not expected to be a detached, balanced account of events in sequence, but an object lesson, an exemplary narrative that derived its didactic authority from its veracity. Its most important subject was human character, and the most proper historical examples of desirable character traits were those of the men and women who made history: rulers, royalty, aristocrats, and military heroes.[108] The *anekdot* collection as a historiographic document also served to "portray and, by extension, promote stability," since there was no discernible temporal progression from text to text, which gave the impression of static time. The behavior of the protagonists was also stable, even predictable, from one *anekdot* to the next.[109]

Aware of the appeal of lively storytelling and the limited effect of overly tendentious (and "stable") didacticism, compilers sometimes included colloquial, humorous, and even obscene texts in their collections. The anthologized texts typically had an unambiguous moral added on, but not always:

> An old woman places two candles in church: one in front of an icon of St. Michael, another one in front of an image of the devil. The deacon notices this and says to her: "Hey, what are you doing, old woman? You're putting that candle in front of the devil." And she says to him: "Don't touch it, father. It's

not a bad idea to have friends everywhere, in heaven and in hell. After all, we don't know where we're going to end up."[110]

The popular reception of these texts was highly discriminating, writes Pel'ttser: "People were not interested in the moral of the story, and retained only the *anekdot,* as a form of amusement."[111] Especially popular texts from anthologies subsequently became part of the Russian oral tradition, a process which, considered alongside the fact that many of the anthologized texts themselves descended from the oral traditions of European and Eastern antiquity, testifies to the increasingly complicated relationship between oral and written culture that emerged during the Petrine era. That process also exemplifies what Bogatyrev and Jakobson dubbed "prophylactic censorship," a sort of textual analog to natural selection that characterizes a community's engagement with its own corpus of oral culture; texts of little or diminished interest to the folk are not rehearsed and therefore fade into oblivion.[112] In the Soviet period, people would also engage in selective consumption of cultural forms—for example, immortalizing certain film protagonists or literary icons in discrete *anekdot* cycles while ignoring others.

Although the didactic function of the *anekdot* and its thematic emphasis on factual events from the lives of historical figures remained strong in Russia well into the nineteenth century, even by the late eighteenth century the scope of the term was expanding to include "interesting, isolated facts and short, witty little stories notable for their freshness and levity."[113] The change in its semantic sphere of reference was in part a synecdochic reemphasis on one subcategory of the genre, humorous historical *anekdoty,* which began to increase in number and influence when Russia's first professional writers started composing them. The shift was also partly due to an expansion of the term *"anekdot"* to include humorous texts previously known only by other names such as *kratkie zamyslovatye povesti* (short complex tales).[114] Finally, the change reflected the influence of the folk *anekdot* and other types of folk narrative, which were populated by fictional archetypal characters, on the historical *anekdot* with its real-life personalities. As I shall demonstrate in chapter 2, the mutual superimposition of the protagonists of these two categories of narrative would become a prominent marker of the Soviet-era *anekdot,* a descendant of both.

THE LITERARY *ANEKDOT*

The florescence of Russian literary culture in the late eighteenth and early nineteenth centuries changed the connotative scope of the word *"anekdot"* in ways that set the genre on a path toward its twentieth-century significance as (1) a medium for commentary on domestic current events and issues and (2) the major oral genre of a highly literate population. By the 1790s, *anekdoty* with Russian themes and protagonists had begun to gain ground on the still-more-popular translated European anecdotes. As they strove to develop a truly native literary language, Russian writers also began to encourage the use of native Russian subjects and themes in literature. Oral culture played a significant role in this drive for literary innovation; Nikolai Karamzin's advice to his fellow authors in 1802 was to "write as we speak."[115]

Interest in the particularities of the Russian ethnos competed with the obtaining neoclassical emphasis on universal human character. Proponents of a more nationally introspective literature pointed out that Russia, in this regard, was somewhat behind the West, where Romanticism had already taken root. In 1793, Ivan Krylov, who would later become Russia's most renowned fabulist, cowrote the following with A. I. Klushin in the first issue of Krylov's journal, *The St. Petersburg Mercury:*

> Every nation gives justifiable recognition to the great deeds of its native sons, and every nation passes on to posterity its citizens' smallest adventures, notable for their magnificence or peculiarity: many volumes of French, English, and German anecdotes have been published. Is it really the case that Russians have done so much less, both good and bad, than other nations? Is it really the case that we do not have a single anecdote that in some way captures the character of the nation? Of course we have such anecdotes, but they are not paid any attention. We searched and inquired and found a great many of them. Why not share them with the public? They will doubtlessly provide a certain pleasure for our readers.[116]

The authors who dominated Russian literature at the end of the eighteenth and the first decades of the nineteenth century—most notably (though not exclusively) Pushkin and other representatives of Russian Romanticism—agreed with Krylov and embraced the native historical *anekdot* as a genre capable of expressing both their keen interest in Russian history and their aesthetic values. Poets and prose authors alike increasingly incorporated Russian history into their stories, novels, and verse. Several wrote nonfiction works—for example, Karamzin's multivolume *History of the Russian State* (1818–29), Nikolai Polevoi's *History of the Russian People* (1829–33), and Pushkin's *History of Pugachev* (1833). Writers also began composing and collecting *anekdoty,* the most notable examples being Pushkin's *Table-Talk* (1835–36) and Petr Viazemskii's *Old Notebook* (1870s).

With their conscious departure from the rationalism that characterized the neoclassical period, writers were attracted by the flexibility of the *anekdot* and its potential for artistic representation of real-life events. The literary *anekdot* popular in Pushkin's day was a transitional stage in the genre's evolution, in that it was no longer a presumably factual story, and not yet necessarily a funny one.[117] In the new aesthetic and intellectual atmosphere, "the anecdote's function shift[ed]," wrote Kux, as Pushkin and others began to "use anecdotes to create subjective, if not idiosyncratic, accounts of history and historical figures."[118] Compare the previously cited *anekdoty* about Peter the Great, for example, with the following, from Pushkin's *Table-Talk:*

> One day a black servant boy accompanying Peter I on his walk stopped to attend to certain needs. He suddenly cried out in fright: "Sovereign! Sovereign! My guts are crawling out of me!" Peter went up to him, realized what was happening, [and] said, "That's not true: it's not your guts, it's a tapeworm," and pulled the worm out with his fingers. Not a very clean *anekdot*, but it does depict Peter's mannerisms.[119]

This text is notable not only for the scatological subject matter but also for Pushkin's reflexive authorial commentary at the end of the *anekdot*.

Russian literati began to study traditional folk genres such as the folktale, the ballad, and the *anekdot* in order more authentically to "translate [them] into the language of literary creation."[120] Karamzin and other prominent writers of his day, including Gavrila Derzhavin (1743–1816), Aleksandr Radishchev (1749–1802), Pushkin, and even empress Catherine the Great (r. 1762–96),[121] composed literary folktales. Their retooling of the historical *anekdot* (which literary historians of the period usually called the "literary *anekdot*") was accomplished through the filter of their knowledge of and fondness for native folklore.[122]

The natural habitat of the *anekdot* changed after writers began to adopt the genre. As part of the process of Westernization initiated by Peter and continued by his successors (especially Catherine the Great in the last third of the eighteenth century), Russia imported a salon culture in which oral consumption of historical anecdotes (as well as other "miniature genres" such as the "epigram, fable, aphorism, madrigal, literary letter [and] inscription on portraits"[123]) was common. The European-style salon anecdote "collided" in the literary salons of St. Petersburg and Moscow with the native folk *anekdot*, resulting in a new, distinctly Russian form.[124] Although the new genre still featured real-life protagonists, the range of social and professional categories deserving of immortalization through *anekdoty* expanded to include not only monarchs and generals, but also literati, artists, and composers.

The discursive function of the genre began to change as well, especially as political intellectualism became increasingly associated with writers and artists. The comment by the civic-minded poet and publisher Nikolai Nekrasov cited in the epigraph to this chapter indicates that the *anekdot* had become a favored (indeed, indispensable) medium for critical discourse and opinionated intellectual exchange. The capacity of literary *anekdoty* for automatic knee-jerk contradiction is shared by the traditional folk *anekdot,* for which discursive conflict is also a crucial constituent feature. Roman Jakobson wrote of his encounter early in the twentieth century with a "genuine master of the anecdote" in a village, who told him:

> When I come into an inn and people are arguing, and someone calls, "There is a God!" and I, to him, "You lie, son of a cur,"—then I tell him a tale to prove it, until the *muzhiks* say: "You're right. There is no God." But again I have to fire back: "Nonsense!" And I tell them a tale about God [. . .]. I can tell tales only to get back at folks.[125]

A definition of the word *"anekdot"* from the *Dictionary of Russian Synonyms or Soslovov* (1840) confirms the growing critical and analytical potential of the form, noting that it can "illuminate the secrets of politics and literature or lay bare the hidden springs of events."[126] The Soviet *anekdot* would fulfill a similar function, often on an ironic level, positing possible yet patently absurd springs that might lie beneath the surface of an otherwise inexplicable sociopolitical phenomenon.

As an oral form, *anekdoty* in Russian literary culture of the early nineteenth century represented a prototype of what Borev would later dub—in reference to the Soviet underground *anekdot*—"the folklore of the intelligentsia."[127] The status of the *anekdot* as an oral genre—an ephemeral form "so easily exhaled and forgotten"[128]—in an increasingly literary culture led to efforts by Pushkin and others to record and preserve examples of the *anekdot,* both as aesthetic artifacts and as repositories of information worthy of inscription in the national memory. Their efforts took on a particular urgency, writes Kurganov, after the failed Decembrist overthrow of the Russian monarchy in 1825, which significantly discredited the educated urban nobility whose members had led or supported it. The uprising's aftermath changed the unwritten laws of public behavior and the sociopolitical dynamics of St. Petersburg and Moscow, so the salon culture that had been central to social and intellectual life lost its former influence. The *anekdot* was deprived of its major cultural context and therefore much of its aura as a full-fledged literary genre. It started to become an informal everyday form of expression, and thus less substantial.[129]

Another factor in the decline of the literary *anekdot* was the commercialization of Russian literature, the migration of literary forms and activity "from the salon [. . .] into the marketplace."[130] Consequently, written and folk *anekdoty* were increasingly consumed in the same cultural contexts, resulting in further intermingling of the genre's various evolutionary strands. Pushkin and others recognized these processes and endeavored to rescue the *anekdot* as an example of salon culture, with its refined "art of social intercourse."[131]

As it gained popularity among the creative intelligentsia, the literary *anekdot* grew more reliant on humor than the earlier historical *anekdot* had been, though humor was not yet its defining feature. The changing aesthetic of literary creation and the surging interest in introspection on both national and personal levels created a growing premium on humorous texts, testifying to Henri Bergson's assertion that "the comic comes into being just when society and the individual [. . .] begin to regard themselves as works of art."[132] Like the previously quoted historical *anekdoty* about Peter and Catherine, literary *anekdoty* were often constructed around a *bon mot*, though now uttered by a writer or artist as often as by a monarch:

> Del'vig [poet and close friend of Pushkin] once challenged Bulgarin [another writer] to a duel. Bulgarin declined, saying, "Tell Baron Del'vig that I have seen more blood in my day than he has seen ink."[133]

> One day a family came to [the painter] Briullov's studio and asked to see his student, N. A. Ramazanov. Briullov sent for him. When he arrived Briullov said to the guests, "Allow me to introduce to you a drunkard." Ramazanov pointed to Briullov and said coldly, "And this is my teacher."[134]

In addition to its newfound status as an independent genre, the *anekdot* acquired a new relationship with larger, more traditional literary genres. Definitions of *"anekdot"* in Soviet dictionaries of literary terminology acknowledge this relationship, characterizing the *anekdot* as a sort of neutral "seed" event or situation [*fabula*] that a skilled verbal artist develops into a story, novella, or novel [*siuzhet*].[135] The best-known example of this in Russian literature is Pushkin's donation of two fictional anecdotes to the young Nikolai Gogol', narrative seeds that Gogol' cultivated into his masterpieces, the comedy *Revizor* (The Inspector General, 1836) and the picaresque novel *Mertvye dushi* (Dead Souls, 1842). Gogol' had solicited the contribution in an 1835 letter to Pushkin: "Do me a favor and give me some plot; whether it's amusing or not amusing doesn't matter as long as it's a purely Russian anecdote."[136] In hindsight, it is perhaps no surprise that Soviet reference books would favor this definition of the *anekdot* as a small verbal form, raw material for higher genres. Such a perception underplays the growing power of the term in Soviet everyday culture and describes a process that is the direct opposite of the contemporary unofficial connotation of the term not as an atomistic, preliminary text but as a finished product—a terminal, stylized, and subjective distillation of images, icons, relationships, and speech forms from a larger narrative: the whole of sociopolitical reality. Soviet Marxist teleology would demand that such a potentially mischievous form of discourse be labeled an obsolete proto-genre rather than regarded as a sophisticated culmination of popular creative thought.

The various applications over centuries of the word "*anekdot*" to texts from a range of discursive contexts (history, biography, homiletics, pedagogy, literature, humor) and the various media used to transmit the *anekdot* (books, private manuscripts, verbatim recitation, improvised oral performance) certainly despecified the term. But the legacy of what Kux called the "formal indeterminacy" and "functional plurality"[137] of the *anekdot* would ultimately be to the genre's evolutionary advantage in the environment of aggressively manipulated and manufactured verbal culture that began in earnest in the 1930s. Of no less utility was the root of the *anekdot* in mythology. The engineers of Soviet cultural production understood the power of myth and employed it in the archaic sense, as a grand narrative of origins and a source of comprehensive discursive authority. The Soviet-era *anekdot* would fulfill what one might call a meta-mythological function, a folkloric form that satirized a political mythology that was itself reliant on folkloric models. The rise of the contemporary *anekdot* in Russia was not solely a result of Bolshevism, of course, but also of related earlier (and larger) processes: urbanization and modernization, which had already begun to engender novel cultural forms by the time Marxism-Leninism became the primary influence on the verbal repertoire of Russian culture.

Tradition and Contemporaneity

Power is amorphous; myth gives it form.
—Gilbert Morris Cuthbertson

The more insistent the call for the epic, the
more likely the appearance of *anekdoty.*
—I. Shaitanov

BY THE BEGINNING of the twentieth century, the *anekdot* had evolved into a form of popular expression well suited to the socio-cultural and even the physical environment of the city, with its demographic density, staccato rhythms, and dynamic sensory and cognitive stimuli. The genre was an increasingly prominent part of a generically and stylistically diverse pre-Revolutionary popular culture that Richard Stites described as "an amalgam of folk, high, and light urban entertainment genres of old Russia in a context of commercialism, the quickening of technology, [. . .] and increased contact with foreign culture."[1] The rather motley pedigree of the *anekdot* again broadened its utility and appeal in this environment of cultural amalgamation. The popularity of the literary-historical *anekdot* among Russian literati in the previous century, in combination with the emergent prominence of the oral *anekdot* in the culture of "the folk" (who would have an unprecedented level of participation in and influence on urban verbal culture by the eve of the Revolution), gave the contemporary genre a multifaceted utility and appeal. The wave of sociopolitical sea changes about to beset the country would create an atmosphere in which the rise in the cultural stock of the *anekdot* could only accelerate.

The institutionalization of Bolshevism was predated (and, of course, influenced) by another dramatic change in Russian social reality that made its own contributions to the cultural significance of the *anekdot:* mass urbanization. The total urban population of Russia tripled between 1863 and 1913. The emancipation of the serfs in 1861 had given peasants unprecedented freedom of movement and, by the end of the century, the number of Russian city-dwellers with peasant backgrounds had increased by nearly

400 percent.[2] Many of these urbanized peasants held temporary passports that allowed them to retain land and homes in their villages while working or doing business in the city, which meant that the link between rural and urban was not simply one of historical demographic change but an ongoing physical fact. The respective forms of popular culture associated with the two habitats commingled with an intensity that matched that of the migrations themselves.

The steep rise in the literacy rate following emancipation contributed to the process of cultural intercourse, as well. The decades between emancipation and the October Revolution, wrote Jeffrey Brooks, saw the rapid development of "a popular culture based on common literacy." The literate peasants, Brooks said, "tended [. . .] to divide all books into two categories, the godly and the humorous. The Scriptures were the model for the first sort of text, and the frivolous fairy tale the exemplar of the second. The fairy tale was ungodly, untrue, useless, amusing, and uninstructive."[3] As godliness became less of a necessary element in Russian letters (and completely anathema after 1917), its frivolous counterpart was, if briefly, free to come to the fore of folk (and, increasingly, urban) cultural consumption.

Although the rural-urban connection in Russian culture began to accelerate as never before at the end of the nineteenth century, it certainly did not originate then. The frequency of urban themes and settings in folktales, ballads, historical songs, and other traditional folk genres attests that the cultural symbiosis of village and city is in fact a centuries-old phenomenon (in some part traceable to the traveling minstrels I discussed in chapter 1). The influence of professional written culture (which in Russia, as elsewhere, has always been largely urban) on oral forms such as religious verse, the legend, and the folktale also predates by centuries the mass urban migrations of the peasantry that began after emancipation.[4]

Yet if the influence of the city and its culture on Russian folklore was previously detectable primarily on a thematic level, the large-scale urbanization of the folk created opportunities for new kinds of cross-pollination. The rhythm and structure of newly generated folk texts, for instance, began to reflect the new temporal, spatial, and psychological contexts in which people were performing and consuming oral culture. The oral *anekdot* thrived especially well in an urban environment. Kurganov cited the genre's signature formal features—its "dynamic, compact form" and its efficient "disregard of details, secondary episodes, and extraneous descriptions [in favor of] immediate presentation of the narrative nucleus"—as crucial factors in its big-city success.[5] He likewise attributed to the urban influence the decisive emergence of the modern oral *anekdot* as a separate genre from the venerable master-genre of Russian oral culture, the folktale:[6]

The city reduced and refined the folktale, plucked from it a single short episode, gave it a tight energetic rhythm, made the text dynamic (increasingly so as it approaches the end), and trained it to orient itself within and sense the pulse, the essence, of conversation. And the folktale gradually fell away, but the *anekdot* remained, better suited to the tempo of city life.[7]

Even the temporal and climatic environment in which city-dwellers lived hastened what Kurganov calls the reduction of the tale to *anekdot* size; in rural Russia, the tale was traditionally a winter genre, a means to pass time indoors during the cold months. The elasticity and repetitiveness of the tale, along with other so-called retardation devices, enhanced its value as such a pastime. The temporal and spatial categories of city life were sufficiently novel to shift the evolutionary advantage to different types of oral texts and different circumstances for their consumption.[8]

The influence on verbal culture of the natural and social environment, of course, had always been significant, even determining. According to Pel'ttser, the original function of the myths and other forms of narrative that lay at the source of folkloric expression was to respond collectively to natural elemental forces outside human control: "The questions that primitive man posed to himself regarding his natural environment could not be answered by dispassionate reason, which did not yet have a foundation in positivistic knowledge; answers came instead in the form of youthfully naive fantasy, at times playful and at times lofty."[9] Often the playful impulse took its semantic cues not directly from the natural environment, but from other extant textual material, and specifically material representing the opposite end of Pel'ttser's implied stylistic continuum: texts that aspire to discursive "loftiness." As the ludic element of cultural expression grew stronger over time, that element came to serve as a sort of internal control (or purgative) mechanism by which a culture could turn back on itself—reflexivity, in its etymologically literal meaning—and critically regard its own formative tropes, images, and premises. Humor, as contained in short genres such as the *anekdot* in particular, was a key mode for this type of cultural redaction. Meletinskii interpreted folk *anekdoty* as "a comic reaction to the mythological impressions of primitive folklore. They discredit the obsolete and moribund features of primitive ideology."[10]

The verbal performance of the ideology of the radiant future was deeply invested in the past. The new authoritative knowledge after 1917 was articulated using linguistic devices, archetypes, imagery, and motifs informed by the same representational fount to which the *anekdot* had ready access: the folkloric tradition and its origins in myth. The vestigial presence in latter-day folklore (such as the *anekdot*) of *its* own myth-oriented heritage in turn "genetically" predisposed it to be a medium for critical engagement

46

of mythological—and neomythological—discourse. Thus folklore had a new point of critical reference, one for the engagement of which the archetypes and motifs of the *anekdot* proved highly useful.

Although some have interpreted the Soviets' political use of folkloric language primarily as a calculated appeal to the peasantry,[11] Julia Latynina saw a more fundamental link between Soviet ideology and archaic oral patterns. She referred to Soviet folkloric discourse as "the ideology's most adequate sublanguage," which she attributed to the fact that "the ideology itself is a pseudomorph of folklore," owing mainly to its similar emphasis on collective over individual creativity.[12] She cited numerous examples, including representations of Joseph Stalin as "the never-setting sun of the Party" and "the greatest gardener" in the "flowering garden of Communism," VDNKh (the Soviet Exhibition of Economic Achievements) as a fairy-tale kingdom, Lenin as a "mountain eagle," and a tale in which "a medal, presented by Stalin, is the magical means that three times saves the head of a collective farm from the machinations of the kulak antagonists."[13] The adoption of such language created an internal paradox within state discourse: the "mythologized form" of official texts "contradict[ed] the postulated rationality of their content."[14] Another way of referring to the same immanent structural tension is in terms of tradition versus contemporaneity, two influences on thought and expression that the *anekdot,* in contrast to the neomythological ideology, successfully united within itself.[15]

The Soviet-era *anekdot* from the beginning merged a defining element of the literary-historical *anekdot*—portrayal of known real-life figures—with motifs and structural features of traditional folk narrative with its fools, devils, tricksters, and attention to everyday situations.[16] In the nineteenth century, *anekdoty* almost exclusively depicted important and famous people—monarchs, politicians, writers, artists—while folk *anekdoty* dealt with everyday events and were populated by fictional stereotypical characters.[17] The Soviet political *anekdot* combined these two strands into a hybrid that often depicted an encounter between the famous and the anonymous, between the extraordinary and the mundane, between power [*vlast'*] and subject [*narod*].

The symbolic crossbreeding of historical personages and folk archetypes served not only to cast the former in a satirical light, but also to engage with the ideology on the level of the ideology's own underlying neomythological representational logic. The guiding influence of that logic is visible in the development of Soviet folklore studies. Early Soviet folklorists had a dual mission: to encourage the composition of (or to themselves compose) folklore that would give credibility to the new ideology's claims of having re-created the world, and to identify those elements of the existing tradition that should be preserved and cultivated. To extend (and do violence to) the botanical metaphor (which itself echoes similar metaphors in the neofolk-loric language used in the epithets cited by Latynina), the collectors and creators of the new folklore were attempting to cultivate on the site of thick old-growth orchards, and they had to cherry-pick among the range of extant folk forms and texts therein to limit the textual harvest to ideologically correct fruit. By contrast, as a vehicle for meta-folklore the *anekdot* could harvest entire orchards or even burn them down, for its discursive potency is not diminished at all by the threat of internal contradiction. In fact, its potency is largely based on contradiction.

Soviet "fakelore" was far from the only species of official discourse to draw on the Russian oral tradition. Like other zealously ideological states, the Soviet Union committed its culture industry to aggressive mythmaking projects in the interest of defining and inscribing, in its own terms, the origins of contemporaneity, and also in the interest of shoring up the discursive authority of its leaders and other emblematic personalities. In doing so, of course, it guaranteed a reliable fount of material for the *anekdot* for more than seventy years:

> "Let's have a drink, Vladimir Il'ich!"
> "I can't, old man, I'm on the wagon. Yesterday I drank a lot at the Finland Station, climbed up onto an armored car, and said such nonsense that I still can't figure out what happened!"[18]

> Helmut Schmidt, Giscard d'Estaing, and Leonid Brezhnev are show-ing off their expensive gifts. Schmidt displays an exquisite snuff box with an inscription reading "To dear Helmut, from your loving wife." D'Estaing has a distinctive pipe that reads "To dear Giscard, from a patriotic French-woman." Brezhnev pulls out a gold cigarette box encrusted with diamonds, with an inscription that reads "To Count Uvarov from Grand Prince Sergei Aleksandrovich."[19]

Anekdoty about political leaders and other Soviet heroes satirically demonstrated that official textual production had assigned them to the wrong genres, that Lenin, Feliks Dzerzhinskii, Mikhail Kalinin, Chapaev, Stalin, Nikita Khrushchev, Brezhnev, and others are characters more at home in the *anekdot* than in the heroic epic, the didactic parable, the exemplary tale, or the instructive proverb.[20] In this regard, the *anekdot* rehearsed one of the earliest processes in the evolution of verbal culture: the creation of "demonic/comic doubles" in response to, and in imitation of, the "cultural heroes" who populate myths.[21]

Political myth, like other varieties of myth, is often constructed as a formulaic expression of secret authoritative knowledge held by an enhanced individual whose authority is largely derived from his status as emblematic of a collective ("We say Lenin, we mean the Party"). It is a form of discourse that "comes into play when rite, ceremony, or a social or moral rule demands justification, warrant of antiquity, reality or sanctity."[22] Myth narrates cultural origins, and in particular the agency of "supernatural beings" present at— and responsible for—the creation of a reality or a specific category or detail within that reality.[23] In its turn, the popular response frequently seizes on not only the overstated self-importance and other discursive excesses of political myth, but also on the neglected signifieds, the body of common knowledge that the myth must actively ignore in order to sustain itself. That response can be both discursive (verbal engagement with the myth) and behavioral (demonstrative evidence of the inaccuracy of the model of reality contained in the myth).

Oral satire typically exposes political myths as incomplete or inadequate information and offers a facetious, yet plausible, alternative chain of causation (ironically fulfilling the function attributed to humor by proponents of "incongruity-resolved" theories).[24] Satirical engagement with myth symbolically subverts the mythmakers' aspirations to comprehensive discursive authority, which in the Soviet case was substantially derived from the purported grassroots nature of revolutionary events. The *anekdot* credits other organic values and forces with inspiring the masses to change their destiny:

> Liski Station calls Moscow:
> "Chairman of the Revolutionary Military Committee Trotskii calling."
> "This is Chairman of the Soviet People's Committee Lenin."
> "Vladimir Il'ich, immediately dispatch two tankers of grain alcohol to Liski Station."
> "What for, Lev Davidovich?"
> "The peasants have sobered up. They want to know what happened to the Tsar."

Folk humor also has a variety of ways of toggling between collective and individual patterns of thinking, thereby destabilizing the key neomythological premise of the leader's (or the leader's words') status as an agent for collective volition:

> A Chukchi comes home after a trip to Moscow and says, "I saw Moscow, I saw the slogan 'All in the Name of Man, All for the Good of Man,' and I even got to see that man."

This joke plays on an implicit theme that was common in nonconformist culture (especially Soviet conceptualism) in the 1960s and 1970s: the idolized

Leader no longer represented as a dread demiurge but as a fetish object, a risible marker of the de facto lack of popular support for the ideology.

The Chukchi's conflation of "Man" and "a man" (specifically, the current leader, or perhaps Lenin in the Mausoleum) hints not only at the corrupting nature of power, but also at a symptom of attempts to alter contemporaneity according to neomythological paradigms: when a living person (or select group) is equated with an abstract collective, the actual members of that collective become irrelevant.[25] This observation may repeat an antitotalitarianist truism, but it also reveals an important function of the *anekdot:* engagement with the paradoxes inherent in hegemonic discourse and simultaneous exposure of that discourse as retrograde, even archaic. At the same time, the generic and perspectival contemporaneity of the *anekdot* is contrastively displayed.

The folkloric fool in the Chukchi joke (characteristically, he is an outsider) fulfills his traditional role of articulating a truth in the form of a misapprehension. That role in the *anekdot* can be performed by any number of characters, not excluding the leader's immediate family:

> Brezhnev's mother comes to visit her son. When she sees how he lives, she bursts into tears and says, "What if the Reds come back?"

As representatives of alien contexts (one geographical, the other generational), the Chukchi and Mrs. Brezhnev are carriers of perceptions that both conflict with contemporaneity and expose contemporaneity's own internal conflicts. The two *anekdoty* illustrate the genre's capacity simultaneously to depict a "verbal communication disturbance" on the level of plot and to cause such a disturbance by exposing internal contradictions in the prevailing discourse of the society.[26] Such contradictions are a product not only of aggressive neomythologization, but also of accelerated social change in general.

NOVELTIES

The utility of the *anekdot* as a medium for parodying political mythmaking emerged slightly after another, related function: as a form of commentary on the profound and ubiquitous novelty of urban life. In his 1922 article about the nature of the comic, particularly the (still very young) Soviet *anekdot,* Viktor Shklovskii writes that the genre's attention to new linguistic and other social formations was more central to its comic essence than its utility as political satire: "The abundance of Soviet *anekdoty* in Russia is explained not by a particularly hostile relationship to the powers that be [*k vlasti*], but by the fact that new phenomena and contradictions in everyday life are perceived as comic."[27]

One of the new phenomena that affected perceptions of everyday life was the multicultural atmosphere of the Russian city. The influx into Moscow and St. Petersburg of "foreigners" from within the Russian empire—Jews, Gypsies, and people from the Caucasus—was a particularly strong influence on the cultural forms extant in cities. The presence of these new participants in the culture appealed to the "appetite for [the] exotic" that helped to make up the new urban patterns of consumption.[28] Their presence also affected the linguistic atmosphere, which had long been a source of material for the *anekdot:*

> A German is seeing off a guest. He says to him, "Vasil' Vasil'evich, why did you stay for such a short time? You barely had time to *zdokhnut'* and now you're leaving!"[29]

Shklovskii wrote that such conflicts between two differing versions of the same language are a more common and reliable source of humor than a conflict between two languages.[30] The new political sublanguage introduced by the Bolsheviks was itself akin to an alien dialect, and oral humor satirized it in ways similar to its treatment of the speech of non-Russians in ethnic jokes. Describing a later period, Maksim Krongauz characterized with particular succinctness the dichotomous nature of the Soviet-era linguistic landscape as a "diglossia" in which two parallel idioms—Russian and Soviet Russian—coexisted and served distinct communicative functions.[31]

Linguistic novelty—as the stories of Mikhail Zoshchenko from the 1920s illustrate[32]—was certainly a major impetus for early Soviet popular humor. The *anekdot* provided an ironic running commentary on the new, often opaque, verbal environment and satirized the state's enthusiastic revisions of the language:

> Soon after the death of Lenin, the State Publishing House issues a popular guide to astronomy. Krupskaia [Lenin's widow], who holds the post of literary censor regarding sociopolitical questions, reads the book and writes a letter to the publishers: "Comrades, I draw your attention to an inadmissible political blunder. I suggest that you immediately recall this book and issue a corrected edition in accordance with the decision by the People's Commissariat to change the name of Jupiter to JuLenin."[33]

The acronym was an especially prolific new form. There is a whole subgenre devoted to it: the *rasshifrovka* (decoded acronym),[34] which is well represented in an anthology of early post-Revolutionary *anekdoty* published in Munich in 1951 by one Evgenii Andreevich:

VKP(b) [*Vsesoiuznaia Kommunisticheskaia Partiia (bol'shevikov)*] [All-Union Communist Party (of Bolsheviks)]—Vory [Thieves], Kaznokrady [Embezzlers], Prostitutki [Prostitutes] [the "b" in parentheses clarifies the third, foreign word (implying *bliad'*, "whore")].[35]

The politicization of everyday words and everyday acts was also a common motif, especially in *anekdoty* that rely on political puns:

"The sun has set! [*Solnyshko selo!*]"
"Now, that's just too much!"[36]

The state's aggressive manipulation of symbols, which shows an appreciation for the mythological power of naming, was represented in *anekdoty* as a compensatory impulse for the insatiability of the state's desire to control every aspect of the physical environment. Here are two early Soviet *anekdoty* that acknowledge both the state's elemental aspirations and its use of signifying systems to compensate for an inadequate reality:

Word has it in Moscow that the People's Commissar has ordered that, due to the fuel shortage, all thermometers are to be set four degrees higher.[37]

[Politburo member] Kalinin is giving a speech about industrialization and animatedly describing for his audience the new twenty-story skyscrapers recently built on Karl Marx Street in Kharkov. Suddenly one of the listeners interrupts him: "Comrade Kalinin, I am from Kharkov. I walk down that street nearly every day, but I have not seen any skyscrapers!" "Comrade," replies Kalinin, "if you read newspapers instead of loitering on the streets, you'd find out what's going on in your city. . . ."[38]

Any unfamiliar sensory stimulus, including a purely visual one, could be ironically attributed to the new status quo:

An old woman is looking at a camel: "Those Bolsheviks! Look what they did to this horse! It's shameful!"[39]

Oral culture also registered changes in the actual physical environment and the circadian rhythms of city life. The traditional categories of control under which rural Russians had lived were temporal—the church calendar and the seasons of the year—and folk expression was intimately bound to people's awareness of those cyclical forces. The urbanized folk found themselves in new circumstances that changed not only their physical behavior, but also the ways in which they produced, performed, and consumed cultural forms. Sergei Nekliudov wrote:

> In the city, human dependence on natural conditions (first and foremost the change of seasons) steadily diminishes, leading to the obsolescence of calendar- and ritual-based folklore, to the desemanticization, deritualization, and temporal displacement of holidays, to their transformation into "ceremonial" forms, [. . .] and to the decisive predominance of verbal over nonverbal forms.[40]

With time the types of external conditions affecting human life (and thus reflected in cultural forms) changed to include "unnatural" phenomena such as crime and living conditions. Urbanization and ideologization, moreover, transformed Russian society into one in which spatial categories were central (living space, residency concerns, daily traversal of the distance between home and work, and so on). Popular expressions of the carnival impulse, too, were determined in the city (and under conditions of censorship) by spatial considerations rather than temporal constraints (feast days defined by the church calendar or older festivals organized according to the change of seasons).

In representations of reality as itself a fairy tale, time meant little, since carnival time was permanent.[41] So actual carnivalesque impulses were given vent in spatially defined contexts. Sergei Averintsev criticized Mikhail Bakhtin for overstating the freedom inherent in traditional carnival behavior by understating the strict temporal limits on the carnival impulse: "If freedom regulates itself according to the church calendar and seeks out a place for itself within the conventional system, its status as freedom is subject to clarification."[42] The spatial carnival of the Soviet period is arguably closer to Averintsev's notion of freedom, but in his criticism he misses an important point about carnival: the permission of the authorities does not diminish the carnivalesque; that permission is an intrinsic part of it. For this reason, it is perhaps not accurate to speak of "Soviet carnival" for the entire Soviet period. For stretches of Soviet history, the officially affirmed rule suspension characteristic of carnival simply did not happen.

Stalin-era jokes reflected the unpredictable state violence in ways that demonstrate the joke's status as a modern-day descendant of traditional folklore, one of the primeval functions of which, again, was to articulate responses to natural and supernatural forces at the mercy of which the folk lived. One canonical *anekdot* from the 1930s in particular reflects the new atmosphere and the new hierarchy of catastrophes:

At midnight in a bourgeois apartment there is a loud knocking at the door. The mistress of the house goes into hysterics and starts stuffing letters behind the wallpaper and under the couch upholstery, and even tries to swallow some papers. . . . Suddenly someone on the stairway outside the door whispers through the keyhole: "Madame! Don't be afraid . . . we're not here to search your place; we're just burglars."[43]

Like the natural elements, the new controlling forces could be treacherously unpredictable:

Stalin is giving a speech. Suddenly someone in the audience sneezes. "Who sneezed?" demands Stalin. (Silence.) "First row, stand up. Take them out and shoot them all!" (Thunderous applause.) "Who sneezed?" (Silence.) "Second row, stand up. Take them out and shoot them all!" (A long ovation.) "Who sneezed?" (Silence.) "Third row, stand up. To the firing squads!" (Thunderous applause, the whole audience is on its feet, shouts of "Glory to the Great Stalin!") "Now, who sneezed?" At the back of the audience, a man says "I did! I did!" and collapses in tears. Stalin looks at him and says: "Gesundheit, comrade!"[44]

Three gulag inmates are telling each other what they're in for. The first one says: "I was five minutes late for work, and they charged me with sabotage." The second says: "For me it was just the opposite: I was five minutes early for work, and they charged me with espionage." The third one says: "I got to work right on time, and they charged me with harming the Soviet economy by acquiring a watch in a capitalist country."

Anekdoty specifically about arrests and purges are not as numerous as one might expect.[45] More common were jokes about Soviet life more generally. A subgenre that is well represented in collections of early Soviet *anekdoty* (Karachevtsev, Andreevich) is what might be called the reverse riddle, in which the answer to the question—a simile—is announced before its relevance to the question posed is explained. Such texts indicate a search for familiar images and conceptual categories with which to characterize the new social reality:

"What do you think of Soviet power?" First response: "It's like my wife—I don't love her, but I tolerate her." Second response: "It's like my wife—I kind of love her, I'm kind of afraid of her, and I desperately want a different one."[46]

"How's life under Soviet power?" First response: "Like riding the bus: some people are sitting [in prison], the rest are shaking." Second response: "Like being on an ocean liner: vast horizons, nausea, and you can't leave."[47]

Tradition and Contemporaneity

Later, this type of *anekdot* would be used to express a more diachronic perspective on Soviet history:

> Under Lenin it was like being in a tunnel: darkness all around and light ahead. Under Stalin it was like riding the bus: one driver, half are "sitting," the rest are shaking. Under Khrushchev it was like being at the circus: one man speaks, everyone else laughs. Under Brezhnev it's like being at the movies: everyone is waiting for the show to end.

The extensive use of metaphor in official discourse, documented by Latynina, gave such satirical texts an additional parodic connotation, thereby enhancing their commentarial potency.

Let us return to the image of leaders. The concept of a cult of personality smacks of archaic ritual and secret wisdom handed down by a dread anthropomorphic embodiment of a value system. The will of the leader and the unanimity of the collective trump other values in the system, especially faith in empirical knowledge:

> Stalin loses his pipe. Beriia opens an investigation. By that evening, 100 people have been arrested, but in the morning, a maid finds the pipe. Stalin calls Beriia: "Lavrentii, the pipe's been found." "All right, Comrade Stalin, but everyone I arrested, except one, have confessed to stealing the pipe." "Except one? Continue the investigation."

It is appropriate that the Stalin cult was demystified by Khrushchev, a figure who resembled the prosaic folk archetypes that populate tales and *anekdoty* rather than a mythic demiurge, an epic knight, or an anointed ruler. If the image of Stalin in folklore (as opposed to fakelore) was that of a sinister, supernatural creature and drew on traditional images of folk devils (or later, historical-*anekdot* depictions of omnipotent tsars), the *anekdot*-al Khrushchev was cast from a different die, the archetypal bumpkin:

> Khrushchev writes his own speech before an appearance and shows it to a friend: "None of those bootlickers will tell me the truth if there's something wrong with it." His friend reads it and says: "I'll be blunt, Nikita. You made two mistakes. 'Shit-ass' [*zasranets*] should be hyphenated, and 'up yours' [*v zhopu*] is written as two separate words."[48]

Khrushchev's simple earthiness is portrayed as comic,[49] especially in contrast to the larger-than-life historic figures who preceded him in the Kremlin:[50]

55

Khrushchev dies. He is being escorted along a corridor in the afterworld. There is a sign on one of the doors that reads "Lenin TC." "What does TC mean?" he asks. "Lenin, Theorist of Communism." Another door reads "Stalin TC." "And that one?" "Stalin, Tyrant of Communism." Finally they reach a door that reads "Khrushchev TC." "And what am I?" "You're Khrushchev, The Corn-babbler."[51]

Khrushchev was initially rewarded by the vox populi with a few specimens of that rarest of verbal forms, the sympathetic political joke:

A question to Radio Armenia: "Is it possible to write *stal'* (steel)?" "Yes, but *khru-stal'* is better."[52]

Before his speech denouncing the cult of personality, Khrushchev ran into the Mausoleum to check Stalin for a pulse.

At the Twentieth Party Congress, Khrushchev is handed a written question from the audience: "Where were you when Stalin was in power?" Khrushchev asks, "Who wrote this?" Nobody answers. "That's where I was, too," he says.

After the unsuccessful coup against Khrushchev by the "anti-Party group," Kaganovich calls him: "Comrade Khrushchev, please don't have me shot." "Comrade Kaganovich, your words show what kind of measures you would have taken if you had won. We are not going to take such measures."

The *anekdot* was a sharp tool for the exposure of the basic incongruity inherent in the manifest ideology because it thrives on incongruity, paradox, and jolting eclecticism. The myth, on the other hand, relies on unity, unanimity, and consistency of vision and register. The clash between the ludic and lofty modes of cultural expression would dominate evolution of the *anekdot* for decades. Khrushchev briefly tapped into the discursive stream ruled by the former mode (ritualistic purgative laughter), but when it became clear he was a servant of the latter neomythological mode, he squandered whatever folk credibility he had earned.

A question to Radio Armenia: "What is Khrushchev's hairstyle called?" "Harvest of 1963."

Khrushchev arrives at the Manezh exhibit, accompanied by undercover KGB agents posing as art scholars. "What sort of abstractionism is this?! It's a naked

broad lying there like some kind of lazy hussy." "That's a painting by Falk."
"And what is that, the ass with ears?" "That's a mirror, Nikita Sergeevich."

The Soviet personality cult was resurrected under Brezhnev, whom
the *anekdot* could portray as Stalin in disguise:

"A joke's a joke, but that's enough!" says Brezhnev, moving his eyebrows back
down to his upper lip.

Or as an aspiring Lenin:

"Comrade Brezhnev, you've become General Secretary. How should we ad-
dress you now?" "You can just call me Il'ich."[53]

Brezhnev says, "After I die I would like to lie in the Mausoleum. Start working on it." The next day, on the Mausoleum there are two dots above the *e* in
"Lenin."[54]

Again, a key reason for the efficacy of folk humor for commentary
on political myth (especially about leaders) is the fact that both types of
discourse are ultimately rooted in a common tradition: oral culture. Folk
humor is a part of the cultural realm that myth must leave unsaid: the profane, the carnivalesque, the physiological, the low. Political *anekdoty,* then,
are in a sense meta-folkloric. Iurii Borev called them anti-myths,[55] although
they might also be characterized as ironic, corrective myths, like the folk
explanation for the Russian Revolution cited earlier ("the peasants have so-
bered up"). That *anekdot* tells a story of origins based on knowledge—that
peasants are inclined to drink and can in fact be rather conservative ("why
was the tsar deposed?")—for which state creation myths had no place. The
question inherent in such texts is this: if the Revolution was carried out by
and for the common folk, why do the Revolution's verbal manifestations eschew essential elements of folk discourse in favor of other formations that
are associated with the other end of the social and stylistic hierarchy?[56] The
answer, which may be obvious from a Sovietological perspective, in fact lies
in that same realm of the ever-present determining unsaid of political mythology. The very question, once posed, is a threat to that mythology.[57]
Soviet discourse, like other political discourse, was particularly invested
in epic modes of speech. Walter Ong wrote that Soviet political clichés such
as "enemy of the people" or "capitalist warmongers" are "residual formulary
essentials of oral thought processes" and that the phrase "Glorious Revolution of October 25" is an "epithetic formula" that effects an "obligatory

stabilization, [as did] Homeric epithetic formulas 'wise Nestor' or 'clever Odysseus.'"[58] The use of epic language was a constant source of parody for the *anekdot,* which itself has been characterized—from as early as 1927—as an "industrial, urban 'epic.'"[59] Shaitanov wrote that the *anekdot* "is opposed, yet akin, to the epic,"[60] a clue to its capacity for elaborating connections by exploiting contradictions (and vice versa). Leonid Stolovich tapped into that same capacity to productively merge tradition and contemporaneity when he stated that "under the totalitarian regime, the *anekdot* took on the function not only of a newspaper, but also of an epic."[61] Indeed, the *anekdot* corpus might be said collectively to comprise an enormous epic cycle, as that corpus is indifferent to the laws of chronological, historical time; in *anekdoty,* long-dead heroes regularly consort with the current leader or engage in similarly anachronistic behavior in the service of drawing metaphorical or other connections.

The subgeneric division between political *anekdoty* and *anekdoty* about daily life (noted in the 1926 encyclopedia article[62] cited in the Introduction) became increasingly blurred as that life became more and more politicized. In another encounter between tradition and contemporaneity, the politicization of the lower classes had brought into contact two traditionally separate spheres of human activity and thought: folk culture and political consciousness.[63] The (omni)presence of political and ideological formations was itself a novelty that provoked a variety of satirical responses. The hyperpoliticized abstract tone of state discourse, for example, was satirized for its neglect or ignorance of more natural categories of human existence:

> Lenin and Krupskaia are lying in bed. Lenin says: "Nadia, let's do it one more time." "No way, Volodia. Feliks Edmundovich [Dzerzhinskii] is sleeping on the other side of the wall. It wouldn't be right." "Come on, Nadia, it was so good last time." "Volodia, Feliks Edmundovich will hear us! We can't!" "Please, Nadia, we can do it quietly." "Oh, all right." They sing in unison: "Stoke the bonfires, blue nights. We're pioneers, children of the workers . . ."

> An American says, "Wow, listen to what happened in the States! A man caught his wife with her lover and killed the guy!" A Frenchman says, "Well, in France there was also a man who caught his wife with her lover, and he shot ten people!" The Russian says, "We had a guy who turned the whole country on its head because his brother was executed, and we still can't sort it out."

A related motif was the state's tendency to politicize those biological categories to a ridiculous degree:

The 1930s. A peasant man is filling out a questionnaire, which asks: "How do you sleep with your wife?" What to write? If he writes "on the left," they'll get him for leftist tendencies. "On the right," he'll be pegged as a rightist. "On top," and they'll accuse him of lording it over the masses. "On the bottom," of sucking up to the masses. So he writes, "I sleep alone and masturbate," and they give him a ten-year sentence "for associating with a *kulak* (double entendre meaning both a well-off peasant and a fist) and wasting surplus seed."

In a converse impulse, political speech was abducted from the sphere of collective lofty myth into the individualistic and crude realm of the *anek-dot,* for instance in the following joke that circulated in 1922:

A young Red Army soldier is assigned to Lenin, who tells him: "Wake me up at seven sharp, brother." "Yes, sir, your . . ." Morning arrives. The soldier goes to the door. Quarter to seven. How should he wake Lenin? He whispers: "Your Eminence . . . Mister Lenin . . . No, not Eminence . . . Your Excellency . . . No, dammit. What sort of Excellency could he be, with the proletariat. Comrade? No, where do I get off calling him my comrade! Your . . . Cripes! It's seven o'clock!" The soldier rushes to the door, but he still doesn't know what to call him. So he shouts at the top of his lungs: "Arise, O curse-branded, Arise!"[64]

While the *anekdot* flaunted its symbiosis with other texts (such as the "Internationale"), the compositional and stylistic logic of official verbal production demanded concealment, suppression, or preemptive denial of (through nonreference to) the possibility of alternative discourse. This is not to say that official texts ignored two-way exchange as a model of communication; indeed, dialogue between the Party (or its embodiment, the Leader) and the People was a format used in official texts of all kinds. Explications of the Party's position on a particular subject often took the form of a response to a question from the public, "proof" of an ongoing exchange of ideas between benefactor and beneficiary, teacher and learner, father and child.[65] The Radio Armenia cycle (canonical example: A listener asks: "What is the difference between capitalism and socialism?" Radio Armenia answers: "Under capitalism, man exploits man. Under socialism, it's just the opposite") is the most sustained engagement of this communicative model, but the broader motif of a brief logical or verbal or behavioral duel between subject and power is ubiquitous in the *anekdot* corpus. For example:

A telegram: "To Lenin, the Kremlin, Moscow. Comrade Lenin, I request material assistance. Ivanov." They summon Ivanov to the KGB: "Have you lost your mind? Lenin died long ago." "It's always the same with you people. When you need him, he 'lives eternally,' but when I need him, he 'died long ago.'"

Meetings and conversations between leaders and citizens were a common trope in socialist-realist literature, film, and art. The many *anekdoty* that depict encounters between anonymous ordinary citizens and political or military figures, as well as those in which state discourse (a leader's words, Party slogans, quotations from official texts) is contaminated via conflation with popular discourse, are, again, not only satirical commentaries on the content of state ideology, but also parodies of the state's model of harmonious state-popular dialogue.

THE OMNIVOROUS *ANEKDOT*

Anekdot analysts and commentators of all stripes (from scholars to popular journalists) are fond of using metaphors to describe the genre and its place in Soviet culture. Often such metaphors refer to the omnibus scope of the *anekdot,* to its capacity to represent and/or comment on virtually any aspect or sphere of life, without exception or taboo. Enrid Alaev, for example, called the *anekdot* a "people's encyclopedia."[66] Siniavskii referred to the genre as a "spore [. . .] containing a model of reality in its entirety" (compare this image with Pertsov's seed metaphor cited previously) and also likened it to the periodic table and to "an endless chain [that] encompasses every existing and potential human condition on earth."[67] In the introduction to their impressive collection *Sovetskii soiuz v zerkale politicheskogo anekdota* (The Soviet Union in the Mirror of the Political *Anekdot*), Shturman and Tiktin wrote that one of the genre's organizing principles is the "absence of [a single] personality, theme or situation that [is not subject] to criticism," that it is marked by "an allness [*vseobshchnost'*] of skepticism and nihilism, an all-penetrating [*vsepronikaiushchee*] and all-encompassing [*vseob"emliushchee*] negation."[68] While I find the engagement of "personalities, themes, and situations" in the *anekdot* to be more nuanced, I appreciate the intertextuality of Shturman and Tiktin's use, three times in one short sentence, of the totalizing prefix "all-" [*vse-*], which is reminiscent of the ubiquitous Soviet-era adjective *vsesoiuznyi* meaning "all-Union" (and its current heir, *vserossiiskii* [all-Russian]).

Indeed, the exhaustive reach of the *anekdot* itself represented an implicit (and more successful) rehearsal of the existential totalism to which state ideology aspired. Caroline Humphrey wrote that Soviet ideology was "intended to deal with virtually every aspect of life, and enormous effort [was] devoted to seeing there [was] an ideological instruction for every social phenomenon."[69] Aleksandr Zinov'ev referred to Communism's "eagerness to penetrate every possible nook and cranny, [. . .] to control its environment and make it identical to itself."[70] Note Zinov'ev's use of the phrase "control its environment," recalling the primordial link between the physical surroundings and the production of verbal culture, and the state's awareness of that link.

Although such literal totalitarianism is most closely associated with the Stalin years, the state periodically and publicly reaffirmed the omnirelevance of the ideology even after Stalin's death, right up to the end of Soviet power. For example, the criterion of *ideinost'* (idea-mindedness)—which stipulated that all cultural texts must reflect the primary ideological views and policies of the Party—was added to the list of Socialist Realism's constituent features at the Second Congress of the Soviet Writers' Union in December 1954. The Third Party Program, adopted at the Twenty-First Party Congress in 1961,[71] is a "constructive generalization of the experience of Socialist development" that announces triumphantly that the Party has "extended its guiding influence to all spheres of social life."[72]

The universalist ambition—particularly in the absence of the gulag—ultimately subverted the ideology's credibility and authority by "despecifying" it.[73] Semantically diffuse and deflated, the omnibus aspirations of ideological oversight were increasingly manifested in mechanistic, ceremonial performances that nonetheless retained the neomythological structuring logic elaborated at the dawn of the Soviet age.

The mechanistic nature of the ideology is often depicted in the person of the ideology's standard-bearer, Brezhnev, who frequently appears as an automaton, a mannequin, or a zombie:

> Brezhnev arrives in Bonn. His plane is met by an honor guard with an orchestra. But Leonid Il'ich does not notice any of it and walks purposefully toward a flower bed, puts a clump of soil in his pocket, gets right back on the plane, and heads back to the motherland. Afterward, the Soviet Ministry of Foreign Affairs sends the following note to Germany: "We apologize for the misunderstanding. Instead of loading the Peace program into the head of the leader, we mistakenly loaded the Lunar Module program."

> TASS reports: "Today there was an assassination attempt on the General Secretary of the CPSU Central Committee and Chair of the Presidium of the Supreme Soviet of the USSR, Leonid Il'ich Brezhnev. The bullet struck him in the forehead, ricocheted, and killed the driver. Leonid Il'ich was not injured."

> Brezhnev is giving a speech over the radio: "I was recently informed [pause] that everyone believes [pause] that a dummy rides in the car in my

place. . . . I hereby officially announce [pause] that it is I who ride in place of the dummy."

Brezhnev is dead. But his body [*telo*] lives on.[74]

As textual production continued to stake ideological claims in and/or take credit for every area of individual and collective behavior in the country, the connotative scope of *anekdoty* changed accordingly, reaching a point where virtually any type of *anekdot*—from leader cycles to jokes about the most mundane and superficially apolitical aspects of everyday life—implicitly engaged the obtaining models of reality in critical dialogue.

Transitional social, economic, and political periods, wrote one cultural analyst, engender "new forms of cultural and literary expression that embody, in more or less thematically explicit and formally articulated ways, the social forces contending for power in the world."[75] A discursively potent embodiment of underlying processes can also occur through the agency of existing forms, particularly if those forms resonate with the overall cultural atmosphere, i.e., with the various circumstances informing the use of symbols in the society. The *anekdot* has served as such a resonance chamber at different moments in Russo-Soviet history, including—as I have discussed here—the early twentieth century, when demographic, technological, and ideological changes provoked equally striking changes in popular verbal culture. It was not until the 1960s, however, that the links of the *anekdot* with latent and manifest textual and extratextual formations alike became so extensive that it resulted in a golden age for the genre and made it a vanguard form of popular expression. During the so-called Stagnation period—which is the focus of the following chapter—the engagement of the *anekdot* with prevailing myths continued, but that engagement acquired a new significance and new forms when the use of verbal and other kinds of symbols came to dominate the range of ideological behavior in the country. The phenomenological blind spots of state myth left the state vulnerable to constant outflanking by the *anekdot*, with its authentically panoramic scope, especially as the battlefield of ideas shifted more and more to the purely textual realm.

Chapter Three

The *Anekdot* and Stagnation

> Where there is a common sense, there will be a
> common nonsense.
> —Susan Stewart

JOURNALIST Dmitrii Makarov repeated an apocryphal account in 1999 that the KGB had conducted an experiment in the 1970s to determine the speed at which *anekdoty* circulated. It reportedly found that a joke could discursively saturate a city the size of Moscow within six to eight hours.[1] Makarov offers no evidence for this satisfying bit of apocrypha, but the mere existence of such legends indicates the lasting view of the importance of the *anekdot*. It is abundantly clear that a particular convergence of sociocultural and political circumstances in the 1960s and 1970s abetted its steady rise to prominence and ubiquity in the quotidian speech of Soviet city-dwellers.

The genre's storied heyday coincided with the years known in retrospect as the era of Stagnation.[2] Looking back in 1990, scholar Miron Petrovskii coined a new term in declaring the unofficial culture of the recently bygone period "*anekdot*-centric," and he wrote that the entire society had been composed of "potential *anekdot* tellers and listeners."[3] The genre was recognized as a leading verbal symptom of the age even (or especially) by those in the top echelons of political power. As he tried to "destagnate" both the economy and the Communist Party's credibility, Mikhail Gorbachev was warned by a deputy, "If we don't keep our promises, the people will go back to the bottle [*v stakan*] and the *anekdot*."[4] Gorbachev himself (a famous teetotaler) reportedly stated on television in 1989 that "*anekdoty* were always our salvation."[5]

Yet the view of the *anekdot* as merely the latest symbolic opiate for a desperate and disillusioned population, or as a salvatory recourse in the absence of other expressive outlets, is overly focused on discursive negative space. It neglects the genre's immanent appeal as a form of popular expression and entertainment and as the national pastime of an informed citizenry, and thus it amounts to a fundamentally incomplete insight. At its peak, the *anekdot* enjoyed the status of a carnivalesque genre-laureate in the organic hierarchy of popular discursive forms that had developed concomitantly with the state-prescribed *ars poetica*. The opiate view also neglects the crucial interactions of the *anekdot* with other cultural forms. An important reason for the genre's storied fecundity was its capacity to outflank, mimic, debunk, deconstruct, and otherwise critically engage other genres and texts of all stripes and at all presumed points on the spectrum from resistance to complicity (or from unofficial to official). The *anekdot* was able to so function in large part because of the number and variety of contact points between its distinctive generic features and the constituent epochal features that defined the cultural moment and informed textual production therein. This chapter is a survey of those contact points and a continuation of my discussion of *anekdot* culture's nuanced apprehension of the structuring logic of other strategies of representation.

The putative KGB-confirmed speed with which the *anekdot* passed from person to person was matched by the genre's appearance in and mobility among other forms of expression, including prose fiction, poetry, film, and songs.[6] The genre's brevity and formal malleability enhanced this tendency to itinerancy. In many respects, the *anekdot* is a genre-picaro. In its functions and contexts, it straddles several generic categories, including *publitsistika* (essayistic current-affairs journalism), small oral genres such as the toast and the rumor, and the language of the variety stage. Kurganov dubbed it a *zhanr-brodiaga* (wandering genre). Sounding ironically like an ideologue doing battle with a social ill, Kurganov also likened the *anekdot* to a "parasitic insect" that can only survive by feeding off of larger "organisms." He went on to say, however, that the *anekdot* in fact does not so much feed off other genres, but feeds them, "enriches and refreshes" them,[7] thus rescuing the concept of agency for a genre often considered "merely" responsive.[8] The genre does both, of course—feeds off of and feeds—in a symbiosis that suggests an integral, even privileged, connection to the underlying symbolic reservoir of Soviet culture.

Kurganov's point also implicitly supports the view of the Stagnation era as a barren cultural desert, an environment in which mass culture was like a bland punch, unconsumable unless spiked with jiggers of irony. Yet while part of the status of the *anekdot* as a touchstone genre of the Soviet imperial twilight was its tendency to infiltrate other discourses that proved susceptible to "*anekdot*-ization" in various ways, the essential appeal of *anekdoty* based on mass-media texts was not so much compensatory as commentarial, as a kind of performed consumption, and—again—was far from limited to cycles grounded in popular entertainment. In this respect, the *anekdot* no doubt did make the purported desert a more hospitable environment for the cultural consumer, who otherwise was relegated to the role of passive, mute recipient of texts and images.

CULTURE-BEARING GENRES

The history of Soviet cultural production testifies to how different genres at different historical moments come to the fore as the popular means of choice for expressing inchoate values, priorities, and conflicts.[9] The fact that specific genres—and not only different topics of discourse—dominate particular cultural milieux suggests that the links between a verbal culture and its available referents need not be merely, or even primarily, semantic. The elevation of a genre to widespread acceptance and consumption by a cultural collective can be the result of various factors: (1) resonance between the genre's defining attributes (formal, pragmatic, thematic) and the latent material to be manifested; (2) dissonance between the genre and other extant manifestations of that material that are judged inadequate and thus deserving of critical attention; (3) the logistical potential for texts in the genre to reach a broad base of cultural consumers (a potential that was often limited in the USSR, for example, in the case of underground lyric poetry during the Stalin period or, in a very different way, auteur cinema during the 1960s, 1970s, and 1980s); and (4) the number and variety of functions (psychological, social, aesthetic) the genre fulfills for its consumers. Another such factor, of a somewhat different nature, is the extent to which the genre is championed and propagated by the state (a factor that can work both ways—that is, a genre can become popular precisely because it is taboo).

At times, the state-sanctioned range of genres in the USSR substantially coincided with the unofficial organic generic hierarchy: for example, nationalistic songs, literature, visual art, and even folk humor during the Great Patriotic War (World War II); lyric poetry and certain forms of youth culture at the height of the Thaw; and documentary film and *publitsistika* during perestroika. During such moments, popular sentiment and state ideological priorities shared constituent tropes. The episodes of apparent polar harmony were typically precipitated by a weakening of ideological supervision of cultural production by the Party, which had the wisdom to modify its cultural policies periodically for politically pragmatic reasons. In all three periods just mentioned, the liberalization of cultural policy was undertaken at least in part to give cultural producers (and consumers or "reproducers") creative latitude to express a newly emergent idea in the ruling ideology, with the ultimate goal of alleviating a crisis in, fortifying, and/or preserving that ideology. In the case of the Thaw, for example, the new values originating from the Party under Khrushchev were fundamentally aimed at reinvigorating the progressive socialist society after the anomalous reactionary Stalinist period. The new idea was de-Stalinization, with a concomitant adjustment of aesthetic emphasis from the epic to the lyrical, from the fathers to the sons (that is, to those who came of age after Stalin's death), and in certain limited respects from the masses to the individual. Even during perestroika, reformers hoped that the relaxation of intellectual and artistic prescriptions and proscriptions by the Party would help to rejuvenate a sociopolitical system in crisis,[10] thus preventing the People from once again resorting to the bottle and the *anekdot*.

Genres, of course, can serve just as readily (or more readily) as means of expressing collective resistance to a new policy turn. The emergence of the *anekdot* as the standard-bearing popular genre of the post-Thaw period reflected the popular disillusionment in the face of renewed quasi-Stalinist manipulation of cultural production, as well as renewed sociopolitical repression—though in a mostly nonlethal form—under Brezhnev.[11] The fact that what came to the fore was a humorous, folkloric genre—a combination of mode and medium that the state had discovered to be ideologically problematic decades earlier—indicated the end of the fragile accord between Party and populace. The transition from a palpable sense of optimism and enthusiasm on the part of citizens in the wake of de-Stalinization during the late 1950s to a widespread penchant for cynicism, irony, and satire by the late 1960s[12]—as well as a palpable reining in of artistic experimentation and variety in the mass media—gave the *anekdot* increasing cachet as a form of expression and entertainment.

The popular cynicism characteristic of Stagnation was in particularly stark contrast to the preceding period of enthusiasm and consensus, with its celebration of youth and especially its premium on sincerity and good humor. Vail' and Genis use the term *"vesel'e"* (joviality) to characterize the general public mood during the Thaw, a time when "official slogans coincided with popular mottos."[13] The heady enthusiasm of the Thaw made adaptation to the subsequent period of reactionism all the more complex a maneuver for the Soviet cultural consumer, who had to effect an intellectual and behavioral retreat from public *vesel'e* and sincere self-expression as the state itself retreated from reformism. To put it another way, the Thaw mentality lingered (festered?), but with ever fewer discursive outlets; Lev Anninskii contrasted the "open freedom" of the Thaw to the "secret freedom" of Stagnation.[14] The latter period saw a revised understanding of the concept of "public," a widespread formation of smaller collectives, and the emergence of more hermetic chronotopes, both within cultural texts (on the level of plot) and as the favored environments for cultural consumption itself. All of these changes affected the functionality of the *anekdot*.

The Stagnation years were followed by another period characterized by a significant measure of official-popular harmony: perestroika. The belief that Gorbachev's liberal policies were a continuation or a belated completion of Thaw-era reforms is one reason for the relative dearth of scholarly attention to Stagnation popular culture. That culture is considered by some to be merely the uninteresting product of an age of bitterness and falsity bookended by two periods of optimism and sincerity, a span of congealed time in which Russo-Soviet culture was in a state of suspended animation.[15] While such generalizations are unhelpfully broad, there is a definite sense that historical time itself had been suspended by the midpoint of Brezhnev's tenure, when even the official designation for the current period—the "era of developed socialism"[16]—implied with its passive participle a kind of open-ended bivouac in the relentlessly progressive march of Soviet history ("life in its revolutionary development").

Predictably, the popular image of the age was less positive; the numerous versions of the stopped-train *anekdot* acknowledge the omnipresent stagnancy of Soviet life using a common official metaphor, a locomotive, and imagine not only Brezhnev's response, but also that of his predecessors:

> Our locomotive races on! Suddenly it stops: the tracks ahead are broken. How do our leaders deal with the problem? Lenin: everyone goes out on a voluntary workday to fix the tracks. Stalin: shoot everyone in the first car, and have the second car shot if the rails aren't fixed by the next day. Khrushchev: pull up tracks behind the train and put them in front. Brezhnev: draw the curtains, shake the train as if it's moving, and keep announcing station stops.[17]

The image of announcing a sequence of stations while on a curtained stopped train is a shrewd metaphor for official strategies of representation that predate the Soviet period (recall Potemkin villages), one that Mikhail Epstein (after Jean Baudrillard) has dubbed "simulation."[18] The Soviet use of such phantom signifiers entailed not merely affixing a signifier to an absent signified, but also composing complex narrative signifiers to mask the myriad signs of a de facto temporal, historical stasis.

The popular image of Brezhnev himself commonly questioned his awareness of the passage of time; there are several *anekdoty* that begin by quoting the general secretary as he addresses the politburo following the death of one of its geriatric members: "Na pokhoronakh Suslova . . . kstati, gde on?" (At Suslov's funeral . . . by the way, where is he?). Another joke intimates just how deeply the concept of stasis was ingrained in the worldview of the political elite:

Brezhnev is playing with his grandson.
"What do you want to be when you grow up?"
"General secretary!"
"What do we need two general secretaries for?"

The creeping stagnation that ultimately became the label for an entire period of Soviet history, however, was not merely the result of the conservatism (or catatonia) of the geriatric Party leadership; the relative lull
in life-shattering historical cataclysms after decades of war and revolution
nourished the Stagnation zeitgeist almost as fundamentally as did the state's
antiprogressivism and rollback of Thaw-era reforms. Temporal tropes were
in flux; a general sense of historical teleology and/or eschatology was giving
way to a common perception of time as cyclical, like the workweek or the
television schedule (not to mention the *anekdot*). In this respect, a genre
that in its cyclicity and scope resembles a latter-day parodic form of epic
seems an appropriate medium for a description of the age, considering that
epic time, too, is static.

Anatoly Vishevsky identified the definitive characteristics of the period
as "the strengthening of the bureaucratic apparatus [another mechanism that
subverted the flow of time—SG] and [. . .] a dull and eventless routine in
art and everyday life."[19] Andrei Nemzer had a similar, if slightly more positive, spin on the Stagnation sociocultural environment, which he described
as a sort of posthistorical parodic idyll marked by an atmosphere of "tender
gloom [in which] it seemed that everything in this world (and especially in
this country) had already passed, and you could quietly live your own life (sav-
ing up for a car, reading *samizdat,* sipping port wine, or combining these and
other pleasant activities)."[20] One such pleasant activity was telling *anekdoty*
in small gatherings in homes, at universities or the workplace (often during
cigarette breaks), on trains, in food lines, and so on. The popularity of joke
telling—and the snowball effect an initial joke had among a group of *anekdot*
aficionados—led to the coinage of the term *"travit' anekdoty,"* meaning to
reel out or to feed out (as in a rope) *anekdoty.*[21] Reeling out *anekdoty* became one of the signal pastimes of urban life during Stagnation. The practice
of reeling evokes the generic heritage of the *anekdot* as a folkloric form in a
most primal sense. Oral forms such as the folktale and the folk song, as mentioned previously, were primarily winter or fallow genres,[22] means of passing
time when the exterior atmosphere precluded other activities or when there
was no pressing work to be done. The Soviet-era *anekdot* also implied the
presence of a hostile exterior atmosphere and thus preserved—in a modern urban way—the ritualistic significance of collective oral performance.

The ways in which *anekdot* telling is typically initiated are constitutive elements of its generic nature. The first *anekdot* is most commonly

articulated in one of two communicative contexts: either a participant in a conversation makes an associative link between something in his own or an interlocutor's speech and an *anekdot* in his personal repertoire, or a new or *svezhii* (fresh) *anekdot* is explicitly offered or solicited, often during the phatic phase of the conversation.[23] The ensuing conversation then takes the form of a chain of *anekdoty;* the participants in the conversation begin to reel out *anekdoty* in turns.[24] The exaggerated closure of each *anekdot*—the punch line—is a clear marker of the end of a particular utterance and the expectation of one in response: laughter and another *anekdot.*

The ritual aspects of *anekdot* culture had a subtle parodic significance. Krongauz has referred to official discursive performances as "verbal rituals,"[25] a point that suggests a functional affinity between the *anekdot* and one of its aboveground discursive counterparts.[26] Nekliudov has pointed out that a better term for the phenomenon Krongauz referred to as "ritual" would be "ceremony," since as an anthropological/folkloristic term, ritual denotes something of genuine and profound meaning, while ceremony refers to the now-empty shell that occupies the discursive location of a former ritual (Nekliudov, personal communication, March 1999).[27] Moreover, ritual has a temporal element, an implication of passage from one stage to the next, that was absent in the atemporal environment of the Brezhnevian USSR, which privileged rites of stasis over rites of passage.

The well-documented public mood of the Brezhnev period notwithstanding, the links between the *anekdot* and the Stagnation environment as a cultural chronotope are by no means limited to the genre's capacity for parody and ironic expression. The retreat of cultural consumers from the Thaw's public settings (poetry "concerts," youth festivals, cafés, and so on) to private activities (reading *samizdat,* attending intimate gatherings in apartments, and especially watching television) also contributed to the genre's florescence. In this regard, it is worth recalling that among the generic ancestors of the *anekdot* is an eighteenth- and nineteenth-century salon genre. The very nature (chronotopic circumstances) of popular cultural consumption and the range of genres consumed by the populace at a given moment are mutually influential. The insular gatherings characteristic of the Brezhnev period (like the intimate circles of urban intellectuals in Pushkin's St. Petersburg) were highly amenable to *anekdot* telling as a social practice. The individual cellular collectives of the Stagnation era together constituted a larger, more abstract popular collective whose cohesion was defined by the uniformity of its members' life experiences and also by their common exposure—and response—to mass-media texts.

Although there are certainly causal links between the Soviet citizenry's disillusionment with public forms of cultural expression and that citizenry's cocooning impulse, the latter tendency was not exclusively a consequence of the former. Television ownership boomed in the 1960s,[28] a development that also influenced the thematic emphases of the *anekdot*, which increasingly drew on (primarily visual) mass-media texts for its source material. Several jokes explicitly acknowledge the role of the mass media in contemporary Soviet life:

"Is it true that under Communism we'll be able to order food by telephone?"
"Yes, but it will be delivered by television."

"They announced on the radio that there is a surplus of food in the country, but our refrigerator is empty. What gives?"
"Plug your refrigerator into your radio receiver."

The state adds a fourth television channel. On the day it begins broadcasting, a citizen turns on channel one and sees Brezhnev giving a speech. He switches to channel two: Brezhnev again. Brezhnev on channel three, as well. The citizen switches to channel four and sees a KGB colonel wagging his finger and saying: "keep going, one more click!"

The extremely standardized familiarity with cultural texts stands in contrast to the more politicized "common knowledge" of previous periods of Soviet history, especially the Stalin years.[29] The citizen's position vis-à-vis the state, obviously, had changed with the end of Stalinism, and it continued to evolve. K. N. Rogov wrote, "The relationship to the political regime, to social 'reality,' became an existentialist problem"[30]—that is, a question not merely of one's own physical safety or professional security, but a philosophical and moral issue, specifically in the aftermath of 1968. Rogov attributed the fundamental condition of the collective consciousness during Stagnation to the Soviet invasion of Czechoslovakia, but he wrote that the Soviet citizen's experience of the events in Prague was textual; the "text" *Tanki idut po Prage* (tanks roll through Prague) "became a direct cause of that complete break with 'reality,' that distinctive 'revolution of pessimism,' that in large measure defined the intellectual axis of the entire era."[31]

The dissident movement that began in earnest following the 1968 invasion relied substantially on unofficial textual responses: letters, petitions, periodicals, novels, and so on. A major indicator of the wider popular discursive relationship with the state, however, is the *anekdot*. Official state discourse acquired new semantic and pragmatic associations in the relatively "vegetarian" atmosphere of post-Stalinist Soviet society, which was in contrast to the "cannibalistic" excesses of the 1930s and the late 1940s to early 1950s.[32] Official statements of ideological goals and principles were no longer routinely

70

accompanied by institutionalized violence (that is, gulag sentences and executions). Rather, they remained largely in the linguistic symbolic realm.[33] The state no longer aggressively mutilated social reality to conform to the official model. The notorious persecutions of Boris Pasternak, Iosif Brodskii, Andrei Siniavskii and Iulii Daniel', Aleksandr Solzhenitsyn, and others notwithstanding, the Party's struggle after Stalin to harness the intelligentsia in the service of ideology was waged largely via ideological institutions (the culture industry, schools, mass media) rather than repressive organs (police and military).[34] More accurately, the sphere of activities of what once were strictly political organs (the KGB and the Central Committee, for example) was expanded to include the monitoring of cultural production for "ideological deviations."[35] This is another development traceable at least in part to the 1961 Party Program.

The popular response to state policies and behaviors likewise remained largely in the realm of the symbolic. The official idiom, which Krongauz labeled "Soviet Russian,"[36] was a form of discourse whose informative and ludic functions had been superseded by various ritualistic (or, Nekliudov would say, ceremonial) functions. Those functions included testing the loyalty of the members of the society (level of participation or nonparticipation in the ceremony) and "maintaining the illusion of public life or, more precisely, imitating it."[37] Such "dead language" (also called *langue du bois*, newspeak, and so on) is simultaneously enslaved to and severed from its referents; thus other nonsemantic functions—pragmatics, for instance—are vulnerable to satirical reinterpretation of precisely the sort favored by the *anekdot*. If popular and official speech were the two incompatible idioms in a diglossic society, the affinity of the *anekdot* for irony—a mode of discourse defined by an encounter between two incompatible idioms—made it an ideal medium for speaking about that diglossia.

The values the *anekdot* explicitly and implicitly expressed did not coincide, and indeed often directly conflicted, with the values informing Soviet dissident literature and art. Dissident pathos was frequently manifested in prosaic, explicit, testimonial accounts of the effects of totalitarianism on the individual psyche and body. What little irony there is to be found in such accounts is tendentious and directed at the regime and its servants. Dissident classics are personal in tone (first-person or quasidirect narrators being the norm). The *anekdot* implicitly parodied pathos and self-righteousness, occupying a discursive position outside both the official ideology and the morally indignant opposition. The writings of Solzhenitsyn and others sought to bear witness, to record and propagate the damning evidence of the official ideology's criminal illegitimacy. But the iconoclasm of such inscribed anti-Soviet sentiments was rarely effected on the level of textual form, and such artists did not eschew the uncritical use of models of discourse that the official ideology itself championed as highly appropriate for the expression of essential truths: the novel, the letter, the memoir, and so on.

If dissident culture represented a strategic opposition to the institutionalized ideology, the *anekdot* was an instrument for tactical engagement with specific performances of that ideology. *Anekdoty* were concrete manifestations of an abstract reservoir of irony at the core of popular sentiment.[38] The *anekdot* was the chief medium by which the public at large (not professional authors) participated in the overall irony pageant.

DISTINCTIVE FEATURES

Mikhail Bakhtin wrote that carnival "belongs to the borderline between art and life. In reality, it is life itself, but shaped according to a certain pattern of play."[39] The *anekdot* itself, as a genre, is a pattern of play that can be isolated generically by identifying its distinctive characteristics. As stated previously, the strategically broad and eclectic referential scope of the *anekdot* allowed it to outflank totalitarian aspirations to discursive omnipresence. Here I want to touch on features and devices of a more formal (that is, stylistic) nature. Several attributes of the *anekdot* found particular resonance (or equally productive dissonance) with more or less abstract qualities of the Stagnation cultural environment itself. Those attributes include orality, the punch line, brevity, third-person narration, present tense, and performativity. The two chapters that follow this one examine a defining feature of the *anekdot* that is more difficult to place on the venerable form-content continuum: reflexivity.

The rise of an oral genre like the *anekdot* as a medium for contrarianism in an environment in which inscribing nonconformist utterances was dangerous (although no longer a certain health risk) is hardly surprising. Whereas folklore in its most traditional sense is viewed as a phenomenon of a preliterate stage—that is, a corpus of texts that predate the onset of a literary heritage—the urban *anekdot* in the USSR partly *supplanted* a literary tradition; the creators and caretakers of that tradition by necessity turned to an oral medium.[40] After it did resort to such forms, the educated stratum assimilated other oral forms as well, such as rumors, urban legends, and anecdotes in the broader meaning of personal, oral testimonies of events and personalities.[41] Zhanna Dolgopolova discussed the *anekdot* as the oral counterpart to another form of unofficial culture: *samizdat* literature. However, Dolgopolova did not concur with Borev that the *anekdot* was an exclusively intellectual genre; whereas *samizdat* was largely associated with the intelligentsia, she wrote, the *anekdot* "operate[d] at all cultural levels."[42]

The genre is among the shortest oral forms. Abdullaeva compared the *anekdot* to a koan, giving its signature brevity a ritualistic, even mystical significance.[43] The succinctness of the genre also had a practical value: it made it portable, and thus, in an environment of censorship, safer than other forms for expressing certain things. The length of the genre is itself the subject of a series of jokes prefaced as "the shortest *anekdot*": *Kolobok povesilsia* (Kolobok hanged himself);[44] *Negr zagoraet* (a black man is sunbathing); *Evrei-dvornik* (a Jewish janitor); *Rodil* (he gave birth); *Odnazhdy vstretilis' utrom v trolleibuse dva chlena politbiuro* . . . (One morning two members of the politburo meet on the bus . . .), and so on. All of these examples distill the text to an essential comic core; the fact that in each case the effect is reliant on a paradoxical image or concept lends credence to incongruity theories of humor.

The allusive power of the *anekdot* relies not on an external ideology that states that all artistic images are stand-ins for the constituent parts of an ideal reality, but on the common knowledge shared by *anekdot* consumers. Soviet citizens' common experiences, again thanks to aggressive standardization in education and the mass media, were more common than usual, which made the shorthand style of the *anekdot* very potent. The enormous print runs of popular books, the high cinema attendance rate, and the ubiquity of televisions made knowledge of cultural codes during Stagnation very standardized indeed, which allowed for concentrated, concise *anekdoty* to carry a heavy semantic load. The signifying power of terse utterances was acknowledged in *anekdoty* themselves:

> Two writers are walking down the street when a "black Maria" passes by. One sighs. "I agree completely," says the other.

> A man is handing out leaflets at a busy pedestrian intersection. Passersby cautiously take them, quickly stuff them in their pockets, and pull them out to read them only when they've covered a bit of distance. Having done so, they come back, incensed:
> "There's nothing written on these! You're handing out blank leaflets!"
> "What's there to write? It's all perfectly clear anyway."

The brevity of the *anekdot* is responsible as well for the overall atomism of the genre, the piecemeal way in which it engages social life and culture. This characteristic of the joke allowed it to refute mainstream culture's sweeping generalities, privileging of high culture (at the expense of low/street/popular culture), and soft-focus perspective on social reality. The *anekdot* was a disassembled epic stored in the minds of its millions of performers and consumers, just as Anna Akhmatova's "Requiem" was preserved orally during the Stalin years by a group of her close friends, each of whom memorized a small section of the long poem.

The fact that a joke tends to be mono-episodic (although the episode frequently contains within it some sort of trebling) is also significant: the joke is a synchronic slice of time, a discrete chronotope, containing no suggestion of how the moment fits in the diachronic sweep of history. The *anekdot* rejects both origins and destinations/destinies in its implicit disregard for teleology. It defies us to explain how that moment is related to the glorious past or the radiant future. In fact, it constantly blurs time by placing figures from the past in contemporary settings or vice versa.

In another sense, though, *anekdoty* are impeccably teleological; the punch line is one of the most stable, reliable features of the genre. David Navon described the punch line as a "violation of expectations" and wrote that it is "probably crucial" to the joke genre that that violation "can be blamed on the absence, disuse or misuse of knowledge."[45] In this sense, the punch line represents an implicit travesty of Marxist teleology; a punch line is a crescendo based not on progression through stages, but on a sudden derailment of predictable forward progress. It is also a retrograde entropic subversion of the evolution from spontaneity to consciousness. Even on an apolitical level, the punch line jibes with Russian-language discourse; the important information in a Russian sentence typically comes at the end.

The capacity of the *anekdot* to outflank other forms is also apparent on the level of grammar: it is predominantly a third-person present-tense form of discourse. Pathos-based unofficial discourse was typically narrated in the first-person singular or by a quasidirect narrator, indicating its partial reliance on notions of martyrdom, testimony, and kenosis.[46] Official rhetoric favored the first-person plural (we the Party, we the socialist brotherhood) or second person (Workers of the world . . .): *we* are all in this together as a collective, but *you,* the People, need the guidance of *us,* the Party. The grammatical tense of the *anekdot* amplifies its topical contemporaneity. The entire past lay open for interpretation through the prism of the most recent authoritative version of history. The future was clear (and bright). The present, however, was more problematic and difficult to engineer and to represent. The Party's curious, paradoxical 1932 exhortation to "depict life in its revolutionary development" seems to demand a simultaneously synchronic ("depict life in") and diachronic ("development") approach to narrative. As Katerina Clark wrote, the synchronic texts of official culture (specifically, socialist-realist novels) were engineered to represent metaphorically the diachrony of Soviet history.[47] The *anekdot* seems to capture that paradoxical temporality: it describes an occurrence that never happened and never will happen but could feasibly happen at any moment. It is typically told in the present tense for a simpler reason, as well: it is a form of drama in which the sole performer—the *anekdot* teller—recites both the dialogue and the stage directions, which, in Russian as in other languages, are rendered in the present tense.

Although folklorists have traditionally categorized the *anekdot* as a variety of oral prose (more specifically as one of the genres of *neskazoch-naia proza* [nonfolktale prose]), it is clearly a dramatic genre. Shmeleva and Shmelev insightfully characterized it as a "production for a single actor."[48] James von Geldern and Richard Stites called *anekdoty* "the script in the private theater of friends in small groups."[49] The genre's fundamental dramatic nature is closely related to its orality. Smolitskaia examined as the key distinctive feature of the Soviet *anekdot* its *performativnost'* (performativity), that is, its status as an oral genre whose discursive habitat is defined by a single teller and one or more listeners who, in turn, themselves may take on the role of teller.[50] She further refined her definition by noting the status of the *anekdot* as the only exclusively oral genre of the Soviet period (by contrast, the performance of songs and *chastushki* was directly informed by written texts). Furthermore, the *anekdot* is a free-floating genre, as opposed to, say, toasts (tied to table culture) and certain wedding songs. It is encountered in a wide variety of everyday situations and locations. A joke-telling session can serve as a bonding mechanism for a group of people (on a train, at the beach) or to reinforce existing bonds, based on "common values" articulated in *anekdoty*, within an established collective.[51]

The purely communicative nature of the "mask" worn by the *anekdot* performer (speech + gestures + facial expressions) has associative links to two characteristic features of Stagnation-era popular culture and discourse. The first is the prevalence of verbal or behavioral disingenuousness, a phenomenon that contrasts directly with the oft-discussed sincerity of the Thaw period. Dissembling speech or other behaviors were often indistinguishable from good-faith participation in public discourse, and they were performed with such seamless irony or inner indifference that they entailed little risk of exposure for the insincere citizen in question. Yurchak discussed this phenomenon in terms of Peter Sloterdijk's notion of "cynical reason," viewing the *anekdot* as the marker of a behavioral middle path between the two undesirable extremes of Communist activism and overt anti-Communist dissidence.[52] The detached savvy irony exhibited by the *anekdot* teller allows him or her to reject the conformity of the activist without participating in the pathos-driven logic of the dissident. Recall the Dovlatov anecdote I cited earlier.

The naturalistic performance of an *anekdot* in the context of everyday communication has another link—this time a contrastive one—to the markedly theatrical professional nature of official entertainment during the Stagnation period. The frames surrounding popular-culture performances—especially comedic performances—were overdetermined in various ways.

The *estrada* theater, for example, which had been a cultural form open to amateur innovation during the Thaw, was reinstitutionalized in the 1970s as a highly professional form of entertainment with a robust fourth wall; plenty of costumes, makeup, and sets; and a highly marked space in which to be consumed (the distance between performers and audiences at the theater was enhanced in televised *estrada* concerts). There were multiple markers of difference between the discourse of vetted popular entertainment and everyday public discourse. The distance between these two realms was alternately bridged and blurred by one of Stagnation's most seminal performers and most recognizable cultural icons: Mikhail Zhvanetskii.

NASH CHELOVEK ONSTAGE: MIKHAIL ZHVANETSKII

Mary Douglas described the cultural figure of the joker as follows:

[A] privileged person who can say certain things in a certain way which confers immunity. . . . He has a firm hold on his own position in the structure and the disruptive comments which he makes upon it are in a sense the comments of the social group upon itself. He merely expresses consensus. Safe within the permitted range of attack, he lightens for everyone the oppressiveness of social reality, demonstrates its arbitrariness by making light of formality in general, and expresses the creative possibilities of the situation.[53]

Although Mikhail Zhvanetskii constantly tested the boundaries of the permitted range of attack, Douglas's description captured his role in late Soviet culture quite well. Despite his reputation as a latter-day heir to Mikhail Zoshchenko as Russia's satirist of record and the fact that his works have been the most fertile source of "winged words" since the early Soviet-era novels of Il'ia Il'f and Evgenii Petrov, Zhvanetskii has received scant attention from scholars. The neglect contrasts with the extensive commentary on other contemporary satirists such as Sergei Dovlatov, Fazil' Iskander, and Vladimir Voinovich. Zhvanetskii's association with television and the *estrada* tradition partly accounts for the lacuna, as does the aphoristic nature of his output, which seems to have inspired a similarly aphoristic (and anecdotal) response from most of those who *have* written about him.[54]

The links between Zhvanetskii's distinctive idiom and the *anekdot* are many. Briker and Vishevskii wrote that his short monologues and sketches are all "pieces of a single text,"[55] recalling characterizations of the *anekdot* as an epic in thousands of small pieces. Although he is a writer, he is better known as a performer of his own work (until recently,[56] most of his writing was seldom read from the page by anyone else). While preparing a series of concerts for NTV's televised anthology of his works in 1998, Zhvanetskii had to transcribe recordings of many pieces from the 1960s because there were no extant manuscripts or printed copies. He does, however, self-identify primarily as a writer—"Concerts are my print runs," he says—and he expressed surprise at being named a People's Performing Artist of Ukraine in 1999. It is surely Zhvanetskii's hybrid status as an *avtor-ispolnitel'* (author-performer) that most clearly distinguishes him from his literary contemporaries and predecessors and places him in the same discursive mode as the *anekdot*. Even a preliminary analysis of his style (like that of the *anekdot*) must incorporate both verbal and performative poetics.

Zhvanetskii's success in four sociocultural milieus—the Thaw, Stagnation, perestroika, and the post-Soviet period—raises a question: what was Zhvanetskii's place in Soviet culture and, considering his symbiotic relationship with the Soviet sociocultural environment, how did he manage to outlive that chronotope and remain both creative and successful? The *anekdot*, by contrast, declined precipitously in productivity and popularity when the Soviet Union collapsed (see chapter 6). The post-Stagnation divergence of two signature phenomena of the period warrants a closer look.

Zhvanetskii's creative origins lie in the amateur student theater movement that began soon after Stalin's death. Those theaters, especially the ones that specialized in comic forms like the monologue or the sketch, had to create their own repertoires virtually from scratch.[57] So by the time Zhvanetskii moved to Leningrad in 1964 to write for Arkadii Raikin's Leningrad Miniatures Theater, he had already cut his teeth writing short comic pieces for his fellow Odessites, the actors Roman Kartsev and Viktor Il'chenko.

In Zhvanetskii's output during his years with Raikin, the themes that would come to define his subsequent solo work are already present, though cast in a more broadly comedic tone than that of his later satire. The monologue V *grecheskom zale* (In the Greek Gallery, 1966), for example, is written from the perspective of a working-class man determined to spend his precious Sunday off in his preferred way—getting drunk, eating canned food from the can, reading the paper—even though his wife has dragged him to the Hermitage art museum. In *Defitsit* (Shortage, 1967), written in a similar style, the narrator defends the beneficial social effects of consumer-goods shortages, which, in the abundant future, he predicts, will themselves be a scarce, prized commodity to be shared behind closed doors with friends. Raikin softened the sociopolitical satirical potential of the piece by transforming it into ethnic *skaz:* he performed it with a Georgian accent.

In 1968, Zhvanetskii began to perform the material not used by Raikin at small readings in houses of scholars, houses of writers, and other such venues. At these events, Zhvanetskii read pieces that he knew skirted the boundaries of the permissible, but he felt that his affiliation with the legendary Raikin afforded him a degree of immunity. In 1969, however, Zhvanetskii heard that Raikin himself was becoming averse to the increasingly pessimistic, politically caustic tone of his satire, not to mention his moonlighting, and wanted him to leave the theater. Zhvanetskii was puzzled to hear this news and even treated it as a joke by slipping an ironic letter of resignation between the pages of the next manuscript he submitted. To Zhvanetskii's amazement and horror, Raikin took the letter seriously and signed it. The circumstances of their split—the mentor's literal interpretation of the disciple's ironic gesture—are emblematic of the ongoing generational shift. It was not merely Zhvanetskii's ironic worldview, however, that helped him thrive during his post-Raikin career in the changed cultural atmosphere. His chosen genre, his stage persona, his thematic range, and his textual style all resonated in the emergent cultural environment of the era of developed socialism. The forms of his atmospheric resonance, so to speak, are similar to those of the *anekdot.*

By the early 1970s, Zhvanetskii had perfected his trademark style: the cherubic author standing alone at the microphone pulling wrinkled marked-up pages out of a worn leather briefcase and reading them aloud in his fast-paced, Odessa-accented patter. From a theatrical point of view, Zhvanetskii performs "naked," without a costume or even a *kostium* (suit).[58] He further eschews stage artifice by reading directly from the page, a demonstrative rejection of stage discourse's customary illusion of extemporaneity (a device used even by Anglophone stand-up comics, with whom Zhvanetskii is sometimes compared). The constant presence of the written text in Zhvanetskii's hands calls to mind another iconic popular-culture image of reading from the page: Brezhnev jokes.[59] The image of the writer reading aloud from the page onstage also brings together the culture of letters and the orality of popular culture.

Another key element of Zhvanetskii's performance style is its rhythmic nature; Zhvanetskii has said that he composes in lines, like verse.[60] Many of his miniatures have a structure reminiscent of songs, especially those written in the reprise form, in which comic lines alternate with nonhumorous narrative.[61] Some of his most famous pieces are built around a refrain, usually a comic line such as *gde nachal'nik transportnogo tsekha?* (Where is the head of the transport guild?) from *Sobranie na likerovodochnom zavode* (Meeting at a Vodka Factory, 1970s[62]) or *v grecheskom zale, v grecheskom zale!* (In the Greek Gallery! In the Greek Gallery!) or *Normal'no, Grigorii! Otlichno, Konstantin!* (OK, Grigorii! Excellent, Konstantin! 1970s) from the monologue of the same name. These telegraphic lines, much like punch lines of certain *anekdoty*, have themselves become discrete bits of oral culture.

Commentators have compared Zhvanetskii's cultural significance to that of the so-called bard singers popular in the USSR beginning in the late

1950s. Andrei Bitov wrote that Zhvanetskii's place in Stagnation-era culture resembled that of his contemporary, Vladimir Vysotskii, whose voice could similarly be heard emanating from thousands of tape recorders in home-made copies.[63] And like Vysotskii, Zhvanetskii for years occupied a place on the boundary between official and unofficial culture. During the 1970s and early 1980s, Zhvanetskii himself was at times treated as a scarce commodity reserved for consumption by elites. Many of his concerts were closed events accessible only through *blat* (connections or clout). He once gave a command performance for the minister of communication in order to have a private phone line installed in his mother's apartment. His most exclusive performance was one he did over two-way radio for cosmonauts in orbit.

Despite categorizations of his texts as *rasskazy* (stories), Zhvanetskii's is essentially a dramatic genre. This is another way in which his work is closely related to the *anekdot*. Zhvanetskii is sometimes professionally categorized as an *artist razgovornogo zhanra* (performer of the conversational genre). The phenomenon of an aesthetic composition performed as everyday communication, as conversation, also evokes the *anekdot*. Vishevsky traces Zhvanetskii's style back to the *konferans'e* (emcee) of the heyday of the Soviet *estrada*. The emcee would appear between performances, and his commentary provided a common thread linking the various numbers together.[64] Zhvanetskii fulfilled a similar role for spectators of the "performance" of Soviet domestic policies; his commentaries bridged the disjunctures in official discourse. As in the society Petrovskii describes as being made up of "potential *anekdot* tellers and listeners,"[65] however, those spectators were also themselves potential performers in the "private theater of friends in small groups."[66]

Zhvanetskii was both a behavioral exemplar and a source of verbal material; lines from his monologues entered the language, where they were used like proverbs or told like *anekdoty*. There was a link between Zhvanetskii and his audience in a broader sense, as well; he was a professional author and performer, yes, but he might also be called the spokesman for a millions-strong *anekdot* subculture within the society. A powerless subject of state discourse like everyone else, he actually performed his response to that discourse in public.[67] Briker and Vishevskii wrote of Zhvanetskii's *sgovor* (conspiracy) with his audience, a common knowledge that is so common it need not be referenced explicitly.[68] The aesthetic value of maximally succinct reference to the tabooed unsaid, of course, is a crucial component of the status of the *anekdot* in the same period.

A characteristic device in Zhvanetskii's work is the metaphorization of one realm of everyday life—or everyday life in general—via another such aspect. In *Beregite biurokratov* (Save the Bureaucrats, 1967), for example, the narrator urges the protection of the bureaucrat as a species, reasoning that in the absence of a bureaucracy with which to struggle daily, the average citizen will become weak. In *Bronia moia!* (Tank of Mine! 1980s) the narrator imagines how much more efficient and enjoyable it would be to make a trip to the market or the doctor's office in a tank. In *Sosredotochenny razmyshleniia* (Concentrated Thoughts, 1960s) he suggests ways in which to harness otherwise wasteful physical activity to the cause of economic production. The drawing of lines between categories of Soviet life ironically evokes the Party's aspirations toward comprehensive influence on Soviet culture and everyday life. Yet Zhvanetskii's lines are ironically metaphorical; their actual effect is to demonstrate metonymical relationships—or, more accurately, disjunctures—among diverse categories of existence. Zhvanetskii's satirical commingling of seemingly disparate realms exemplifies a basic comic device of the period: the production of a comic incongruity via exposure of an unexpected congruity. The *anekdot* often operates on the same principle:

> A joke from 1987: A foreign tourist lights a cigarette on Red Square. A policeman explains to him with gestures that he must put it out immediately. The tourist, a well-disciplined member of a democratic society, does so and says in poor Russian, "Ah! Understand! Aerodrome, Aerodrome!"

> A foreigner falls into a hole while walking down a Soviet street. He climbs out, all filthy:
> "How disgraceful! In my country, they put a little red flag near hazardous areas!"
> "Didn't you see a big red flag when you flew into Sheremet'evo [the airport]?"

The first of these two *anekdoty* posits a logical explanation for the otherwise unmotivated Red Square smoking ban while referring implicitly to an episode embarrassing to the state: Matthias Rust's miraculous landing on Red Square in 1987. This sort of discursive engagement is a more potent form of satire than the light, generalized jabs at isolated social ills characteristic of official satire in the 1960s; a cause-and-effect relationship is depicted between two phenomena or institutions. This is a device that Zhvanetskii's work and the *anekdot* have in common.

Zhvanetskii's colloquial, conversational style and his parade of idiosyncratic narrators evoke the *skaz* tradition, with the past masters of which he is often compared, especially Zoshchenko. The inclusion of Zhvanetskii's work in the *skaz* canon, however, is potentially problematic. *Skaz* in the traditional definition is a literary technique by which the writer creates the illusion of oral speech on the written page for the reader's eye and mind's ear. Zhvanetskii's published works, however, have been described as "almost impossible to read."[69] His role as the performer of his own compositions then becomes not simply one of interpretation, but of decodification, an element indispensable to the consumption and perception of the texts.

Another feature of *skaz* narration is highly relevant to Zhvanetskii: the complexity and significance of the relationship between author and narrator. The absence of a literal mask in Zhvanetskii's performance style is accompanied by a related difference from his earlier work, as well as from his predecessors in the *skaz* tradition. In contrast to early Zoshchenko (and to Raikin, for that matter), Zhvanetskii often collapses the distance between author and narrator. The *skaz* style, then, becomes an instrument not for satirizing a risible narrator's lack of cultural or intellectual sophistication—a sort of verbal slapstick—but a medium for the author's own more or less direct (though stylized) discourse. It is partly this perspectival agility that made Zhvanetskii's work officially suspect.

One of Zhvanetskii's best-known monologues in this regard is *Ikh den'* (Their Day, 1974), inspired by a characteristically optimistic televised speech by the Soviet minister of meat and dairy production. The piece is a good example of the increasingly frequent autobiographical perspective in Zhvanetskii's work, as well as the essayistic tendency that would make his one of the leading voices among the creative intelligentsia during perestroika. In the monologue, Zhvanetskii ironically addresses the incongruity between the everyday reality described in the mass media and that experienced by the average citizen, as well as the privileged lifestyles of state officials.

Unlike many other writers and performers of his generation, Zhvanetskii has enjoyed a successful postcensorship career. One reason for this fact is Zhvanetskii's prescience during the 1970s; his thematic repertoire in the Brezhnev years anticipated (and helped to shape) the topical agenda of public discourse during perestroika: shortages, queues, bureaucracy, alcohol, gender relations, and an only semi-ironic appreciation for the value of hardship and struggle to the physical and social development of *homo sovieticus* (and *homo post-sovieticus*). Another reason for his sustained popularity is the sheer magnitude of his celebrity; Bitov did not exaggerate when he placed Zhvanetskii alongside Vysotskii as an emblem of a cultural epoch. Another factor is the increasingly strong current of lyricism in his work, which distinguishes it from "pure" satire, heavily reliant on the satirical target. His lyricism is particularly apparent in his periodic self-portraits, each titled according to the current year, in which Zhvanetskii mixes light self-reflexive irony with hints at the sociopolitical atmosphere and more serious philosophical sentiments.

Zhvanetskii's modal flexibility from one miniature to the next is a key factor in his professional longevity. It was also part and parcel of his discursive effectiveness during the days of censorship. Not only irony and cynicism were anathema to the logic of official discourse, but also the ease with which the ironic becomes the sincere or the nostalgic and the satirical a performance of humility. Again, this flexibility is related to the complexity of Zhvanetskii's *skaz*, in which the degree of author-narrator identity ranges from the familiar model of the narrator himself as the author's satirical target to texts in which *skaz* stylization serves as the medium for authorial commentary or even self-commentary. His oral *skaz*, of course, also evokes the *anekdot*, a satirical form of orality that relies on a conspiracy between speaker and audience similar to the one that Zhvanetskii himself creates.[70] Zhvanetskii's move toward lyricism echoes an analogous general shift away from cynicism in the direction of ingenuousness, even hope, during the perestroika period, when the *anekdot* began its precipitous decline in popularity. In another sense, however, Zhvanetskii's self-referential impulse rehearses a crucial feature of the *anekdot*, one of the most reflexive genres in contemporary Russian culture. In chapters 4 and 5, I examine the genre's multifaceted capacity for reflexivity.

Chapter Four

Discursive Reflexivity in the *Anekdot*

> Two Chukchi are sitting on the shore of the
>   Pacific in Siberia.
> "Want to hear a joke?"
> "A political joke?"
> "Yes."
> "Better not. You can get exiled for that."

ANDREI SINIAVSKII (writing as Abram Terts) observed in 1978 that the *anekdot* is a rare example of reflexive—or, in his words, "self-conscious"—folklore.[1] Siniavskii limits his discussion of self-consciousness to meta-jokes like the one that serves as the epigraph for this chapter, but the descriptor "reflexive" is in fact applicable to a rather broader variety of *anekdot*, analysis of which reveals how the genre's capacity for self-regard ("self" both in terms of the text and the discursive source of the text, i.e., the joke teller) contributed substantially to its prominence in Soviet culture, especially during the Stagnation years. Its reflexive tendencies distinguished the *anekdot* both diachronically, from its predecessors in the Russian oral tradition,[2] and synchronically, from its generic contemporaries in Soviet culture, whether unofficial (dissident literature) or official (the socialist-realist canon).

In addition to meta-*anekdoty*, the following types of *anekdot* employ reflexivity of one sort or another: (1) intertextual *anekdoty:* texts that make reference to specific texts of other genres (a group that includes not just the classic cycles about Chapaev, the Soviet World War II mole Shtirlits, cartoon characters, and so on, but also many political jokes); (2) texts that evaluate the nature and practice of verbal signification in more or less implicit ways; and (3) self-referential ethnic *anekdoty:* jokes told by Russians in which Russianness is foregrounded. At first glance, this list may seem irresponsibly to conflate two distinct species of reflexivity: meta-textuality, on one hand, and self-reference in the literal sense during an individual or group's discourse, on the other. Russian jokes about stereotypical behaviors and character traits of the Russian (or Russo-Soviet) ethnos, however, are arguably intertextual in their own right, insofar as they often implicate extant textual representations of that ethnos. Their function often overlapped with that of the more obviously intertextual *anekdoty:* to engage critically the normative, inscribed models of social reality that dominated the corpus of texts available for popular consumption. Still, I have separated my analysis of Russian reflexive ethnic jokes (which I examine in chapter 5) from the present chapter, which treats the first two varieties of self-referential *anekdoty* just listed.

In the post-Stalin years, especially during Stagnation, the *anekdot* became more than a ubiquitous form of oral discourse; its tendency to engage with other constituent texts and genres of Soviet culture made it the genre of choice for popular meta-discourse. While *anekdoty* of the period do, naturally, depict actual personalities, relationships, and sociopolitical events, "anecdotal" significations of such things have more immediate referential links to previous significations: concrete textual representations of real-life phenomena. Ol'ga Chirkova wrote that *anekdoty* are constructed on the basis not of "realia as such, but those realia that have moved to the level of idea."[3] Ideas are expressed in the form of discourse and, as Mikhail Bakhtin tells us, every unit of discourse—every utterance—is by definition responsive to previous utterances in the given cultural environment's communicative chain.[4] What is significant about the *anekdot* as a speech genre is its tendency to display its responsive nature, to draw attention to its discursive position vis-à-vis other utterances. *Anekdot* telling is not merely a response, but also a performance of response, just as dance is both movement and a performance of movement.[5] Performance as a cultural practice involves simultaneous use of and commentary on a medium of expression. Its reflective probing of "the formal features of the communicative system"[6] is thus also reflexive; cultural performance is self-evident meta-communication.

Verbal performance is a reflexive form of discourse in the same way that philology is: the discursive medium—language—is also the discursive referent (although in philological analysis the reference is explicit). While this bootstrapping dilemma has the potential to undermine the objectivity (and therefore the credibility) of a scientific endeavor like philology, reflexivity only amplifies the discursive potency of the *anekdot,* a form of utterance that has thrived on "paradoxicality"[7] since long before it became the chief medium for parodying the self-contradictory absurdities of ideological pronouncements. Because it is of the same stuff as its referent, the intertextual *anekdot* is able to assimilate all or part of a text from a different genre and then re-present it through the prism of its own generic logic:

> During a speech by Brezhnev, a man in the audience is arrested. He turns out to be a spy. "How did you know he was a CIA agent?" Brezhnev asks the famous KGB Major Pronin. "As you constantly remind us, Leonid Il'ich, the enemy never sleeps."

This text and others like it exploit the full potential of quotation as a discursive mode that "mark[s] discourse as the 'so-called,' [. . .] give[s] the discourse a suspicious integrity."[8] *Anekdoty* such as this are not mere quotations, but quotations "in drag," a form of oral philology that operates (and annotates) from a position not of scholarly detachment, but of satirical condescension. In the USSR, the *anekdot* became an outlet for the otherwise restricted commentarial impulse of the educated urban cultural consumer. The genre was also, of course, a means of expressing collective contempt for the source of the restriction—the state's illegitimate monopoly on textual production—and the resulting crisis of representation.

ANEKDOTY ABOUT ANEKDOTY

As Siniavskii/Terts pointed out, the *anekdot* itself is not immune to its own predilection for critical meta-discourse. Except for a text that openly refers to itself, the most direct form of textual reflexivity is representation of other texts of the same genre, or explicit reference to that genre as a whole. The meta-*anekdot* was a significant generic subcategory that made just such reference and that itself existed in several variants.

The *anekdot* engaged critically with the prevailing ideology on a direct thematic level, and here, too, its capacity for generic reflexivity played a role. The genre became grist for its own mill initially as a result of its politicization by the state, that is, when arrests for telling or transcribing *anekdoty* became an element of the Soviet popular consciousness and experience. As I mention in chapter 2, jokes about the political consequences of careless joke telling became commonplace beginning in the 1930s, when the sentence for propagating or transcribing *anekdoty* was up to ten years' imprisonment under Article 58 of the penal code. An example of such a joke: The state announces a contest for the best political joke. First prize: fifteen years.[9] Or: A Soviet leader (sometimes Stalin, sometimes Brezhnev[10]) boasts to an adviser that he himself has a large collection of *anekdoty,* and when asked how large, answers "nearly two and a half camps' worth."

Another venerable *anekdot* references not only the illicit status of the genre, but also the universality of its appeal and consumption:

A judge walks out of a courtroom chuckling.
"What's so funny?" a colleague asks.
"I just heard a hilarious *anekdot*!"
"Let me hear it!"
"I can't. I just gave someone fifteen years for it."

The practice of *anekdot* telling is a narrative theme in Soviet *anekdoty* themselves for the simple reason that the practice was a part of everyday life [*byt*], a central medium for the representation of which is the *anekdot*. Common among this type of meta-*anekdot* are variations on the numbered-*anekdoty* motif:

> In a prison all the jokes have been told a thousand times, so the inmates number them so as not to waste time.
> "Number 67!" Laughter.
> "Number 52!" Laughter.
> "Number 41!" One of the inmates starts laughing like mad.
> "What's the matter with you?"
> "I never heard that one before!"

In other versions a newcomer shouts out a random number, prompting a reprimand for telling such a filthy joke in the presence of women, a dismissive rebuke that "he doesn't know how to tell a joke," or a gestured warning that there is a hidden microphone or a police informant in the room. The notion of a numerical shorthand for *anekdoty* is an implicit commentary on the status of the *anekdot* itself as a kind of shorthand, a distilled observation on a particular aspect of public or private life. The jokes-by-numbers motif also implies the shortage, and therefore the value, of fresh *anekdoty,* something addressed in the brief *anekdot* "Why did Cain kill Abel? Because he told old jokes."[11]

Anekdoty about the culture of *anekdot* telling were also an outlet for the popular impulse not only to violate taboos but also to reproduce the pleasure therein in a symbolic way by *talking* about the violation of taboos.[12] Such texts are semantically akin to representations of other illicit activities, such as drinking, swearing, and fornication. A joke circulating in Moscow in 1999 acknowledged the simple truth that talking about transgressive acts (especially transgressive acts involving supermodels) can be almost as appealing as the acts themselves:

> A man is shipwrecked on a desert island with Claudia Schiffer. After some time has passed, he says to her, "Um, I was wondering. You're a woman, I'm a man. We might be stuck here for the rest of our lives. Why don't we . . . you know . . ." She agrees. Afterward she asks him how he liked it. "Well, it was great," he answers, "but . . ." "But what? What else do you want?" she says. "Um, could you do one more thing for me," he says, "could you put on my hat? And my suit?" "What, you don't like women?" she says. "Of course I do, but please, just put them on," he implores. She obliges. He looks at her, puts his hand on her shoulder, and says, "Dude! Guess who I just had sex with!"

Another category of meta-*anekdoty* depicts *anekdot* characters (or other folkloric characters) acknowledging their own textual status or telling *anekdoty;* the already tongue-in-cheek pretense of mimesis is demonstratively abandoned.[13] Textual self-reference of this sort amounts to an exaggerated corrective to the hypermimetic transparent texts of mass culture, which subordinated form to content while rigidly prescribing both. The formal exhibitionism of the *anekdot* was anathema to the representational system of Socialist Realism, which had little tolerance for self-referential art. Once a text acknowledges its status as a text, its signifying link to reality—and its potential as a medium for the equation of reality with myth—is damaged or lost. The playful complication of the relationship between text and reality is sometimes an explicit narrative theme in an *anekdot,* for example:

> Shtirlits wakes up in a jail cell. "If a soldier in a Nazi uniform comes in, I'll say I'm SS officer von Shtirlits. If he's in a Soviet uniform, I'll say I'm Colonel Isaev." A policeman comes in and says: "Well, well, comrade Tikhonov, you sure tied one on last night, didn't you?"[14]

Another example of generic reflexivity is the super-*anekdot* motif, in which a Soviet computer is programmed to generate the most typical *anekdot* possible, with results in which recognizable characters and situations randomly converge:

> A woman is in bed with her lover. The doorbell rings. Vovochka runs to get it and there stand Vasilii Ivanovich Chapaev and Pet'ka, both Jewish.

> Rabinovich asks a Chukchi: "Vasilii Ivanovich, have you been to the visa office?" "The girls there even saw Lenin himself in person once."

Some meta-*anekdoty* are part of a generic feedback mechanism that identifies particularly hyperproductive (and/or hackneyed) cycles or motifs by ironically laying bare their textuality:

> Chapaev is walking through the village drunk and covered in mud, straw, and shit. "What happened, Vasilii Ivanovich?" "The *anekdoty,* Pet'ka, it's from the *anekdoty.*"

> A Jew is running along Nevsky Avenue in Leningrad. He meets an acquaintance:
> "Where are you running from?"
> "From the *anekdot*! The generals squeezed me out!"[15]

Such reflexive treatment of jokelore in danger of losing its novelty served to "make strange" thematic or compositional patterns repeated in so many permutations that the only remaining direction for innovation was up, to the meta level.

THE ABSTRACT *ANEKDOT*

The most extreme example of generic self-criticism in the *anekdot* is the so-called abstract or absurd *anekdot*. For example:

> Bear and Fox are sitting on the river bank. Hare comes up and asks: "Guys! Do you have any glue?" "No," they answer. Hare runs off for a minute, comes back with a bottle of glue, and says: "Here you go."

Such jokes are reflexive in an etymologically literal sense: they turn back on themselves by inflicting the genre's signature device—a sharp, terminal disruption of the logical flow of discourse—on the genre's own expected discursive trajectory, toward a punch line.[16] They display awareness of the genre's conventions by ostentatiously violating them. Paradoxically, however, they are no less successful as *anekdoty* than normative texts of the genre; they fulfill the genre's most basic function—to evoke laughter. They are, then, simultaneously generically self-critical and generically self-regenerative.

Other *anekdoty* of this type pour absurd narrative content into an *anekdot*-shaped shell:[17]

> A guy goes out onto his balcony with a case of kefir and pours one bottle after another onto the street below. A man from the balcony below asks: "What, are you playing chess?" "How'd you guess?" "See that bicycle over there?"[18]

> A customer in a restaurant:
> "Bring me a pot of soup."
> He takes the pot and pours it over his head. The waiter says:
> "What are you doing? That's soup!"
> "Oh, I thought it was compote."

> A cow is climbing a tree.
> "Hey, Cow, where are you going?" asks Crow.
> "Well, I wanted some apples."
> "Apples? But that's a birch tree!"
> "I have some with me."

"Hey, Crow! How many legs do you have?"
"Two, especially the right one."

Two crocodiles were flying: one red, the other to Africa.

Even absurd *anekdoty* are not immune to becoming hackneyed and formulaic, and thus require periodic prophylactic defamiliarization [*ostranenie*]. Consider, for example, the following hyperabsurd embellished variants on two of the *anekdoty* just cited:

> A naked man stands in the middle of the street. Every other minute he pours a glass of kissel over his head and says "Cuckoo!" Another man comes up to him:
> "What are you doing?"
> "Playing chess."
> "Can I play?"
> "Sure!"
> They stand across from each other saying "Cuckoo!" A third man walks by:
> "You playing chess?"
> "How'd you guess?"
> "Because there's a Zaporozhets [cheap car] parked around the corner."

> There flew two crocodiles: one green, the other to the right. How much does a kilogram of herring weigh? (Who the hell knows!)

Such texts fulfill on the level of form the comic utterance's role to which I refer in the Introduction: as "a remark on the indignity of any closed system."[19] Pavel Borodin wrote that their purpose is "to expose the laws of the communicative act."[20] In a logocentric, hyperrational society, they amounted to symbolic "holy foolishness" [*iurodstvo*].

ANEKDOT TELLERS AS MEDIA CRITICS

Briker and Vishevskii wrote of a common awareness among the educated populace that there was an abstract paradigm of the typical life shared by the members of that stratum.[21] They called this model a "cultural text" and wrote that it has an almost

> generic structure [. . .] at the basis of [which] lies a schematic description of the life of [. . .] the average person. All the elements of the description are so characteristic of all the participants that any one of them can superimpose

it onto their own personal life and see that the two correspond. Moreover, the person will be surprised to discover that even the private, personal, individual, and inimitable features of his life are already programmed into the overall schema.[22]

The links between that text and cultural texts in a more literal sense affirm Jaeger and Selznick's definition of culture as "everything that is produced by and capable of sustaining shared symbolic experience."[23] Language was a crucial medium for sharing symbolic experience within the educated collective to which Briker and Vishevskii referred. The lexicographer Vladimir Elistratov identified a tendency of social subgroups to use "linguistic doubles" of the standard language.[24] The *anekdot* was part of such a discursive doppelgänger (sometimes called an "anti-language"[25]), and the collective used it to comment on—and define itself in relation to institutions associated with—the "parent" language.[26]

The major conduit via which material passed from one pole of the Soviet diglossia to the other was the mass media, and prominent among the instantiations of mass culture that provoked popular response in the form of *anekdoty* are several films and television programs of the 1960s and 1970s. They provided thematic, compositional, and linguistic source material for the topical *anekdot* cycles that to this day account for a large portion of the generic corpus: Lieutenant Rzhevskii,[27] Shtirlits, Cheburashka, Sherlock Holmes and Watson, Vinni-Pukh (the Russian rendition of Winnie-the-Pooh, which has little in common with the Disney version except being based on the book by A. A. Milne), and even the Chukchi cycle. The Chapaev cycle also dates from this period; the 1934 film enjoyed a renewed surge of publicity and popularity beginning with the celebration of its thirtieth anniversary in 1964.

Although these cycles were inspired by texts in visual media, the engagement of them by the *anekdot* was primarily meta-linguistic. In the post-Thaw years, visual culture had begun to reflect the resurgent logocentrism of official culture. Moreover, the *anekdot* favors dialogue as its chief compositional form, so it typically co-opts specific examples of dialogue from the source texts (for example, the famous bedtime chat between Chapaev and Pet'ka). The only major cycle that does not rely heavily on dialogue between characters—the Shtirlits cycle—is based on a different verbal device: Emil Kopel'ian's voice-over narration in *Semnadtsat' mgnovenii vesny*. *Anekdoty* such as the following should be told using Kopel'ian's deadpan intonation:

Shtirlits arrived at Himmler's house in a red Russian shirt and carrying an accordion. He played a Russian folk song and danced squatting while whistling.

Kopel'ian's voice-over commentary: "Yes, never before had Shtirlits been as close to blowing his cover as on that night."

Film and television narratives also lent themselves to strip mining by the *anekdot* because, like it, they are performance genres. The raconteur does not quote from the film *Chapaev* or a *Vinni-Pukh* cartoon; he momentarily becomes Vasilii Ivanovich or Piatachok. Finally, with the rise of television viewership and the sky-high cinema attendance figures, the film and television media—part of an electronic-age phenomenon that Walter Ong called "secondary orality"[28]—themselves functioned as generators of discrete bits of oral culture that quickly became common knowledge. In other words, Soviet mass culture itself became a prominent source of folkloric material, part of the cultural langue of an urban "folk." Occasionally *anekdoty* were referred to by joke tellers as "communications of OBS" [*odna baba skazala*, "some woman said"], a reference to the ubiquitous phrase "communications of TASS" (the Soviet news bureau),[29] a parodic gesture that highlights the status of oral humor as competition for the mass media.

A better term than "citation" or "allusion" for the engagement of the *anekdot* with material from other texts in that reservoir might be "abduction," the most typical trajectory of which is from the realm of irony-deficient solemnity to one of pure irony. This is one reason that certain very popular films and television programs did not provoke *anekdot* cycles: because they themselves already privilege the ironic mode. Some examples are the films *Beloe solntse pustyni* [White Sun of the Desert, 1969], *Tot samyi Miunkhgauzen* [That Munchausen, 1979], and *Dvenadtsat' stul'ev* [The Twelve Chairs, 1971] and the cartoon series *Nu pogodi!* [Just You Wait! 1970s–1980s].[30]

Another reason certain visual texts inspired *anekdot* cycles more readily than others is that the source texts themselves resemble common *anekdot* structures and motifs. *Semnadtsat' mgnovenii vesny*, about a Russian among non-Russians, has a link to comparative ethnic jokes, for example, about a Frenchman, an Italian, and a Russian on a desert island, in a plane about to crash, and so on.[31] The film *Chapaev*, as I shall discuss in chapter 5, is constructed as a series of brief episodes with simple dialogues, many of which end with (humorous or nonhumorous) punch lines.

The intertextual links of the *anekdot* are certainly not limited to popular culture; political discourse figured in the Soviet *anekdot* early in its history. Stalin-era *anekdoty*, like later ones, found comic material in Soviet leaders' use of language. Unlike Stagnation political jokes, however, which tend to portray members of the political elite as incompetent, Ivan-the-fool-like abusers of language, the older ones frequently emphasize the tricksteresque or even diabolical nature of official discourse and manipulation of texts:

"Aleksei Maksimovich [i.e., Maxim Gorky], you should write my biography!"

"Please, Iosif Vissarionovich [Stalin]. It's been a long time since I kept up with what's going on in the Party. There's so much that I don't know, it's not even worth trying."

"Give it a try. As Lavrentii Pavlovich [Beriia, Stalin's feared head of the secret police] says, it doesn't hurt to try!" [In Russian the proverb is *Popytka— ne pytka,* literally "making an attempt is not torture."]

Contrast the image of crafty Stalin transforming a proverb into gallows humor with the many jokes about Brezhnev's simultaneous dependence on and incomprehension of texts:

Brezhnev is giving a speech: "Who says that I always read from a piece of paper? Ha, hyphen, ha, hyphen, ha, hyphen."

Brezhnev in Central Asia: "Salaam aleekum!" the workers shout to him. "Aleekum es-salaam!" Brezhnev replies, having been coached in the custom. "Salaam aleekum!" they shout. "Aleekum es-salaam!" he replies. Suddenly a dissident jumps out and shouts "Arkhipelag gulag!" [Gulag archipelago!] to which Leonid Il'ich replies, "Gulag arkhipelag!" [Archipelago Gulag!].

A speech by Brezhnev: "Nasha strana idet na govno . . . na govno . . . noga v nogu so vsemi tsivilizovannymi stranami mira."[32]

The critical engagement of state discourse by the *anekdot* often involved isolating and excising a discrete unit of that discourse (slogan, neologism, acronym, quotation) from its communicative frame (speech at a state ceremony, political banner, socialist-realist film or novel, history book) and transplanting it into an incongruous context (Chapaev and Pet'ka in Africa; a Marxist slogan uttered in a whorehouse; the first line of the "Internationale" in a telegram addressed to Lenin in the Mausoleum). As Krongauz pointed out, Soviet state utterances were particularly susceptible to this basic comic device—incongruity between discursive content and context—because they were maximally reliant on their communicative environments.[33] Thus even a verbatim quotation of a political utterance amounted to a drastic reinterpretation of its meaning.

A good example of the popular perception of the political during Stagnation is the well-known *anekdot* about an encyclopedia of the future that contains the following entry: "Brezhnev, Leonid Il'ich—Minor political figure of the [pop singer Alla] Pugacheva era," which Tat'iana Cherednichenko tapped for the subtitle of her 1994 book *Tipologiia sovetskoi massovoi kul'tury: Mezhdu "Brezhnevym" i "Pugachevoi"* [A Typology of Soviet Mass Culture: Between "Brezhnev" and "Pugacheva"]. Those two figures, she argued, represent the "public and private poles of the cultural continuum" during Stagnation.[34] As the joke indicates, the sphere of the "minor political figure" was less and less able to compete for the public's attention with the popular-culture realm ruled by icons such as Pugacheva. In fact, according to Cherednichenko, the populace perceived and consumed political texts and images the same way they consumed mass culture: as pure form with nonexistent or irrelevant content. It was all, she wrote, "la-la-la."[35] Another *anekdot* suggests that the Soviet subject's tendency to conflate popular and political culture begins in childhood:

> During a class trip to the park, the teacher points at a hedgehog and says, "Look, children, this is who I've told you so many stories and sung so many songs about." One of the kids picks up the hedgehog and says in a sweet voice, "So *that's* what you look like, Vladimir Il'ich."

> Lenin comes back to life and is walking around in the city. He wonders if he will be recognized or not. He sees a drunk worker lying on the sidewalk and approaches him: "Comrade, do you recognize me?" "Nope." "Look carefully!" "Oh, yeah! I know you! You're that commemorative ruble!"

The nature of the rehearsal of other texts by the *anekdot* distinguishes it from the traditional uncritical performances by a "folk" of its native cultural reservoir. An intertextual *anekdot* removes discourse from its original context to exploit it in a new signifying performance. In this respect the *anekdot* resembles ritual, which, according to Richard Schechner, is a performance constructed from pieces of existing signifying acts (specific movements, gestures, and invocations) that the performer treats "as a film editor treats strips of film" to create a new signifying act.[36] Susan Stewart discussed in similar terms the performer of riddles, jokes, and puns, whom she called a *"bricoleur"* who transforms old knowledge in specific ways to produce "new meanings."[37] Unlike a shaman, whose ritualistic use of "recovered behaviors"[38] as material for the new performance typically either affirms the original meanings of the material or uses it unreflectively, the *anekdot* performer's discourse is often directed in a triangulated fashion toward both the source text and the source text's own original referent to comment critically on one or both.

Sometimes, however, the mobilization of a prior text—especially if it is a text from traditional folklore or pre-Revolutionary literature—implies a positive commentary on that text as a useful discursively legitimate tool for sociopolitical criticism. *Anekdoty* frequently modify folkloric texts such as proverbs and tales to comment on a contemporary issue. This device has been used in the post-Soviet period, as well, for example in the recent proverb/*anekdot* "Putina boiat'sia—v sortir ne khodit'" [If you're afraid of Putin don't go into the outhouse], which combines the folk proverb "volkov boiat'sia—v lcs ne khodit'" [If you're afraid of wolves don't go into the forest] with the new president's widely reported promise to "mochit'" [waste] Chechen terrorists "v sortire" [in the outhouse].

The use of literary allusions in political *anekdoty* is nearly as old as the Soviet *anekdot* in general. In her notebooks from the mid-1930s, the writer Natal'ia Sokolova recorded an *anekdot* about the productions being staged at new Moscow theaters that season: at the Lenin Theater, *Gore ot uma* [Woe from Wit]; at the Stalin Theater, *Ne v svoi sani ne sadis'* [Don't Sit in Someone Else's Sleigh]; at the Kalinin Theater, *Ivanushka-durachok* [Ivan the Fool]; at the GPU (later known as the KGB) Theater, *Iskateli zhemchuga* [Hunting for Pearls] in the morning and *Bez viny vinovaty* [Guilty Without Guilt] at night.[39]

Despite its ostentatious, ludic exposé of signifying practices (including its own), the *anekdot* cannot historically be confined to the project of postmodernism (especially the Soviet variety), much of the cultural production of which is premised on language's essential failure to signify anything except other signifiers. *Anekdoty* certainly impugned the representational capacity of a particular language—the language of official Soviet culture—making the genre a kind of postmodernism in one country. Its symbolic undermining of the representational authority of state discourse, however, was accompanied by a complementary project: the composition of an alternative credible representation of popular experience. As Richard Bauman wrote: "Cultural performances may be primary modes of discourse in their own right, casting in sensuous images and performative action rather than in ordered sets of explicit, verbally articulated values or beliefs, people's understandings of ultimate realities and the implications of those realities for action."[40]

Anekdoty were performances of a discursive schism in Soviet culture: the incongruity between official narratives of the collective life of the society on one hand and the popular common experience of that life on the other. Whereas official discourse emphasized brotherhood, unanimity, and the infallible word of the Party, the *anekdot* trafficked in conflict, dialogue, and contradiction. The genre's penchant for reflexivity, often critical, demonstrates the ways in which self-sabotage must sometimes precede reconquest. The same process is apparent in *anekdoty* featuring Russian protagonists, to which I turn now.

Ethnic Reflexivity

> Communist ideas and Communist deeds
> should blend organically in the behavior
> of every person and in the activities of all
> collectives and organizations.
> —*Program of the Communist Party of the Soviet
> Union*, 1961

> When news of the Russian conquest of space
> reached the cosmos, Saturn hid his rings, Mars
> mobilized for invasion, and Venus put on a
> chastity belt.
> —*Anekdot* reported by Algis Rusksenas in *Is That
> You Laughing, Comrade?*

RUSSIANS ARE sometimes the butt of their own jokes, as
the second epigraph for this chapter testifies.[1] Although Russia is certainly
not the only cultural space with such a tradition, self-inflicted ethnic satire
is far from universal or even widespread among the peoples of the world. In
The Mirth of Nations, a comparative survey of ethnic jokes, Christie Davies
detects an analogous impulse in the humor of Scots, Jews, Newfoundland-
ers, and Australians. He is silent on Russians, but his explanations for the
presence of reflexive ethnic jokes among those other groups help to illuminate the Russian case, albeit obliquely. Davies writes, for example, that
an ethnic group might tell jokes about itself to maintain ownership of its
stereotypical ethnic image and thus preempt the use of that image by more
powerful and/or potentially hostile out-groups.[2] If (as I argue in this chapter) the image of the Russian in underground *anekdoty* functioned as an implicit rebuttal of state-produced or state-sanctioned representations of the
Russo-Soviet ethnos, then such *anekdoty* do evince a collective awareness
of an out-group. The out-group in question was not an ethnic one, however,
and the representations that the *anekdot* contradicted were not themselves
satirical or openly hostile toward Russians or Russianness. On the contrary,
by privileging a cluster of behaviors and character traits that were anathema

to state discourse, the *anekdot* served as an antidote to the constant self-aggrandizement of official discourse.

Soviet culture was the site of parallel discursive projects with incongruous strategies of representation, including strategies of self-representation. In other words, Russian *anekdoty* about Russians were in critical engagement with another extant fount of textual production that was itself reflexive: the ongoing official autobiography and ethnography of the country and its citizens. That open-ended descriptive (and prescriptive) project was manifested—especially from the 1960s on—in cultural texts, particularly film and television narratives. It also found expression in mass-media treatments of events and processes in which nationality was underscored: references to the "friendship of peoples" in the multiethnic USSR, heroic accounts of Russo-Soviet empire building (past and present), and news reports of the Soviet leader's latest meeting with foreign leaders. All of these motifs, of course, were exploited in the *anekdot*.

In this chapter, I examine some of the implications of the characteristics that Russian urban folk humor has ascribed to the eponymous consumers of that humor. I focus first on *anekdoty* that explicitly feature Russians or Russianness as the comic crux. I then turn to *anekdoty* that do not explicitly reference the Russian as an ethnic category, but that draw from the same general well of character and behavioral traits as the clearly ethnic jokes, locating those traits in specific archetypal heroes. I examine canonical cycles with superficially dissimilar subjects: the Russian Civil War martyr Vasilii Ivanovich Chapaev, the Chukchi of the Siberian arctic, and, briefly, the fictional Soviet World War II spy Shtirlits. What the cycles had in common—in addition to the fact that they are all in one way or another based on cinematic images—was their protagonists' day jobs as anthropomorphic Soviet tropes. The post-Soviet cycle about the so-called New Russians, which I examine in chapter 6, is an instructive epilogue to the story of satirical Russo-Soviet self-regard.

I am aware of the danger of interpreting as reflexive in-group humor a joke that is actually told by one subgroup about another subgroup in the same country (Russian Jewish jokes about ethnic Russians, for example, or jokes about Russians told in the non-Russian Soviet republics). It is often tricky to establish the trajectories of satirical vectors, especially when studying the satire of a previous period so different from the present. Yet there is no doubt that *anekdoty* about Russians circulated and continue to circulate within Russian oral culture, and so they can be analyzed as instantiations (of varying degrees of irony) of Russia's self-image as an ethnic collective. The *anekdoty* in this chapter, like those in other chapters, have been published in Russia, told to me by Russians, or analyzed by others, sometimes explicitly in the context of Russian humor about Russians.[3] Moreover, multinational *anekdoty* (which I discuss in this chapter) typically portray a Russian and two or more representatives of Western (or at least non-Soviet) nationalities. If these jokes were actually intra-Soviet ethnic jokes aimed by a minority ethnicity at the dominant ethnicity, we would expect those minority groups themselves to figure in the jokes, either as victors over or victims of the Russians. They rarely do.[4]

Davies divided ethnic-group joke protagonists into those depicted as stupid and those depicted as "canny" (that is, stingy and calculating) and further wrote that reflexive ethnic jokes tend to emphasize the canniness of the group in question.[5] The jokeloric Russian is certainly not canny, and although there are of course *anekdoty* in which he (or occasionally she) behaves stupidly (in the tradition of Ivan the Fool), he has many other equally canonical traits: drunkenness, belligerence, thievery, laziness, sexual boorishness, a compulsion to use profanity, and a knack for incompetent workmanship and destruction of property.[6] Here are three examples:

The famous Russian singer Vertinskii returns to the Soviet Union after having emigrated years before, under the tsar. He steps off the train, puts his two suitcases down, kisses the earth, and looks around:
"I do not recognize you, O Russia!"
Then he looks behind him and his suitcases are gone.
"Now I recognize you, O Russia!"[7]

At a secret CIA school where they train moles to be planted in the USSR, the instructor says, concluding a lesson, "Today we worked on a very important situation: 'in line at the liquor store.' Are there any questions?" One of the trainees asks: "Sir, I have a question. In the sentence 'Fellas, they're only lettin' us buy two bottles apiece,' where do you put the present-active participle 'fuckin'?" ["Vo fraze 'Muzhiki, daiut tol'ko po dva puzyria na rylo'— gde luchshe vsego postavit' neopredelennyi artikl' 'blia'"?][8]

Question: What is it that doesn't buzz and doesn't fit up your butt?
Answer: A domestically produced [Russian] butt-buzzing apparatus.

The second of these *anekdoty* ironically ascribes one of the markers I mentioned—a penchant for obscenity—not to the behavioral level, but to the grammatical structure itself. *Anekdoty* often code stereotypes in comically pseudoscientific terms (for instance, the comparative ethnic jokes [see next section] that begin "They conduct an experiment to determine . . .").

RUSSIAN OR SOVIET?

The first of the three preceding *anekdoty* cited is noteworthy for a very different reason: its fantasy of continuity between the pre-Soviet and Soviet instantiations of the stereotypical Russian character. In this way the joke defuses an anticipated objection that most of these texts target Sovietness, rather than Russianness, and should thus be considered "mere" political *anekdoty* rather than reflexive ethnic humor. It is an understandable objection; there are many *anekdoty* in which the political system is the obvious target. The systemic features on which they seize, however, are frequently similar, even identical, to the features around which *anekdoty* about Russianness are typically constructed. In other words, the Soviet Union's stereotypical behavior and its personality as a state and a geopolitical entity are extrapolations from the stereotypical Russian self-profile:[9]

> A doctor, an engineer, and a Communist are arguing: who was the first man on earth? The doctor says, "I was the first man, since without me it would have been impossible to make Eve from Adam's rib." The engineer says, "No, I was first, because without an engineer it would have been impossible to create the world out of chaos." The Communist says, "You're both wrong. Without a Communist, where did the chaos come from?"

> The USSR is like Cupid: naked, armed, and ready to offer its love to everyone.

The following *anekdot* implies that the Soviet system itself is a manifestation of a hardwired behavioral template (or gene) that turns the maxim "ontogeny recapitulates phylogeny" on its head:

> They decide to conduct an experiment. Three groups—one English, one French, and one Russian—are put on three desert islands. In each group there are two men and one woman. After a year they send a boat to the English, who are sitting on opposite ends of their island.
> "Why are you sitting like that?"
> "Nobody introduced us."
> They go to the French and ask the woman:
> "How are you doing here?"
> "Wonderfully! One day I live with one man, the next day with the other."
> They go to the Russians and see the two guys. One is sitting behind a table with a red tablecloth and a carafe. The other is sitting across from him on a stool. The first is giving a speech and the second occasionally raises his hand to vote. They ask them:

"Where's the woman?"
"What woman?"
"You were left here a year ago with a woman!"
"Oh, the People! The People are out working in the field."

The reference to Soviet-style "affection" in the joke about Cupid certainly satirizes episodes of Soviet militant imperialism, officially coded as "brotherly support," but it also is closely linked to a motif found in apolitical *anekdoty* about what might be termed the "ruthless hospitality" of Russians:

An American, a Frenchman, and a Russian are marooned on a desert island. They have no food, so they start to fish. Suddenly they catch a golden fish. "Let me go, kind sirs, and I'll grant each of you a wish," says the fish. So the castaways line up and make their wishes. The American says, "I want to be back in America with a luxury home and a million bucks in my pocket." He disappears immediately. The Frenchman says, "I want to be in Paris with a beautiful woman." He, too, disappears as soon as he's made his wish. The Russian says, "A house?! A woman?! Ah, what a great bunch of guys we had! I want a case of vodka and everyone back here right now!"

The self-directed Russian *anekdot* not only predates the October Revolution, but it also has outlived the Soviet Union by more than a decade now. (An example: "What is business, Russian-style? Steal a case of vodka, sell it, and drink up the profits.") Far from creating out of whole cloth a new stereotype, as the Vertinskii joke cited previously testifies, the Soviet context represented a new sociocultural petri dish in which long-standing native images of stereotypical Russianness could flourish with particular fecundity.

THE POLITICS OF SELF-REGARD

As I wrote in chapter 4, reflexivity was one of the essential differences between the underground *anekdot* and official Soviet humor, which vigorously employed what Mikhail Bakhtin called "the pure satire of modern times," with its culturally external (or isolated and anomalous internal) targets. Bakhtin contrasted modern satire with traditional folk humor, which was often self-directed by a community, a medium for the "laughter of the people at themselves."[10] The folk tradition is but one of the relevant influences on the contemporary *anekdot* and its utility as a self-satirizing medium, however. Other likely candidates include the penchant for self-irony among the intelligentsia,[11] whose folklore the *anekdot* arguably became during the Stalin period, and Jewish humor, whose own self-deprecatory tendencies have often been noted but almost as often rebutted.[12] Both of these influences enhanced the element of reflexivity in folkloric expression after the intelligentsia became prominent producers and consumers of oral culture, in part due to vigorous Soviet censorship of written texts, but also because of the various oral emphases of urban popular culture: radio, cabaret performance, theater, film, and so on.[13]

Of particular relevance here are the substantial ideological connotations of reflexive ethnic satire in Soviet culture, connotations that were—like those of the other types of reflexive jokes I discussed in chapter 4—enthusiastically exploited in *anekdoty*. Comic self-deprecation by groups and individuals in Soviet society had inherent ideological bite, since aspersions cast on the character of citizens represented implicit criticism of the premises and methods of the presumptive engineers of that character. The state's celebration of the "all-around personality" of the Soviet citizen, the image of whom was exploited as a shining example of the superiority of the socialist "way of life,"[14] is contradicted in *anekdoty* in which that citizen is depicted as the polar opposite of his official representation. Such *anekdoty* are not reducible to mere carnivalesque contrariness. In a society in which each member was expected to be a physical, moral, and intellectual example of the systemic legitimacy of "mature socialism," not to mention a synecdoche of the capital-C Collective, any critical or negative representation of a citizen as such amounted to evidence of a desire to sabotage the nation's infrastructure and material resources. Recall the 1982 article from *Komsomol'skaia Pravda* that reminded readers that the "front of the war of ideas" is located within the "heart of every citizen."[15] The *anekdot* suggests that an appropriate response to the myriad ideological intrusions inflicted on the mind and body of the Soviet citizen was a sort of symbolic idiocy (reminiscent of the tradition of *iurodstvo* [holy foolishness]) and self-parody. If the official national self-image was marked by an exaggerated egoism (with episodes of righteous sadism in defense of that image), urban folk consciousness countered with a form of stylized verbal masochism that drew freely on an existing tradition, strategically adapting elements of that tradition to contemporaneity.[16]

Anekdot culture occupied something of a third space. If the state held that all the achievements and noble qualities of the Soviet people were traceable to the fact that they lived in the USSR and were products of the socialist system—and if the mainstream dissident (and anti-Soviet Western) view was that the achievements and nobility of the Soviet people existed despite their "captivity" in the USSR—the *anekdot* manifested the idea that any aspiration to nobility or great achievement plays into the logic of the nonironic (and thus false, or at least unsatisfying) ideological poles.

The strategic self-defamation of Soviet man was accompanied by actual behavior that resembled that of *anekdot* protagonists. Zinoviev wrote that average citizens were "compelled by truths and untruths (especially untruths) to adapt themselves to the conditions of life, repaying the torrent of lies and violence streaming down on them from above with lies, idleness, theft, drunkenness, hack-work, and other phenomena of this kind."[17] Yet the behavior he described did not amount to simple payback; it had elements of classic subcultural use of symbolic gestures. Stagnation was a time of crisis not only for the ideal of the Soviet collective, but also for the tenuous individual identity that had been staked out during the Thaw. The response from the urban populace was to form new kinds of collectives, many of them dominated by irony and/or by forms of alternative consciousness and behavior—alcohol consumption, deviant sex, and "reeling out" *anekdoty*. Engaging in such activities became a means for intragroup commiseration and cohesion, shared quotidian rituals around which more-organic popular collectives could be constituted and sustained. Here is Zinoviev again, describing a kind of anticollective:

> For a man to be recognized as a member of the collective he must possess a certain set of vices permitted by the collective in reality, although often they are officially censured. For example, drunkenness . . . , two-facedness, sycophancy, a quarrelsome disposition and absence of talent. . . . The collective, in fact, is essentially a union of injured, pallid, unhappy creatures which compensates for their defects.[18]

The "injured, pallid, unhappy" protagonists of *anekdoty* frequently defend their right to a squalid or otherwise defective existence, wherein the earth of the Motherland merges with collective feces:

> A man is sitting in a pit full of shit. Only his head, hands, and a book he is reading are visible. A passerby says: "Oh, you poor guy, how did you end up in there? Hold on, I'll pull you out!" "No, that's OK, go on your way." Another person happens by, sees the man in the shit, and reaches out to him: "Here, give me your hand, I'll get you right out of there!" "No, no, move along," says the man, and goes back to his book. Then an old man comes by: "Oh, dear, what are you doing down there in that shit?" "Why is everyone bothering me? This is where I live!"[19]

> Two worms—father and son—are sitting on a pile of manure. The worm-son asks: "Dad, is it nice living in an apple?" "It is, son," sighs the father. "What about in an orange, Dad?" asks the son, not letting up. "It's great to live in an orange, son," says the father, sighing even more deeply. "Then why do we live here, Dad?" "Well, son," says the father with great seriousness, "you don't choose your Motherland!"

In addition to passivity, stubborn indifference to catastrophe is also coded as a tactical and desirable behavioral stance:

> Letit nad derevnei Pizdets Vsemu. Dumaet: "Pizdets derevne!" Svistnul—netu derevni. Letit dal'she . . . Vidit—eshche odna derevnia. Dumaet: "Pizdets derevne!" Svistnul—netu derevni. Letit dal'she . . . Vidit—tret'ia derevnia. Dumaet: "Pizdets derevne!" Svistnul—netu derevni, odin dom stoit. Svistnul eshe raz—dom stoit. Svistnul tretii raz—dom vse ravno stoit. Spustilsia k domu, stuchitsia v dver.' Iz-za dveri:
> "Kto tam?"
> "Pizdets vsemu, a ty kto?"
> "A ia Pokhui vse!"[20]

Both characters in this *anekdot,* in fact, exhibit attributes coded as positive, especially among Russian males. Nancy Ries wrote that many *anekdoty* "glorified and reproduced the image of the Russian male/Russian *narod* as a powerful, menacing, mischievous hooligan, wreaking havoc on the societies and economies he/it touches, contaminating and spoiling everything along the way."[21]

The willingness and capacity to withstand suffering does alternate with a more negatively portrayed quality—abject submissiveness to the state:

> On a visit to the USSR, Nixon asks Brezhnev why Soviet workers never go on strike. Instead of answering him, Brezhnev invites Nixon to a factory. Brezhnev addresses the workers: "Starting tomorrow, wages will be reduced!" (Applause.) "And the workday will be extended!" (Applause.) "And every tenth worker will be hanged!" (Applause and a question from the audience: "Should we bring our own ropes, or will they be provided by the trade union?")[22]

The previous four *anekdoty* demonstrate the genre's role as a site for the negotiation of identity, especially identity in terms of power-subject relations. Because of the dual influences on the *anekdot* of the state's national legitimization myth and the native folk tradition, that negotiation had a strong element of ethnic consciousness. The tradition of self-degradation and self-ridicule in Russian popular culture—in addition to the *iurodivyi* (recall the *skomorokh* and the buffoon)—incorporated visual, behavioral, and verbal aspects, but it became primarily verbal in the urbanized logocentric Soviet century. Yet *anekdoty* are linked to the physical realm in multiple ways and can thus be reminders of the individual subject's "ontological status."[23] Moreover, they can function as assertions of the primacy of that status in relation to the contrived abstract subject posited as genuine and normative by the culture industry and other kinds of mass textual production. Reflexive Russian ethnic jokes emphasize the physical aspects of the stereotype, reflecting the carnality that had long been part of the folk tradition itself but that mass-media discourse and image production did not reflect, despite the traditional elements therein. The visceral associations of the *anekdot* enhanced its value as a medium for expressing this alternative category of identity. Those associations are not only thematic, but also extratextual, and they are present in the communicative process of joke telling itself.

The *anekdot* was doubly transgressive, simultaneously a medium for depicting taboo-breaking behavior and itself a form of taboo-breaking behavior. This combination of verbal and performative nonconformity had particular potency in an atmosphere in which verbal taboos were so highly charged. Also, as Arthur Koestler suggested, laughter is distinctive among human reflexes because it is a physical response triggered by a cognitive stimulus: the comic.[24] Joke telling is thus a point of contact between the visceral and the abstract, between the mundane and the aesthetic, between the realm of the mind and the realm of the mouth. In this sense it is metaphorically (not just metonymically) linked to drinking alcohol, another activity that combines, though in a converse way, the material and the mental (perhaps partly explaining alcohol's status as an obligatory accompaniment to *anekdoty*). Joke telling and drunkenness—along with other pastimes such as sex and fistfighting—are self-induced reminders of the subject's biological existence in a sensory environment dominated by Potemkin stimuli.

Despite their fetish for *diamat* (dialectic materialism), the culture industry and the mass media continued to generate models and texts that resembled less and less the empirically acquired knowledge of the subjects and consumers of those texts. One might object that this is true of mass culture anywhere, but the gap was especially wide in the Soviet case, in part because of the absence of market forces that afford consumer desires—especially physical desires—an influence on the content of mass media.[25] The prevalence of reflexive references to the physical life of *Homo sovieticus* in the *anekdot* was thus compensatory; the genre functioned as an outlet for the otherwise stifled impulse of the "folk" to narrate and perform its ongoing physical biography. Popular behaviors and cultural practices represented a deep-tissue parody of state ideology, which posited in materialist theory an essential link between the physical and the mental/spiritual (expressed in ideas such as base and superstructure and less esoterically in Ludwig Feuerbach's famous statement "You are what you eat") while producing abstract discursive models that were actually diametrical opposites of lived experience.

In a perverse way, Stalinism had demonstrated a keen interest in the links between texts and bodies, since it did violence to so many of the latter for producing the former. In the post-gulag age, ideology squandered its connection with the physical realm in part because ideological proscriptions and prescriptions ceased to be predictably enforced with physical violence. There was a shift in emphasis toward state aggression to texts themselves, rather than to their authors (shelving films, confiscating manuscripts, bull-dozing paintings, and so on).

MULTIETHNIC *ANEKDOTY*

A particularly common type of *anekdot* in which the Russian is featured as a category, and in which his physical and other characteristics are especially prominent, is what might be called the United Nations joke.[26] These involve characters representing two or more nationalities (typically three, but as many as fifteen[27]) most typically depicted in a single extraordinary situation, competition, or controlled experiment that demonstrates the essential character of each group. Such jokes are common in many (perhaps most) countries, but the Russian variant is distinctive for its consistent placement of the Russian himself (or herself) in the final humor-bearing position. The punch line represents a triumph, sometimes lifesaving, for the Russian:

> Three men are abducted by extraterrestrials (a German, a Frenchman, and a Russian). They are locked in separate rooms, given two steel spheres each, and told that the one who does the most amazing thing with them the next morning will be released. Morning. The German is juggling the spheres. The Frenchman is juggling while singing and dancing. They decide to release the Frenchman (what else could be done with the spheres in a room without windows or doors?). Just to complete the experiment, they look in on the Russian. Five minutes later they go to the Frenchman and tell him that the Russian will be sent home. The Frenchman is in shock: "What did he do that I didn't do?" "He lost one sphere and broke the other!!"

> A Russian, a Frenchman, and an Englishman are captured by cannibals. The cannibals tell them: "We're going to eat you all, except for the one who can make an echo in the forest last the longest." The Englishman shouts, "How do you do! . . ." and the echo responds: "do . . . do . . . do . . ." The Frenchman yells even louder: "Cherchez la femme! . . ." and his echo lasts even longer. The Russian calmly steps up and says: "Vodka for sale." "Where? . . . where? . . . where? . . ." comes the echo and doesn't fade for a long time.

> A symposium of thieves from around the world. A thief from France stands up and asks that the lights be dimmed for thirty seconds. After thirty seconds, from the same spot where he stood before, he says, "The gentleman

in the white jacket sitting in the section opposite from where I am standing, please come and get your fountain pen." Next, an American stands up and does a similar trick. After the American, a Russian stands up and says, "No need to dim the lights. Vasia, give everyone back their socks."

Soviet nationalism was frequently expressed in texts lionizing various heroes of the pre-Soviet and Soviet past. A central purpose of the Soviet approach to Russian history was to establish a chain of enlightened countrymen in order to demonstrate the historical inevitability of socialism's triumph. Rapid establishment of a deep native source for the ruling ideology was an important preemptive rebuttal of claims that the October Revolution imposed an imported ideology on Russia from without. Such hurried mythmaking was essential to the still tenuously victorious Bolsheviks, who sensibly felt an urgent need for self-legitimation via epic inscription of their brief past (see chapter 2). From the contemporary historical perspective, every epoch had its heroic (proto-socialist or socialist) representative: Sten'ka Razin, Emel'ian Pugachev, the Decembrists, Alexander Herzen, Nikolai Chernyshevskii, and so on.

The omnihistorical scope of the *anekdot* corpus also serves to establish the presence of native tricksterlike "heroes" throughout the Russian millennium. Accordingly, each period is also associated with an anecdotal "antihero": Lieutenant Rzhevskii, Chapaev, Shtirlits, etc. Since official hagiographies and popular texts about folk heroes often tapped the same cultural tropes, there was overlap and dialogue between the two. The role of the antiheroes is similar, in fact, to the actual mission of Shtirlits the spy: to represent the interests of the Russian people "behind enemy lines," be it Nazi Germany or in a calcified domestic cultural environment that officially denies recognition of identifiable native ethnic features. The state frequently embedded behavioral models and personality features that it advocated inside cultural icons, both historical and fictional. The *anekdot* did, as well.

CHAPAEV

The symbiotic relationship between the *anekdot* and the hothouse fakelore of Soviet myth production that provided a steady supply of models for it is especially evident in the vast corpus of jokes that feature Vasilii Ivanovich Chapaev (1887–1919), commander of the 25th Infantry Division of the Red Army. In the previous chapter, I demonstrated the ways in which the Soviet *anekdot* was a rare form of self-referential folklore. Some time during the heyday of Stagnation, one *anekdot* informs us, the Soviet government

programmed a computer to determine the most popular *anekdot,* with the
following result:

> Vasilii Ivanovich Chapaev is walking on Red Square and he meets Vladimir
> Il'ich Lenin. And Vladimir Il'ich asks Vasillii Ivanovich (with a Jewish accent):
> "So, Abram, isn't it time we left for Israel already?"[28]

If Lenin (along with Stalin for a time) was the dominant figure in the official
national iconography and autobiography, Chapaev—himself a deity in the
Soviet mytho-historical pantheon—fulfilled an analogous role in the popular
imagination, where his relevance seems to have outlived that of the other
two. Since shortly after his death in 1919,[29] Chapaev has enjoyed a legendary reputation in a variety of cultural contexts; he has been a hero of print
and visual media and of fakelore, folklore, and jokelore alike. He remains a
popular icon to a "folk" that is still steeped in a detailed knowledge of (and a
complex and ironic, yet nostalgic, stance toward) Soviet mass culture.

The enormous cycle of *anekdoty* about Chapaev is both a result of
and an engine for the continuation of his popular appeal. His preeminence
as a joke protagonist even today, a dozen years after the end of the Soviet
power that he helped establish, was confirmed by a 1999 survey asking Russians about which subjects they most often tell or hear *anekdoty:* 15 percent
named Chapaev; 14 percent the New Russians (see chapter 6); 11 percent
the foulmouthed class clown Vovochka; 8 percent the Chukchi (see following); 4 percent Jews; 2 percent alcoholics and dystrophics; and 1 percent
Radio Armenia.[30]

Unlike many of the other models for popular Soviet joke cycles, Chapaev was, of course, an actual historical figure, a famed peasant-general who
died in battle while swimming across the Ural River. His canonization was
rapid. Dmitrii Furmanov's 1923 factographic novel *Chapaev* was perennially
listed among workers' favorite books beginning soon after its publication.
The proto-socialist-realist text firmly inscribed Chapaev in the fledgling Soviet state-creation mythology less than four years after his death. His fame is
based primarily, however, on the Vasil'ev Brothers' seminal 1934 film *Chapaev.*[31] Although the *anekdoty* date from three decades after the film's initial
release, they play specifically on the image of Chapaev therein.

In a front-page *Pravda* article published in 1934 not long after the
film's release, the spectators' experience of the film is described for the
benefit of those unfortunate comrades who have not yet seen it:

> The lights go down in the cinema, a blue beam floods out of the projecting
> booth, the equipment makes a noise behind the audience's back and sud-
> denly the dim swarm of shadows on the screen gives way to an animated

story, the stern and proud story of our battle and our victories. The film captivates the audience from the very first moments, it enthralls and moves them with each last shot, it infects them with love and hate, ecstasy and fear, joy and rage from scene to scene.[32]

Over the next several decades, and indeed to the present day, the story and character of Chapaev has inspired countless verbal, visual, and behavioral homages of the most varied sort, across the entire spectrum of regard from ironic mockery to panegyric awe. Osip Mandel'shtam, who would die in the gulag before the decade was out, wrote excitedly of the *Chapaev* film in a 1935 poem:

[. . .] Into our open mouths
Talking Chapaev galloped from the sound screen—
[. . .]
To die and jump onto his horse!
[. . .] V otkrytye rty nam
Govoriashchii Chapaev s kartiny skakal zvukovoi—
[. . .]
Umeret' i vskochit' na konia svoego![33]

Mandel'shtam's appreciation of "talking Chapaev" is a clue to the character's initial appeal; the film was among the first Soviet talkies, and Chapaev was certainly the first Soviet film icon of the sound era. Cinematic positive heroes lent themselves more readily than literary protagonists to immortalization in *anekdoty* because the *anekdot* itself, again, is a dramatic genre, so it easily assimilates filmic forms of discourse such as dialogue and third-person voice-over narration. (The Shtirlits cycle would exploit the latter device, used extensively in its source text.) The Chapaev film, moreover, is constructed from a series of episodes that each has its own miniature narrative or dialogic arc, often ending with a sort of punch line. Like punch lines, several of those bits of dialogue have entered the language as "winged words," for example: "Enema tubes!"; "Alexander of Macedonia? He's a general? Who is he, and how come I don't know him?"; "A psychological attack? Hell, bring on the psychological attack"; "Quiet, citizens! Chapai is going to think!"; "Are you making fun of Chapaev?!"; "Teach me the machine gun, you devil!"; "I didn't go to no academies, I'm no graduate"; "They march beautifully" "They're intelligentsia"; "The Whites came and looted, the Reds came and looted. Where's a peasant s'posed to turn?"[34]

Among the scenes most commonly referenced in jokes is one in which Chapaev and his trusty orderly, Pet'ka, are talking late at night on the eve of a battle. The two warriors have just finished singing a touching duet about trying to thwart the *chernyi voron* (black raven).[35] Pet'ka, appropriately awed by his commander and role model, asks him a series of four questions about the extent of his military prowess. To Pet'ka's first three inquiries, about whether Division Commander Chapaev could command a battalion, an entire army, even the combined Soviet armed forces, the general replies in the affirmative. To the fourth question from the by now enraptured Pet'ka, however—could Chapaev command the combined armies of all the nations in the world—the commander thinks for a moment before answering that no, he could not, because he does not speak any foreign languages.

The bedroom scene itself mimics (yet ultimately violates) one of the cardinal rules of joke composition—the rule of threes—and even has a punch line of sorts. In this respect, the numerous jokes that satirically rehearse the scene are both mocking and corrective, and they satirize both the implied skill of the general and the attempt at folksy humor on the part of the filmmakers. The anecdotal versions of the exchange nudge the situation into the realm of the vulgar and the prosaic (and the Russian) by, for example, substituting alcohol consumption or sex—important cultural behaviors that the film largely ignores—for military planning:

> "Vasilii Ivanovich, could you drink a half-liter?"
> "Sure, Pet'ka, sure!"
> "What about a liter?"
> "Sure, Pet'ka, sure!"
> "What about a barrel of vodka?"
> "Sure, Pet'ka, sure!"
> "How about a whole river of vodka?"
> "No, Pet'ka. Where would I get a pickle big enough to chase it down with?"
>
> "Vasilii Ivanovich, could you drink a liter?"
> "Sure."
> "What about two?"
> "Sure."
> "What about a whole bucketful?"
> "No, Pet'ka. Only Lenin can drink that much!"
>
> "Vasilii Ivanovich, can you do the Baroness?"
> "Sure, Pet'ka."
> "How about the Gypsy Girl?"
> "Sure, Pet'ka."
> "What about the Boogie-Woogie?"
> "Now what kind of whore is that?" [Pet'ka is talking about popular dance steps].

Note that the second *anekdot* begins by playing on Chapaev's capacity for drink but ultimately shifts the satirical focus to a different hero, Lenin.[36] That shift ironically suggests not only the universality of stereotypical behavior among Russians, but also a hierarchy within that stereotype that matches the military/political hierarchy that the *anekdot* mocks.

Again, the film is only the best-known incarnation of Chapaev's renown, which has transcended cultural and generational boundaries. Soviet children played "Chapaev" (a Soviet analogue to "cowboys and Indians") in the 1950s, their imaginations sparked by matinee showings of the film, history textbooks, and the "Chapaev" radio program popular at the time. One of the first avant-garde film groups to form during perestroika dubbed itself *Che-paev,* merging the names of two martyred icons of world revolution. The list goes on: a rock group called The Chapaev Brigade; a 1998 erotic remake of the classic film;[37] a 1995 play by Oleg Danilov entitled *My idem smotret' "Chapaeva"!* (We're Going to See *Chapaev!*). Two recent films— Petr Lutsik's *Okraina* (Borderlands, 1998) and Aleksei Balabanov's *Brat-2* (Brother 2, 2000)—explicitly use motifs from the Vasil'ev Brothers' film. Perhaps the most famous and idiosyncratic piece of recent "Chapaeviana" is Viktor Pelevin's 1995 novel *Chapaev i Pustota* (Chapaev and Void).[38] Vasilii Ivanovich's face has even been drafted for use on products ranging from mustard to vodka to pistachio nuts.

Although Chapaev has been a prominent presence in the jokelore only since the 1960s, there were folkloric elements to his story and image long before he became *anekdot* protagonist number one. The first oral genre to be associated with the martyred hero was the rumor: stories circulated after his death that he in fact suffered only concussive amnesia while crossing the river and that he lived a long subsequent life, isolated and anonymous in a remote psychiatric ward.[39] A 1937 tale entitled "Chapaev zhiv!" (Chapaev Lives!) inscribed such rumors in official Soviet folklore, which also immortalized him in folk songs and legends.[40] Sidel'nikov cites one such legend, entitled "Lektsiia Chapaeva o tom, kak odnomu semerykh ne boiat'sia" (Chapaev's Lecture on How One Man Doesn't Have to Fear Seven):

> In one battle several young fighters ran from the enemy. They chickened out, to put it simply. Vasilii Ivanovich found out after the battle and summoned them so he could give them a lecture about how one man shouldn't be afraid of seven.
>
> "It's good to fight alone against seven men," Chapaev said. "It's hard for the seven. Seven men need to find seven mounds to shoot from behind, but you only need one. You can always find one mound, but it's hard to find seven mounds. So you get down and start shooting: kill one—there'll be six left, kill two—five left . . . When you kill six of them, the one that's left will be afraid

of you. So you make him put his hands up and take him prisoner. Then you bring him to headquarters!"[41]

There was even a short film, directed by Vladimir Petrov and starring Boris Babochkin, the same actor who played Chapaev in 1934, entitled *Chapaev s nami!* (Chapaev Is with Us! 1941), in which Chapaev makes it safely across the river, where he joins Russian soldiers geared up to fight the Nazi invaders.[42]

Chapaev was one of the holy trinity of Soviet jokeloric fools, along with Shtirlits and the Chukchi.[43] Chapaev *anekdoty* fall into several categories, some of which evoke folk portrayals of the traditional Russian fool (and play on features ascribed to "the Russian" in *anekdoty* I cite previously): drunkenness; skirt-chasing; language (i.e., Chapaev or Pet'ka's linguistic shortcomings); cleanliness (e.g., "Pet'ka sees Vasilii Ivanovich sitting by the campfire, chewing, and asks him 'Where'd you get the American chewing gum?' and Chapaev replies, 'It's not gum, Pet'ka; I'm washing my socks'" or "Pet'ka says to Chapaev, 'Vasilii Ivanovich, your feet are much dirtier than mine,' and Chapaev explains, 'Of course, Pet'ka. I'm older than you.'"), and foreign travel (Chapaev in Israel, Chapaev in Paris, Chapaev in Vietnam, Chapaev in America, etc.). The most common motif is linguistic incompetence:

Vasilii Ivanovich! They're bringing in a captured spy!" "Did you find any documents on him?" "Yeah, there's a piece of paper that says . . ." "Read it!" "U-rin-al-y-sis . . ." "Let him go! He's Italian!"[44]

"Vasilii Ivanovich! [The] Gulf Stream is frozen!"
"How many times do I have to tell you: don't send kikes on reconnaissance missions!"

Chapaev asks Furmanov:
"Who's that up on the roof?"
"That's Pet'ka—he's up there messing around with [the] antenna."
"Hmm, Antenna—that's a pretty name!"

On the military academy entry exam in math, Vasilii Ivanovich is given the following problem: from a square trinomial [in Russian *trekhchlen*, which contains the word "*chlen*" (member)] extract a perfect square. He cries, but sharpens his saber!

Several buzzwords specific to the Russian Civil War are among the alien words that Chapaev mangles, in particular the term "white" [*belyi*, plural *belye*], which, as is evident below, can imply a range of white objects:

"Vasilii Ivanovich, there are whites in the forest!"
"OK, Pet'ka, we'll go mushroom picking in the morning."

"Vasilii Ivanovich! They brought [a] white!"
"How many cases?"

Angela Davis saw *Chapaev* in the USSR and really liked it, especially the part when they say "We'll slaughter all the whites and life will be happy."

There is a leitmotif in the *anekdot*-al Chapaev's constant misapprehension of language, and indeed in his behavior in general. He perceives the world through a filter of carnality, rather than ideology or military values. His motivations are food, sleep, drink, tobacco, sex, gambling, and the chance to use profanity. Whereas in the film everyday items are invested with military meanings—potatoes represent soldiers and a tobacco pipe becomes heavy artillery when Chapaev is giving a lesson in battle strategy—in the *anekdoty* all military and political categories of perception are constantly re-presented in a different connotational realm, the stereotypical world of the Russian male:

Vasilii Ivanovich says, "When the war ends, Pet'ka, we'll build a conservatory."
"And we'll put a machine gun on the roof."
"What for?!"
"So the *konservy* (items of canned food) aren't stolen."

Somehow Pet'ka and Vasilii Ivanovich are elected members of the Soviet Academy of Sciences. They're sitting in their office shuffling papers around. Suddenly Pet'ka says, "Oh, Vasilii Ivanovich, this Keldysh [name of the president of the Soviet Academy of Sciences at the time] is bothering me . . ." "Just don't scratch it, you dolt."

Chapaev and Pet'ka are in Spain. Chapaev asks Pet'ka, "What's all that racket on the street?" "Some Dolores is getting *ibarruri*'d and she's shouting "Better standing than kneeling!"[45]

This is not to say that Furmanov or the Vasil'evs completely neglect Chapaev's demographic and cultural background. On the contrary, his simplicity and crude enthusiasm are underscored. The inscribed Chapaev is clearly a *muzhik* (man of the people), but something is missing; he is a folk archetype corrupted in the service of a value system alien to folk traditions. *Anekdoty* are hyperbolic correctives to that bogus use of his image.

The diegetic resurrection of Chapaev in Petrov's 1941 film for an extraordinary cause—the Great Patriotic War—is a rule-affirming exception among official representations of the hero. Both the novel and the original film underscore the indispensable yet ephemeral value of the historical Chapaev, with his primitive and spontaneous brand of Communist enthusiasm. That is, they are careful both to represent spontaneity and to enshrine it into submission.[46] This represents a tactical solution to the problem of what to do with the entropic and visceral urges of the *narod* (the folk)—which were useful to the revolutionary cause—once the revolution was a fait accompli and the status quo became something to be defended rather than attacked. The *Pravda* article cited above betrays such a view of history when it calls the film a "crystallized artistic reproduction of our country's past."[47]

Chapaev jokes are part of a counterimpulse: to rescue the hero from the pedestal, to liberate Chapaev from both the civil war chronotope in which he was "crystallized" by Furmanov and the Vasil'evs and from the abstract epic of Soviet history. The *anekdot*-al Vasilii Ivanovich is a positive cultural figure, a hero.[48] The way the *anekdot* conflates elite and its putative opposite—drunk, dirty, stupid—is not only to the purposeful detriment of the former, and not only exposes the official version of Chapaev's biography as bathetic self-parody, but also it evinces affection for and approval of the latter. Its signature maneuver is a precipitous demotion of the lofty accompanied by a corresponding elevation of the base. It is not difficult to identify moments in the Chapaev joke cycle where he is reclaimed, co-opted, and escorted into a different narrative stream in which it is not consciousness that will overcome spontaneity but, on the contrary, it is marks of spontaneity (and Russianness) such as drunkenness and obscenity, of which Chapaev is a paragon, that are immortal and no match for the limited, ephemeral buzzwords and chronotopes of the engineered Soviet zeitgeist. Nancy Ries wrote that this alternative system of values was affirmative: "Mischief, resistance, envy, and roguery have, in fact, been popularly treated if not as unambiguously positive values, then at least affectionately—as amusing, refreshing, spontaneous, and free."[49] What emerges from an analysis of the cycle is an image of Chapaev as a kind of an unwitting spy behind enemy lines, a comfortingly recognizable *muzhik* who drinks and whores and thereby affirms both his gender credentials and his ethnic credentials. In the logic of the *anekdot,* his vices are distinctive ethnographic features that stand out with particular clarity in the incongruous environment of ideology and abstract rationality.

The same is true of another *anekdot*-al Russian in uniform: the fictional hero of Lioznova's miniseries *Semnadtsat' mgnovenii vesny,* SS Standartenführer Max Otto von Shtirlits, the cover identity of Colonel Maksim Maksimovich Isaev, a Soviet Army spy living in Nazi Germany. Shtirlits, in the words of M. Timofeev, "plays the role of an elegant German officer, but remains a Russian man in the depths of his soul."[50] At times the pressure from within that soul becomes so great that Shtirlits cannot refrain from reflexively performing his ethnic behavioral birthright:

> The Reichstag. A meeting of the top Nazi officials. Shtirlits is there. At the moment when the others are bent over a map spread out on the table, Shtirlits quietly blows his nose on the drapes. Kopelian's voice-over commentary: "Shtirlits knew, of course, that it was not proper to do that, and thus very dangerous. But he wanted, he really wanted, here in the very bowels of fascism, to be himself, if just for a moment."

> They find Shtirlits passed out drunk on the floor amidst vodka bottles, with his fly undone and his red underwear sticking out of it, in a pool of vomit, a brassiere in his left hand and a torn piece of a message in his right that reads: "You can relax a bit. Signed, Center." [Center is Shtirlits's Soviet contact who sends him instructions in code over the radio.][51]

Shtirlits is a "carrier" of Russianness abroad.[52] His Russianness is an irresistible internal force, a sort of ethnic Tourette's syndrome.

One reason for the incredible popularity of both the miniseries and the *anekdoty* is Shtirlits's status as an impostor-by-necessity, a basically decent Russian forced to stifle his identity and convictions in public while living in a repressive ideological state. The motif of daily strategic role-playing found resonance in a society in which there existed a similar incongruity between public and private performances of self. Indeed, the telling of *anekdoty* itself implicitly parodied the requisite disingenuousness of Soviet social life.

One target of satire in the Chapaev cycle is the premium placed by the authors of the Chapaev novel and film, and by Soviet culture in general, on factography, on the accurate recording and immediate validation of historical facts. For example, Chapaev is talking to Pet'ka and recalling a particularly fierce battle:

> "I look to the right: Holy motherfucker! I look to the left: Motherfucking hell!"
> "Wow, what a memory you have, Vasilii Ivanovich!"

Another battle reminiscence, from Chapaev's diary:

> There was a battle. We drove the whites from the forest. The next day there was another battle and the whites drove us from the forest. On the third day the forest ranger showed up and chased us all out of the forest.

Driven from the battlefield by the angry forest ranger, the *anekdot*-al Chapaev, unlike Furmanov's or the Vasil'evs' Chapaev, can move away from the battlefield, away from the civil war, away from any hope of achieving consciousness, even away from the USSR.[53] Both the official and unofficial branches of the Chapaev legacy led, albeit by different paths and with different results, to quasimythic spaces: one to the sterile pantheon of Soviet epic heroes, the other to the carnivalesque, native chronotopes of Anecdotia. The cycle responds to the mythologization of the hero not through demythologizing, but by remythologizing him. This remythologization testifies once again to the presence in Russo-Soviet culture of competing yet interdependent approaches to iconic choreography, one of which employs the ironic mode, while the other privileges the epic or romantic. A rather different icon—though one similarly invested with symbolic significance by both state textual producers and *anekdot* culture—is the Chukchi.

THE CHUKCHI CYCLE: *OTKUDA, ODNAKO?*

Connoisseurs of the Soviet *anekdot* will recognize a 2001 American joke in which space tourist Dennis Tito learned just two Russian phrases during his stay on the International Space Station—"Welcome aboard. Don't touch anything"—as an adaptation of a similar joke from the 1970s about the first Chukchi cosmonaut. Among the canonical cycles of Russo-Soviet jokelore, the Chukchi cycle stands out as enigmatic. When and why did the Chukchi—an ethnic group with a population of about thirteen thousand indigenous to the arctic northeast of Siberia—acquire their "privileged" position in the *anekdot* corpus? Other famous cycles of the 1960s, 1970s, and 1980s—Chapaev, Shtirlits, Winnie-the-Pooh, Cheburashka, and so on— have singular concrete textual sources in popular culture. Ethnic jokes are told about nationalities with whom urban Russians have real-life contact (especially Jews, Georgians, and Ukrainians). The Chukchi, however, are relatively scarce in both Soviet cultural production and Russian cities.

While claims made by some that Chukchi jokes are not ethnic jokes at all[54] are excessive, the cycle clearly differs from other ethnic-themed cycles, typically motivated by historical and/or sociopolitical factors. The *anekdoty* about Ukrainians that flourished during the first post-Soviet decade, for example, are legible as parting shots directed at the closest inhabitants of a lost empire. Jokes about Georgians as wealthy conspicuous consumers, according to Emil Draitser, boomed in the 1950s, when people from the Caucasus began coming to Russian cities to take advantage of a new law permitting the sale of flowers and produce in street markets.[55] Jokes about Jews, of course, predate and outnumber all other Russian ethnic *anekdot* cycles.

The Chukchi are unlike most other ethnicities conscripted into joke-lore in that their history, ethnography, and especially their relations with the Russians are largely irrelevant to the functions and content of the jokes. Of the twenty-six nationalities known as the *malye narody severa* (small peoples of the north), the Chukchi are the fifth most populous. Traditionally they are nomadic reindeer herders or marine hunters and fishermen. The word "Chukchi" is a Russian coinage based on the native word *chavchi* (or *chauchi*), meaning "rich with reindeer." The Chukchi's name for themselves is *Lyg'oravetlan* (or *Lugora Vetlat*), "the true people."

In 1778, after more than a century of contact during which the Chukchi proved resistant to subjugation, the Russian empire made peace and began trading with them. The Chukchi also traded with the Ameri-cans, Norwegians, British, and Japanese until the Soviets closed Chukotka to foreign trade in the early 1920s. In the 1930s, the Chukchi put up a brief but fierce armed resistance to collectivization.[56] In the post-Soviet period, Chukotka has suffered from the environmental legacy of industrial pollution and nearby nuclear tests in the 1950s and 1960s and has experienced grave shortages of heating fuel, food, and labor, especially after the 1998 Russian financial crisis. While economically disastrous, however, the mass exodus of Russian and other Slavic settlers from Chukotka in recent years has proved to be something of a stimulus for renewed emphasis on and interest in local native cultural traditions.

Again, those traditions tend to figure in the *anekdot* cycle mostly as superficial descriptive details and not as targets for ethnic condescension or hostility. In composition and setting, Chukchi jokes are in the tradition of Russian folk *anekdoty* and tales about simpletons.[57] Many Chukchi jokes in fact are old chestnuts from that tradition, with the detail of the Chukchi pro-tagonist superimposed. The physical image of the Chukchi contains several elements characteristic of the fool across cultures. He wears a fool's "uni-form," with baggy clothing that exaggerates his small stature. He frequently wears distinctive headwear and carries some kind of stick (in the Chukchi's case, a fishing pole, a spear, or a rifle). Draitser points out that the jokeloric Chukchi, like Ivan the Fool, exhibits a naive and persistent belief in magic.[58] For example:

> A Chukchi is sitting in a tree and sawing through the branch he's sitting on. A passing geologist looks at him and says: "Watch out, you're going to fall!" The Chukchi keeps sawing. The branch falls and the Chukchi along with it. He gets up and says: "A shaman!"[59]

This is a variant of a venerable folk motif with the traditional Russian peas-ant protagonist transformed into a Chukchi and the sorcerer into a shaman.

115

As in the Chapaev cycle, a common source of humor is misinterpretation or overly literal interpretation of a word or phrase, especially concepts related to modern technology:

> A Chukchi goes into a store:
> "Do you have color televisions?"
> "Yes."
> "I'll take a green one, please."

> A Chukchi is at the Aeroflot counter:
> "How long is the flight to Chukotka?"
> "Just a minute . . ."
> "Thank you."

> Two Chukchi are lost in the taiga. One says, "Why don't you shoot into the air? Maybe someone will hear us." The other one shoots, but nobody answers. "Shoot again." The second one takes another shot, but still nothing. "One more time," says the first Chukchi. "I can't," says the second; "I'm out of arrows."

He is also sometimes naively self-destructive, especially when dealing with technology:

> Two Chukchi are taking apart an unexploded bomb. A passerby says: "Are you insane? It could blow up!" "We have another one!"

Another traditional folk motif common in Chukchi jokes is the bumpkin in the big city.[60] The motif was exploited as a device to ridicule Soviet tropes (the fool's traditional role of speaking truth to power) and to expose as a hopeless failure or fraud the socialist project of enlightening the backward masses:

> A Chukchi submits a novel for publication. The editor reads it and tells him, "Well, it's not very good, I'm afraid. . . . You should read the classics. Have you read Turgenev? Tolstoy? Dostoevsky?" "No," says the Chukchi, "Chukchi not reader. Chukchi writer."

> A Chukchi returns home after graduating from the Institute of Foreign Affairs in Moscow. His friends ask him what he learned. "Oh, I learned a lot," he says. "Now I know that Marx-Engels are two different people, Ul'ianov and Lenin are the same person, and Slava KPSS [glory to the CPSU; the word "Slava" is also a first name] is not a person at all."

So why did the collective Soviet consciousness, sometime in the late 1960s or early 1970s, graft the image of the Chukchi onto an existing folkloric template? The periodic replacement of one joke protagonist with others is a natural process in the evolution of the genre—every generation has its canonical jokeloric idiot—but why the Chukchi? One not immediately evident reason for the cycle's emergence may be found in the "extremity" (in various senses) of the Chukchi and Chukotka, which were exploited in official texts as well as in *anekdoty*. Geographically, for example, Chukotka is the farthest Russian point from Moscow, more than thirty-six hundred miles and nine time zones away. It is also the closest point in Russia to the United States, a fact that itself has inspired at least one *anekdot:*

Two Chukchi are talking:
"That emperor Nikolashka [Nikolai I] was an idiot . . ."
"Why?"
"Because he sold Alaska to the Americans, but he didn't sell Chukotka."

As one of the most economically primitive and geographically peripheral nationalities in the Soviet family of peoples, the Chukchi were useful guinea pigs on which to demonstrate the effectiveness of Sovietization. As Galya Diment and Yuri Slezkine wrote, "The 'small peoples' represented the most remote past on the Marxist evolutionary scale. Hence their march into modernity and beyond was the most arduous and most heroic of all."[61] The harsh climate of Chukotka added an element of physical heroism to the ideological heroism exhibited by the brave men and women who brought Communism to the "savages." Stories about Chukotka in the 1930s underscore both the bravery of commissars and geologists in Chukotka and the civilizing influence of Soviet power, especially the exposure of the Chukchi shaman as a fraud.[62]

Another, more visceral reason for the cycle's appearance is phonetic. Several people[63] have pointed out the inherent humorousness of the word "Chukchi,"[64] which not only has alliterative syllables, but also abounds in the "funniest phonemes": voiceless fricatives, the affricate *ch,* and stops (/ch/, /k/, /kh/, and /th/ are especially common in humor). We find the same principle at work in the names of other major *anekdot* cycles: Cheburashka, Chapaev, Vinni-Pukh and Piatachok, and Vovochka, not to mention Ivanushka-Durachok. Belousov and Draitser have also suggested the influence of the popular Soviet children's book *Chuk i Gek* by Arkadii Gaidar.[65] As Draitser wrote, the Russian lexicon itself predisposed the poor Chukchi to immortalization in jokelore; words that use the syllables *chu* and/or *cha*[66] often evoke absurdity (*chush,' chepukha*), stupidity or other undesirable traits (*chuchelo, churka, chainik*),[67] or simply non-Russianness (*chukhonets, chu-*

vash, and the nonspecific slur *chuchmek,* which refers to any Asian in the USSR[68]). The word *"chukcha"* itself has entered Russian slang as simply a term for a stupid person (note this particularly offensive mini-*anekdot:* "Chukcha—eto ne natsional'nost,' a diagnoz" [Chukchi is not a nationality, but a diagnosis]).[69]

Another phonetic reason for the popularity of the Chukchi cycle is the stereotypical Asian accent that is de rigueur when performing Chukchi jokes. The comic use of this accent was familiar in Russian and Soviet culture long before the Chukchi joke caught on (for example, the Chinese servants in Mikhail Bulgakov's play *Zoikina kvartira* [Zoika's Apartment]). This ethnic stereotype was uncontroversial perhaps because it was considered purely comedic rather than satirical, even in the land of "friendship of the peoples." Ethnic accents could even serve in approved cultural texts as comedic filters to camouflage otherwise risky satirical content (the Georgian accent adopted by Arkadii Raikin to perform Zhvanetskii's monologue "Defitsit," for example). In underground humor, of course, in which the Chukchi by the 1980s was the major representative of Soviet Asians, the accent could be openly exploited to satirical ends, for example:

> They ask a Chukchi: which space program is the best in the world? He proudly replies: "NASA!" [mispronunciation of *nasha* (ours)]

Or in obscene puns:

> One day a Chukchi is asked what kinds of ambassador [*posol*] he can name. "Well, there's ambassador extraordinary [*posol chrezvychainyi*], there's ambassador plenipotentiary [*posol upolnomochennyi*], and there's *posol ty na khui*" (mispronunciation of *poshel ty na khui,* "fuck off").

No discussion of the Chukchi cycle is complete without a mention of a curious, if tiny, subcycle: Jewish-Chukchi jokes. The reasons for the emergence of the odd hybrid are both historical and textual. Two images in Soviet unofficial culture closely associated with Siberia are Chukchi and the gulag. Jews in the USSR were a nationality disproportionately familiar with the gulag, and they are the "anecdotal comrades" of the Chukchi.[70] A joke book published in 1997 makes the link explicit and includes the following preface:

> What is Rabinovich doing during his terrible exile in Chukotka? Nothing bad: he married a Chukcha woman and is breeding frost-resistant Jews. We can hope that in the twenty-first century Chukotka will be inhabited by Jews as crafty as Chukchi and Chukchi as trusting as Jews. Buy this book. If you're a

Jew, you'll laugh at the Chukchi, if you're a Chukchi, laugh at the Jews, and if you're neither one nor the other, you can laugh at both of them.[71]

This excerpt, however tongue in cheek, suggests that the logic of the "Chukcho-Semitic" *anekdot* is not devoid of anti-Semitism (or anti-Chukchism, for that matter). Yet the main impulse for the forced cohabitation of the two nationalities in post-Soviet jokelore seems to be the concentration of incongruities between the stereotypes of the two groups: dumb/smart, rural/urban, uneducated/intellectual, Asian/Western. Draitser wrote that the Chukchi is "an 'anti-Jew' of sorts."[72]

In a sense, the previous comment to the effect that urban Russians have no contact with Chukchi is false; the "fool" in the late twentieth century still comes to the city and is immortalized in folk humor, but he does so electronically, via mass-media images. By far the most sustained depiction of the Chukchi in Soviet mass culture, and a catalogue of stereotypes that later informed the *anekdot* cycle, is Vitalii Mel'nikov's 1966 film *Nachal'nik Chukotki* (The Head of Chukotka),[73] about a young revolutionary who comes to Chukotka in 1922 as the scribe of a Bolshevik commissar, but who has to take on the responsibilities of being the only representative of Soviet power in Chukotka himself (and becoming the eponymous "head of Chukotka") when the commissar dies of typhoid en route.[74] Despite Mel'nikov's extended treatment of the Chukchi theme, however, the most immediate impetus for the Chukchi joke cycle was almost certainly a 1972 pop song by a singer named Nikolai (a.k.a. Kola) Bil'dy (refrain: "Samolet—khorosho, a oleni luchshee-e-e!" [An airplane's good, but reindeer are better!"]).[75] Other images of Chukchi in Soviet culture include the works of Chukchi novelist Iurii Rytkheu and a 1972 textbook of English containing a story that contrasts the charmed lives of the Chukchi under socialism with the misery of the Eskimos across the Bering Strait in Alaska.[76]

The Chukchi's name, physical size, and stereotypical accent contribute to their folkloric image as naive and childlike simpletons. Inevitably, therefore, there was also a counterimpulse in the cycle: to represent the Chukchi as wise, crafty, or even secretly brilliant:

A group of geologists is trying to pull their stuck ATV out of the snow. A Chukchi rides by on a reindeer sleigh. He stops, looks at the geologists, takes a drag on his pipe, and says: "Hey, chief! I know what you need to do! Give me a bottle of vodka and I'll tell you." "Get outta here. We'll manage fine without you." The Chukchi goes home, and in the evening comes back. The geologists and their ATV are still stuck. This time the head geologist goes to the Chukchi and says: "OK, here's your bottle. Tell us what we need to do." "Eh, chief. It'll cost you two bottles now." The chief gives him a second bottle. The Chukchi puts the vodka in his pack, whips his reindeer into motion, and says: "You need a tractor, chief!"

A Chukchi sits fishing on the easternmost tip of the Chukotka peninsula. Suddenly a submarine with foreign markings surfaces right in front of him. The hatch opens and the captain looks out and says: "Do you speak English, sir?" "Yes, I do," replies the Chukchi, "but what the hell good does it do me in this idiotic country?"

The image of the overeducated Chukchi who nonetheless lives a third-world material existence suggests the cycle's function as an oblique outlet for Russian self-satire, as observers including Barskii and Draitser have pointed out.[77] Chukotka in this respect is a hyperbolic synecdoche for Russia. The Chukchi and Chukotka are prominent in the jokelore for the same reason they were used in official Soviet texts: they represent a concentration of extremes—geographic, meteorological, cultural, political—that amount to a potent metaphor for a range of discursive agendas. The mockery that underlies many Chukchi jokes contradicts images of the privileged New Soviet Man and also reflects an older, deeper national anxiety regarding Russia's self-image vis-à-vis the West. Chukotka is to Russia as Russia is to Europe:[78] peripheral, freezing, dark, impoverished, Asiatic, and inhabited by furry ursine simpletons. In this respect, *anekdoty* about Chukchi are as much defensive as they are offensive ethnic humor; the Russian subconscious ethnos exports negative aspects of its self-image onto a geographically remote Other.[79] In the past, this Other could be much closer; in the eighteenth and nineteenth centuries it was represented by the *poshekhontsy*, residents of the backwater town of Poshekhon'e (immortalized by Saltykov-Shchedrin). In the new multinational state and after the onset of widespread cultural uniformity in Soviet Russia, there were no more *poshekhontsy;* the "fooltown"[80] to which undesirable traits must be relegated had to be farther away. If the "we-say-Chukchi-but-mean-Russian" thesis is to be believed, however, that "town" was also much closer to home than it had ever been. In this respect, the Chukchi cycle may well execute a maneuver similar to the one Davies ascribed to reflexive ethnic humor: stereotypical self-representation to preempt stereotyping from without. Yet if Draitser, Barskii, and Davies are correct (I believe they are), the cycle adds a bit of legerdemain that deflects that potential external appraisal toward another group that is (in more ways than one) as remote as can be, but is nevertheless (also in more ways than one) *nashi* (our own kind).

Chapter Six

Post-Stagnation Deflation, or the Afterlife of the Soviet *Anekdot*

> It is as if the *anekdot* wants to be banned,
> liquidated, and survives on this expectation.
> Give it its freedom, remove the ban, and it will
> croak.
> —Abram Terts, 1978

ALTHOUGH THE PREDICTION in this epigraph proved to be hyperbolic, the end of Soviet censorship (and of Soviet power itself a few years later), as expected, dealt a severe blow to the cultural currency of the *anekdot*. By the early 1990s, the generic corpus was in quantitative and qualitative decline. The disappearance of an ever-present monolithic target for satire deprived the *anekdot* of at least the political aspect of what Sigmund Freud considered a joke's central purpose: to help people "evade restrictions and open sources of pleasure that have become inaccessible."[1] With the removal of state proscriptions on the pursuit of "pleasure" and on free expression, the substantial weight the genre had borne for decades as an outlet for such impulses was quickly distributed among other forms. The history of the *anekdot* in the post-Soviet period is inextricable from the history of where humor and satire "went," in terms of genres and media, when the formidable potency of the *anekdot* was suddenly replaced by a humbling absence of rhetorical tumescence. This final chapter examines the redistribution of the functional portfolio of the *anekdot,* as well as new mutations in the genre's evolution, that followed the obsolescence of its taboo status.

The value of the Soviet *anekdot* had never been limited to making Russians laugh, of course. As Krongauz pointed out, most of the forbidden spheres of life for which *anekdot* telling had previously been a sublimation—independent political activism, ethnic self-expression, and sex—acquired new expressive venues: political party formation, nationalist movements, and erotica.[2] The *anekdot* had also been the use that mass-media consumers found for otherwise useless material extant in the popular consciousness.

121

That consciousness suddenly found itself overstimulated by novel and compelling material.

Its small size and attention to detail had made the *anekdot* a potent tool for expressing values alternative to those championed in the large generalizing texts of the Soviet period, and after that period *anekdoty* lost much of their utility. Such a "trivial" reactive form of expression was not a viable genre-*dominanta* in a period devoid of a clearly hegemonic ideology during which many found themselves searching for precisely the kind of sweeping explanations of reality that were so soundly repudiated by the events of 1989–91. If the *anekdot* during the predictable and dull news environment of the 1970s had provided an alternative source of information and entertainment—one that focused not on dry production statistics or inflated rhetoric about the brotherhood of socialist nations, but on television characters, daily life, and Generalissimus Brezhnev's stroke-slurred and eminently risible speeches—in Yeltsin-era Russia the public consumed a constant stream of small news stories with little mention, or even implication, of higher national significance.

Indeed, many such stories themselves read as naive *anekdoty.* For example, a string of reports on the various consumer products (including coffins, watches, and dildos) given to factory workers in lieu of wages became a sort of tragicomic nonfiction news miniseries.[3] In a late 1990s cartoon by Andrei Bil'zho, one man asks another if he wants to "hear the latest presidential decree." Bil'zho's quip reflects the increasingly cynical public view of Yeltsin, of course (as well as a certain measure of giddiness at the still-novel idea of democracy), but it also indicates the extent to which the shock-therapy-economics phase of Russian history was an unpredictable discursive free-for-all in which the myriad "speech subjects" that took part in it did not have to rely on concentrated, portable, and ephemeral forms like the *anekdot* to express (and entertain) themselves.

THE *ANEKDOT* IN PRINT

In the late 1980s, no longer confined by censorship to oral propagation, *anekdoty* began circulating widely in published form.[4] The glut of published *anekdoty* initially served a historiographic purpose: the *anekdoty* comprised a written record of a lost underground folk culture. In this respect, *anekdot* compilers and publishers participated in a central project of perestroika: filling in the *belye piatna* (white spots) of Soviet history. Many of those white spots are part of the realm of the cultural unsaid that I identified in chapter 2. Perestroika-era joke compilers and publishers were caught up in what A. V. Voznesenskii called the "pathos of publishing previously forbidden texts," the literary counterpart to the many posthumous political rehabilitations of the Gorbachev years.[5] Newly mobilized for a project based on pathos, the *anekdot* seemed to undergo a fundamental change in both its primary function and its primary medium of propagation.

From the beginning, *anekdoty* were published most often by topic, again reflecting the taxonomical approach to publishing the mountains of previously illicit information. The largest and most visible joke-book series was one compiled by Tat'iana Nichiporovich and published by the Minsk publishing house Literatura beginning in 1997. By the end of 1998, there were forty volumes (350 to 500 pages each) and counting, plus numerous small brochures. Titles include the following (in alphabetical order):

Anekdoty About Alcoholics and Drug Addicts
Anekdoty About the Army
Anekdoty About Bandits
Anekdoty About [Religious] Believers and Non-Believers
Anekdoty About Chapaev and Shtirlits
Anekdoty from the Circus
Anekdoty from Computer Networks
Anekdoty About the Criminal World
Anekdoty About Doctors
Anekdoty About Dummies (*chainiki,* used here in reference to Chukchi and other Asian peoples)
Anekdoty from England
Anekdoty About English Lords
Anekdoty About Great Personages
Anekdoty About Hunters, Fishermen, and Athletes
Anekdoty About Husbands and [Their Wives'] Lovers
Anekdoty About the Intelligentsia
Anekdoty from Italy
Anekdoty About Jews and Non-Jews
Anekdoty About Love
Anekdoty About the Militia and the Police
Anekdoty About Money
Anekdoty About New Russians (three volumes)
Anekdoty from the Other World (Supernatural *Anekdoty*)
Anekdoty from the Parrot
Anekdoty About Piglet [Piatachok], Il'ia Muromets, and Baba Iaga
Anekdoty About Politicians
Anekdoty from the Restaurant
Anekdoty That Rhyme and Don't Rhyme
Anekdoty About Russians and Non-Russians

Anekdoty from the Television Screen
Anekdoty About Vovochka
Black Humor (*Anekdoty* About Blacks)
Laughter Through Tears
Literary *Anekdoty*

Even after the *anekdot* publishing craze began, the genre continued to exist on the boundary between literature and folklore, in the realm of ephemera: cheap brochures, fliers, and four-page newspapers. The texts of the genre were thus fixed in a less permanent form than other varieties of verbal art. This was in part a cost-cutting strategy, of course, but it also resonated with the nature of the genre itself: it is portable, it exists in numerous variants, and so on. Various periodicals have regularly published *anekdoty,* including even such laugh-a-minute publications as the trade-union newspaper *Trud* (Labor) and ultranationalist politician Vladimir Zhirinovskii's party organ, *Sokol* (Falcon). Some periodicals—for example, the entertainment weekly *MK-Bul'var* and the student magazine *Studencheskii meridian*—solicit and publish *anekdoty* from their readers.[6]

In contrast to early perestroika joke anthologies, in which the jokes were packaged as newly emergent testimonies to the formerly unprintable realities of Soviet society,[7] by the mid-1990s anthologies were more frequently packaged and marketed together with other forms of light entertainment such as crossword puzzles, or as crib sheets to enhance the reader's social skills (a marketing strategy that is also used with collections of toasts, which, like crosswords, frequently appear with *anekdoty*).

The most recent step in the evolution of the genre has been its tremendous success on the Internet, especially in *anekdot* archives on the World Wide Web.[8] The best-known and largest such archive is Dima Verner's *Anekdoty iz Rossii* (*Anekdoty* from Russia, http://www.anekdot.ru). Verner, a Soviet-born astrophysicist working at the University of Kentucky, is a modern-day Afanas'ev who does not have to be physically present in the field—or even in Russia—to collect his texts.

The rise of the *anekdot* and other forms of satire on the Internet was predated by the emergence in the early 1990s of satirical television programs such as *Oba-na* (Take Both), *Ostorozhno, modern!* (Look Out! Moderne!), *Klub "Belyi popugai"* (The White Parrot Club, which featured famous performers sitting around a table telling *anekdoty* and was hosted by Iurii Nikulin from 1993 to 1997), and especially *Kukly* (Puppets), a political-satire program created by writer Viktor Shenderovich based on the British program *Spitting Images.*

RESURGENT PHYSICALITY

The incarnation (and commodification) of the oral genre in concrete re-corded forms rehearsed in a way a more general process of "materialization" in post-Soviet culture, which began in a literal sense the moment the USSR was dissolved on Christmas Day in 1991 but had a running start. The year 1986 marked the beginning of Gorbachev's liberalizing reforms, a beginning symbolized in retrospect by a specific event: the Fifth Congress of the Soviet Filmmakers' Union in May of that year. The Congress was notable not only for the triumph of the liberal faction of the union—the first official organ of creative intelligentsia to embrace the nascent openness—but also for an incident at the Congress when a speaker, in the presence of Gorbachev, mentioned the recent nuclear accident at Chernobyl, which to that point had not been publicly acknowledged by the state. One attendee reported that Gorbachev responded to the unexpected exposure of the disaster by silently covering his face with his hand (Irina Shilova, personal communica-tion, June 1999). The government made its first public statement about the accident the following day.

The explosion at Chernobyl is significant in the history of the *anekdot*, as well; the first transcribed political *anekdoty* to be published openly were a handful of Chernobyl jokes included in an article by Iurii Shcherbak in the journal *Iunost'* (Youth) in 1988. Here is one of the best-known texts in that cycle:

> A grandfather and his grandson are sitting on the bank of the Pripiat River [in Chernobyl] fishing. "Grandpa! Is it true that an atomic power plant once stood on this spot?" "It's true, grandson," says the old man, patting the boy on the head. "And is it true that it exploded?" "It's true, grandson," says the old man, patting the boy on his other head.[9]

The year before Chernobyl saw the beginning of the last official Soviet initiative to inspire a discrete cycle of *anekdoty,* Gorbachev's infamous anti-alcohol campaign:

> A Moscow bus driver announces: "This stop—liquor store. Next stop—end of the queue for the liquor store."

Both of these vintage late Soviet cycles manifest a larger impulse: to bring to the public forum critical discourse about the everyday lives of the urban Soviet folk and to make explicit the links between ideology and physiology, between the Motherland and irradiated soil, between the Party line and the vodka line. These are links that the culture industry had previously worked hard to obfuscate. Reasserting the presence of the body in the social life of the nation was one of the first corrective projects of post-Soviet culture. The newly permissible self-referential variety of collective discourse had a prominent physical aspect across genres and media, but one popular form, the *anekdot,* had long been a medium for such visceral subject matter.

POST-SOVIET (AND POST-POST-SOVIET) POLITICAL HUMOR

Although the political joke, for obvious reasons, had an especially minuscule amount of cultural cachet after the collapse of the USSR, the images of Russian leaders continued to inspire engagement by the *anekdot.* For a time after the unsuccessful coup attempt in August 1991, which thrust Boris Yeltsin into the public eye as the heroic defender of the People against Communist retrenchment, Yeltsin was the subject of sympathetic *anekdoty,* much as Khrushchev had been in the early de-Stalinizing stages of his premiership. For example:

> During the first Congress of People's Deputies of the USSR [in 1989], a guy with a machine gun suddenly bursts into the meeting hall: "Which one of you is Yeltsin?" Everyone points in the direction of Boris Nikolaevich [Yeltsin]. "Boris, duck!" says the guy.

> Radio Armenia describes Yeltsin's favorite "sporting activities": tank rallies, hurdles, and hammer-and-sickle toss.

Like Khrushchev, Yeltsin's reputation eventually plummeted, and his image in the *anekdot* was juxtaposed with the images of his predecessors, especially Lenin, whose literally moribund condition became a point of comparison with the current leader as that leader's health drifted southward:

> Two demonstrations are being held outside the State Duma in Moscow: one by the communists and one by the democrats. The communists are holding an enormous portrait of Lenin with the slogan "Lenin's Forever Alive." The democrats are holding an enormous portrait of Yeltsin with the slogan "Yeltsin's Forever Healthy."[10]

> What's the difference between Yeltsin and Lenin? The intravenous drip.

The rise of über-capitalists in post-Soviet Russia and the concomitant demographic swelling of the impoverished population ensured that economic, rather than political, categories would dominate the shrunken range of *anekdot* archetypes (see the following section on the New Russians). Still, an early indication that Vladimir Putin's Russia might see a mini-renaissance in popular oral political humor was the reappearance of the meta-*anekdot:*

> The Russian government has announced that beginning March 26, 2000, all *anekdoty* about Vovochka will be treated as political.

March 26, 2000, was the day Putin was elected president, and Vovochka is, of course, the archetypal foulmouthed class clown of Russian jokelore.[11] Those who argue that Russia has entered a neo-Soviet phase might point out this joke's resemblance to one from 1984 about a government ban on all "jokes beginning with the letter *ch:* Chapaev, Chukchi, Cheburashka, and Chernenko." The depiction of political leaders as inhabitants of the same imaginative plane as popular-culture characters is a tradition that is clearly alive and well, and it is enhanced today not only by Putin's physical resemblance to an impish schoolboy (and the fact that Putin is also a Vovochka [a diminutive of Vladimir]), but also his stint as a KGB spy in Germany and his somber demeanor, which have prompted comparisons with another jokeloric hero from the Brezhnev period: Shtirlits.[12] As I reported in chapter 4 in the "Putina boiat'sia" *anekdot,* Putin's words have also been enshrined in Russian folk humor, once again via the agency of a recognizable oral text:

> Putin gets into bed with his wife and says, "I'll make this brief" [*Budu kratok*].[13]

Another Putin joke draws on a different traditional genre, the fable, to express popular cynicism toward (or passive acceptance of) the new political system:

> A crow is sitting in a tree with a piece of cheese in its mouth. A fox runs by: "Crow, crow, are you politically aware?"
> The crow is silent.
> "Crow, crow, are you going to vote in the presidential election?"
> The crow is silent.
> "Crow, crow, are you going to vote for Putin?"
> The crow caws with all its might:
> "Yeeeees!"

127

The cheese, naturally, falls out, and ends up in the mouth of the impudent red-snouted fox. The crow sits in the tree and thinks:
"And if I had said no, would it have changed anything?"

Despite the widely reported publication of a slim volume of Putin jokes in 2001, the *anekdot* in print has entered a new period of dormancy. The scarcity of the genre is perhaps a sign of creeping neo-Brezhnevism on the part of the state, a reflection of market forces, and a symptom of a new less cynical Russian zeitgeist. The costumed buffoon of a carnival culture presided over by Yeltsin, Communist Party leader Gennadii Ziuganov, and Zhirinovskii has apparently given way to austere Putinism. The first phase of the post-Soviet period, however, produced an *anekdot* protagonist whose fame as a comic archetype began to approach that of his predecessors in Russian jokelore: the so-called New Russian.

THE "NEW RUSSIAN" JOKE: A NEW RUSSIAN JOKE?

Despite its bout of doldrums in the early post-Soviet years, the utility of the *anekdot* as a medium for instantaneous collective reaction to current events and trends was intact, if dormant, and new cycles did manage to condense in the transformed sociocultural atmosphere. This was especially true as it became clear who the beneficiaries and victims of the transformations were (or, as Russians might say, *kto kogo*). The most productive thematic species of post-Soviet humor is certainly the series of jokes about New Russians, that filthy-rich, amorphous, quasimythical social-class-*cum*-criminal subculture that bore the brunt of popular discontent with the shock-therapy economic policies of the 1990s. The New Russians were not the only fledgling joke protagonists of the period—drug addicts and computer programmers, for example, also "enjoyed" ample representation—but the emerging post-Communist wealthy quickly became the *anekdot* entrée du jour. The prominence of the New Russian in public discourse and popular culture has diminished considerably in recent years, however, partly because of the Russian financial collapse of August 1998.

From the present historical vantage point, well into the Putin era, it is probably safe to regard the New Russian cycle as a discrete corpus of texts associated with a discrete sociopolitical chronotope: Yeltsin-era Russia. The current second Russian president's consistently high approval ratings (Putin jokes like the pair I have cited notwithstanding) are but the most quantitative indicator of a tendency in Russian society toward ingenuous civic engagement and support for the government. This tendency is something Russia has not seen since before Yeltsin squandered his own popular mandate remarkably soon after his triumphant ascension to the Kremlin on the cusp of 1991–92.[14] In the "post-post-Soviet" period that arguably began on the first day of 2000, even the New Russians have reportedly become conscientious citizens.[15] According to journalist Darya Aslamova, "There is no doubt that today's 'New Russians' are very different from those of the 1990s [. . .]. As I see it, they have become ennobled, cleverer and more experienced. It may sound pompous, but I believe they really care about the fate of their motherland" (quoted in Mozheitov). Aslamova's comments appeared in an article reporting an event called "New Russians Day" [*sic*] held at the Casablanca Casino in Moscow in July 2000. The aim of this celebration "was to demonstrate that there are witty and intelligent people among today's 'New Russians' and that they deserve to be called 'New Russians of the 21st century.'" The event included a competition pitting five wealthy Russian businessmen against each other in contests ranging from *pel'meni* eating and arm wrestling to "distinguishing cocktails" and "counting cash without looking."[16]

The satirical popular-culture depiction of the New Russian, as Aslamova acknowledged, is indeed the image that the rest of the Russian population associates most readily with its recently moneyed countrymen, and the willingness of the businessmen to participate in a mildly self-parodic performance hardly suggests a widespread attempt from within to dispel the negative stereotype.[17] What it does suggest, though, is an awareness on the part of flesh-and-blood rich Russians of their own representation in the popular and/or mass media. That awareness is hardly a recent development (one that might indicate, for example, that the concept of the New Russian has merely been around long enough for media stereotypes and social reality to begin influencing each other); members of the new economic elite have carefully modeled their behavior and lifestyles on media characterizations of their particular demographic group ever since the post-Soviet renaissance of Russian capitalism began.

Aleksei Levinson wrote in an early 1995 article that the nascent capitalists in Russia, much like immigrants experiencing culture shock in a new environment, were at a complete loss regarding their own image and place within society: "They're new. And not only to us; they're new to themselves, as well."[18] There was simply no extant model of behavior for a rich person in Russian society, the elites of which had spent the previous seven decades impugning wealth and its trappings as the marks of the (anti-Soviet) beast (the most recent domestic role models for would-be entrepreneurs were the NEPmen of the 1920s).[19] The newspaper *Kommersant"*, says Levinson, shrewdly recognized the unsure culturally unaffiliated nouveaux riches as a highly desirable—and malleable—readership, and began to publish articles actively constructing a paradigmatic lifestyle for that readership: "Thanks to the influence of [*Kommersant"*], the leading factor during the group's formative stage was its way of life."[20] The newspaper's editors understood "way of life" to mean not only questions of fashion, interior decorating, and other consumer status symbols, but also "detailed instructions regarding all questions of everyday existence" [detal'nye instruktsii po vsem bytovym voprosam]. Novice or aspiring New Russians could read the newspaper and learn, for example, that a man of means begins the day with a glass of grapefruit juice and the morning paper (ideally, of course, *Kommersant*").[21] Thus a media-constructed profile of a social group influenced its own supposed real-life referent in that group's earliest formative stages. This was free-market Russia's first encounter with the instant media feedback mechanisms and aggressive targeted image-mongering to which the capitalist West has long been accustomed.

The New Russians' earnest, ostentatious pursuit of the lifestyle described in the media, not to mention their reputation as violent criminals, made them natural targets of resentment on the part of their non-"new" countrymen, that is, the impoverished plurality of the post-Soviet Russian population. This latter collective, hampered by its lack of economic power just as the vast majority of Soviet citizens had been restricted by their lack of political power, responded to its own powerlessness in a familiar, symbolic form; by 1994, the New Russian had become the latest favorite son in a genealogy of joke protagonists going back more than a century.

The use of the epithet "new" in the New Russian *anekdot* reflects not only an ironic adaptation of the Western term, but also, as Draitser wrote, an acknowledgment on the part of the *anekdot* teller of his own "oldness"; Draitser characterized these "'old' Russians"[22] by their own self-image as people "who, despite dramatic political and social changes, remained true to their perception of themselves as a group—as nonmaterialistic people, much more concerned with cultural and spiritual values than with profit making."[23] Draitser is, of course, describing the traditional discursive source of Soviet *anekdoty*—the creative intelligentsia—from whose perspective the New Russians were not merely guilty of theft and violence, but were also morally, culturally, and intellectually offensive. The offense is reflected in the *anekdot*-al New Russian's profound amorality, lack of refinement, and intellectual bankruptcy. In this respect, the New Russian *anekdot* resembles the Soviet-era *anekdoty* that ridiculed similar traits in high-ranking members of the Party or the *nomenklatura*:

An art exhibit in Paris. Picasso has forgotten his invitation, so he is held up at the door. "Do you have any proof that you're Picasso?" they ask him. He draws a dove, and they let him in. Furtseva has also forgotten to bring her invitation. "But I'm the Minister of Culture of the USSR!" she objects. "Prove it," they tell her. "For instance, Picasso was just here and he had to prove his identity by drawing something." "Who's Picasso?" Furtseva asks. "Everything is in order, Madame Minister," they tell her. "Go right in."

Part of the impetus for such *anekdoty* was certainly the ongoing affront experienced by the intelligentsia over the fact that the country's artistic and intellectual life was under the ham-handed (and at times iron-fisted) control of ignorant ideologues. This sentiment had deep roots in Soviet society, as the following joke shows:

> Lenin and Lunacharskii are at an exhibit of futurist art in 1920. Lenin says, "I don't understand this at all." Lunacharskii says, "I don't understand it, either." These were the last two Soviet leaders who didn't understand anything about art.

The New Russian in *anekdoty* is analogous to the Communist official in that his financial position makes him a necessary participant in the newly privatized cultural sphere,[24] despite his gracelessness and cultural incompetence:

> Two New Russians are talking. "Did you hear? Sergei got hit with a big fine up in St. Petersburg! He got drunk and ran into a guy on a horse!" "Poor Sergei! How is he?" "As you'd expect—his Mercedes is wrecked and he's in the hospital." "And the guy with the horse?" "What about him? He's made of bronze" [Sergei has crashed his car into the Bronze Horseman, a famous monument to Peter the Great in St. Petersburg].

His disregard of Russian culture is matched by his blasphemous ignorance of more universal symbols of reverence:

> A New Russian goes into a jewelry store. "Listen, I need a crucifix, you know, like everyone has." "Certainly, sir. We have these gold crosses . . ." "What? . . . don't give me this small stuff! I want a normal cross, 500 or 600 grams. Don't have one? Well, find one!" The salespeople rush around in a panic, searching the entire inventory until finally they find one. "Here you are, sir. A hand-made crucifix. Gold, 620 grams. Highest quality." "Yeah, it's not a bad cross. Listen, can you give me one the same size, but without the gymnast?"

The New Russian is "new" in that he is intellectually isolated from the past by ignorance or indifference. The type, however, is firmly ensconced in a tradition. The social context was not the only factor that contributed to the group's jokeloric immortalization; the New Russians' rapidly congealing image fit remarkably well into the existing templates of several *anekdot* varieties simultaneously, making New Russians worthy successors to protagonists whose representation in popular culture had become hackneyed or even obsolete in post-Communist Russia. Furthermore, the comparatively narrow range of signifiers available to the New Russians (the three or four acceptable models of car, for example) and their uncritical "herd mentality"[25] in following the latest trends made them ideal candidates for exaggerated satirical representation, which employs simplistic, primary-color imagery and thrives on irony-deficient targets. The New Russians were also vulnerable to ridicule by virtue of the mechanistic manner in which they adopted artificial models of behavior; recall Bergson.[26]

The New Russians' early (and—in jokes, at least—lasting) image was also marked by the seemingly haphazard eclecticism of that image, indicating their willingness to incorporate an indiscriminately broad array of stylistic, attitudinal, linguistic, and other influences in the interest of developing a functional in-group identity. Their syncretic principles of self-presentation were as apparent in their behavioral code as in their choice of clothing or hairstyles; Ol'ga Bukharkova wrote that the New Russians at their zenith operated according to a loose but distinctive moral system ("ideology, even," she said) based on a "mish-mash [*kasha*] of criminal-world concepts, merchant traditions, Western values, Communist principles, and biblical commandments."[27] The resulting image, propagated through the hyperbolic prism of popular culture and mass media, had potential associative links with a diversity of existing images in Russo-Soviet culture, and the *anekdot*—a genre in search of new characters—readily exploited those links.

Scholars of Russian urban folklore have neglected the New Russian joke, despite its status as the genre's most productive contemporary instantiation. The cycle's lack of folkloric "credibility" partly explains this phenomenon; as a body of data, the numerous anthologies, periodical publications, and Internet archives that constitute the available corpus of New Russian *anekdoty* are less reliable than the material typically examined in postcensorship urban folkloristics: joke collections compiled clandestinely during the Soviet period and retrospective anthologies of Soviet *anekdoty* published since the perestroika era. Since their genesis as a cultural presence, New Russian *anekdoty* have existed simultaneously in oral and written form (perhaps even primarily in the latter) and are thus ethnographically suspect. From a broader perspective not limited by the disciplinary constraints of folkloristics, however, we can regard the New Russian *anekdot* as a visible, demonstrably influential cultural phenomenon[28] and contextualize it both diachronically, as the latest successful mutation in the rich evolutionary history of the Russo-Soviet *anekdot*, and synchronically, as one of the myriad popular-culture forms engaged with the still-nascent dominant characteristics of post-Communist Russian society. What existing *anekdot* cycles, motifs, and protagonists were conscripted in the creation of the cycle?

Visually the New Russian is among the most recognized Russian social types of the 1990s: he sports a *strizhka-ezhik* (flattop buzz cut);[29] he is clean-shaven; his neck is adorned with gold chains; he is thick (muscular or corpulent) in the torso; and his sport jacket is crimson (the proverbial *malinovyi pidzhak*). He carries a cell phone and/or wears a pager. He has not necessarily mastered the use of them, however:

> A New Russian says to his wife in surprise:
> "My Tamagochi is pregnant!"
> "What?"
> "Look!"
> She reads the display screen and says:
> "That's not your Tamagochi, stupid. That's your pager!"

The New Russian and his brethren communicate using distinctive slang, as well as a nonverbal lexicon (most famously, the *pal'tsy veerom* [fanned fingers], in which the index finger and pinky are extended, with the other fingers tucked under as in a fist). By far his most indispensable accessory is his car, almost always a Mercedes-Benz 600, occasionally a BMW, very rarely a Jeep Cherokee or a Cadillac. He has bodyguards and travels freely around the globe.

The *anekdot*-al New Russian is a type defined by a cluster of behaviors and accessories associated with a single demographic category: the rich. Other standard attributes of the type—stupidity, violence, drunkenness, amorality—are important (but secondary, even optional), but material wealth is de rigueur. The major source of criticism, again, as with nouveaux riches[30] in other contexts, is the "old money," represented in the case of post-Soviet Russia by the impoverished intelligentsia, which previously held, if not enormous amounts of material wealth, at least a measure of discursive capital in Soviet Russia and—just as importantly—in the West's image of Russia. It is this intelligentsia perspective that is responsible for the jokeloric New Russian's lack of grace and refinement; the jokes, wrote Levinson, are "the views of those who are cultured, but poor, towards those who are rich, but uncultured."[31] Like other national varieties of nouveaux riches, the New Russian is not merely wealthy, but incompetently and vulgarly wealthy:

> Two New Russians meet. One says to the other, "Hey, look, I bought a new tie! Paid two hundred bucks!" "You idiot! Just around the corner you can get the same tie for five hundred!"

The New Russian's cavalier attitude toward money is often accompanied by a complete lack of awareness that others do not have such wealth. Again, the New Russian is new in that he has no historical memory, no knowledge of Russia before the Yeltsin reforms that engendered his type:

> A Mercedes collides with a Zaporozhets [ultra-cheap, Russian-made car]. A New Russian gets out of the Mercedes, spits, and says, "Eh, no big deal. Tomorrow I'll buy a new one." But the owner of the Zaporozhets says with tears in his eyes, "I saved up my whole life for this car, and now it's wrecked!" The New Russian replies, "Why'd you buy such an expensive car, stupid?"

This joke also hints at the presence of secretly wealthy people in Soviet times. The image of cars colliding—the most common motif in the cycle—is a transparent metaphor for the collision of old and new. In such encounters the representative of the old typically is forced upon threat of violence to pay the New Russian for the damage inflicted, regardless of who was at fault.[32]

The New Russian in *anekdoty* is not only prone to violence and tastelessly extravagant; he is also undeserving of the wealth and influence he enjoys. Often the subtext of a New Russian joke is the implication that he is ethnically unworthy. Exacerbating the resentment toward the New Russians is the perception that the worst of them are not Russians at all. The term, then, takes on ironic implications. The frequency of Jewish and Caucasian protagonists in the cycle indicates that the use of the word "Russian" in the phrase "New Russian" is often an ironic reference to the perceived usurpation of Russian wealth by non-Russians. The premise underlying that perception is that the elites of a particular society define and even represent the normative image of the society's dominant ethnic profile.

An element of the jokeloric New Russian's image that is particularly reminiscent of ethnic humor is his distinctive speech. Predictably, it is judged poorly, especially so because the New Russian is the member of the society who should have the most experiences and impressions about which to wax eloquent; for example, about foreign travel:

> A New Russian comes home after a trip to Paris. His wife asks him, "So how was it over there in Paris?" "Friggin' cool, I mean, shit, that Feiffel Tower and everything, you know, oh man, I mean, friggin' awesome! Vera, why're you crying?" "It sounds so beautiful!"

Draitser writes that many New Russian jokes are "de-ethnicized" versions of previous jokes told by Russians about ethnic minorities, especially people from the Caucasus (Georgians, Armenians, and so on) and Jews.[33]

Levinson and Draitser both note the New Russian cycle's resemblance to an earlier cycle about a suddenly wealthy group: Georgians and other Caucasians in the 1950s, who began to sell flowers and produce in Moscow and other Soviet cities after the strict laws against private enterprise were eased slightly to allow such activities.[34] Draitser cites the following 1996 joke as an example of the persistence of this image into the post-Soviet era:

> A Georgian boy asks his father, "Daddy, what nationality am I?" "You're a Georgian." "And you?" "I'm also a Georgian." "And Mom?" "She's a Georgian as well." "So, Uncle Otar is also a Georgian?" "No. He's a New Russian."[35]

Draitser's point is also supported by "pre–New Russian" texts such as the following, which were later recycled as New Russian jokes, with no mention of Georgians:

> A Georgian college student writes a letter to his parents: "Dear Mom and Dad: I've almost become a real student. But everyone here goes to class by bus, and I take a taxi." His parents write back: "Dear Son: We'll sell a few oranges and send you some money so you can buy yourself a bus."

Levinson also discusses the links between New Russian jokes and similar jokes about the emerging Jewish middle class of late-nineteenth-century Russia. A contemporary *anekdot* illustrates that the stereotypical image of the Jewish businessman informs the New Russian cycle, as well: "What did the New Russian say to the old Jew? 'Papa, can I have some money?'"

Despite the well-documented links to anti-Semitic and anti-Caucasian humor, a no less productive way to approach the cycle is to disregard the ironic implications of the word "Russian" and examine the jokes as reflexive ethnic humor; the name of the cycle includes the same ethnic designation as the language in which the jokes are told, after all. The economic sphere was certainly the major locus of attention and concern for the majority of Russians, and for the government, in the 1990s. The New Russians were not only associated with that sphere, but also they themselves were representations, incarnations of the altered society produced by economic reforms. The inhabitants of post-1991 Russia are "new Russians" quite literally, insofar as it is a new sovereign state, a "new Russia."[36]

Supporting such an interpretation is the fact that the New Russian sometimes appears as the protagonist of so-called everyday *anekdoty,* which satirize not a particular group or socioeconomic phenomenon, but a common recognizable situation (often involving gender conflict) or human foible (for example, drunkenness, adultery). While the substitution of the label "New Russian" for what could just as well be "a man" or "a Russian" certainly has subtle implications regarding the character of the New Russians, it is just as often a device that serves merely to expand the situational potential of the joke. The New Russian's ability to travel, in particular, has made him a useful protagonist in *anekdoty* requiring a foreign beach or a famous landmark in a foreign city. There were Soviet *anekdoty,* of course, in which Soviet citizens were depicted abroad (these were both situationally and sociopolitically ironic, given the impossibility of traveling abroad for most Soviets[37]), but the insertion of the New Russian into the role gives such *anekdoty* a measure of verisimilitude that allows for emphasis on the comedic situation at hand: a New Russian *would* be found on a Mediterranean beach or at the Eiffel Tower. Furthermore, the fact that the New Russian abroad is the latest instantiation of a familiar character in Russian popular and mass culture—"our man in the West"—acknowledges his status as the unofficial representative of the Russian ethnos to the world. This is a jokeloric role previously fulfilled by Shtirlits, the Soviet spy in Nazi Germany, or by Soviet leaders on state visits to Western countries. The New Russian's namelessness, however—he is a type, not a personality—also suggests the cycle's kinship to explicitly ethnic (or other group-directed) humor.

The fact that there are very few *anekdoty* about actual wealthy public figures—Boris Berezovskii, Vladimir Potanin, Vladimir Gusinskii, and so on[38]—indicates that the New Russian *anekdot* is primarily a descendant not of the nineteenth-century historical *anekdot,* whose protagonists were real-life elites (monarchs, aristocrats, military leaders), but of the traditional folk *anekdot,* which trafficked in nameless representatives of social types (peasant, landowner, priest, fool) depicted in a limited number of situational scenarios. In composition and setting, many New Russian jokes are in the tradition of Russian folk *anekdoty* and tales about simpletons. Some are even old chestnuts from that tradition, with the detail of the New Russian protagonist superimposed. The physical image of the New Russian, while not as evocative as other latter-day folkloric Russian dunces, such as the Chukchi, contains several elements characteristic of the fool across cultures. His expansive crimson jacket is a contemporary version of the fool's motley garb. Moreover, the image of the suddenly wealthy Russian who has none of the intangible commodities (common sense, spirituality, ethics) needed to deal with his new material circumstances is akin to that of the bumpkin in the city, a motif whose most recent instantiation in Russian jokelore was the Chukchi cycle.[39]

The New Russian *anekdot* exemplifies a social and demographic displacement rather than a geographic one. The New Russian's hapless and crude participation in the capitalist system is also reminiscent of the Russian peasant's first awkward encounters with the Communist system in the 1920s, a motif exploited most famously by Mikhail Zoshchenko.

As in traditional folk *anekdoty*, and in some Chukchi jokes, the New Russian fool sometimes appears not as a *glupets* (idiot) but a *khitrets* (clever trickster):[40]

> A traffic policeman stops a New Russian and sees that he is under the influence. "Breathe into this, please." The New Russian blows into the breathalyzer and the cop says, "You're drunk!" "No way, I'm sober! I haven't drunk a thing! Your equipment doesn't work! Try it on my wife, you'll see!" The cop gives it to the wife, she blows into it, and he says, "Your wife's drunk, too!" "How can my wife also be drunk? It's your equipment. It doesn't work. Try it one more time, on my five-year-old son, here in the backseat." The cop administers the test to the boy. "Your child is drunk, too!" "Uh-uh, officer. You're off your nut! What are you saying?" "All right, my mistake. I apologize." He lets them go. After they pull away, the New Russian says to his wife, "And you said drinking's bad for him, but it turns out I was right!"

Occasionally the New Russian trickster even demonstrates his adroitness and understanding of the new economic system:

> A New Russian goes into a bank in Geneva and asks whether he can take out a loan using his Mercedes as collateral. The clerks hesitate, nod, and ask what amount. "A hundred dollars," the New Russian replies, "for one year." One year later to the day, the New Russian comes back, pays the fifteen percent interest (for a year), and gets into his car. "Oh, sir," the clerks yell after him, "can you explain why you did that?" "Ha," says the New Russian, turning on the ignition, "where else'll I find a secure parking spot for a year for fifteen dollars?"

If the implication of Soviet jokes was that the Russian character (to which Ries attributed a wide streak of mischievousness and an urge to be a "spoiler"[41]) is poorly suited for Communism, then the implication of most New Russian jokes is that this character is equally out of place under capitalism. It is perhaps this cul-de-sac of cynicism that is the most serious obstacle to the cycle's continued productivity, and the reason that, as Mark Lipovetsky wrote, the New Russian *anekdot* has been substantially "replaced by [. . .] more psychological approach[es] to the enigma of the new class," such as prose fiction.[42]

Another cultural sphere that generated multiple representations of the New Russian—a sphere with strong links to the *anekdot* in Soviet culture—is cinema, though the two media did not conspire to produce the new archetype. A factor in the overall decline of the *anekdot* in the 1990s, in fact, was surely the paucity of material from domestic popular movies—for the *anekdot,* one of the main sources of characters and motifs during the preceding decades.

The New Russian *anekdot* certainly found no prototypes on the silver screen; the cinematic New Russian has had little influence on his jokeloric counterpart. The New Russian in films is often a caricature, but rarely comic or even productively risible. While the profoundly cynical *anekdot* offers little possibility of social reform or redemption—the New Russian in the Mercedes will always be a threat to the *muzhik* in the Zaporozhets—cinema more than once has taken a revisionist view of stereotypical post-Soviet class relations. One of the first cinematic portrayals of the New Russian takes a straightforward dramatic approach to the new socioeconomic environment and its emerging character types. Denis Evstigneev's *Limita* (Limits, 1994) is a simplistic modern tragedy that shows the ultimately lethal effects of the New Russian lifestyle's culture of violence. The wealthy and cynical protagonist of the film is indirectly responsible for the mistaken-identity murder of his old friend, who has retained his integrity and refused to participate in the new shady economy. The implication at the end of the film is that the New Russian has learned a lesson and will begin to fly straight. Even further removed from the joke image is Villen Novak's *Printsessa na bobakh* (The Princess and the Pea, 1997), in which the New Russian protagonist is the romantic hero, a positive and sympathetic figure. Such portrayals underscore the differences between urban folk culture and the culture industry. Unlike publishing and film production, the *anekdot* is outside the new guiding "ideology," market capitalism. It has no profit margin and thus no allegiance to wealthy Russians themselves that might soften its critical perspective.[43]

Several recent films elevate the *anekdot*-al New Russian's perennial victim—the poor *muzhik*—to dominant, even heroic, status. The protagonist of Alla Surikova's *Khochu v tiur'mu!* (I Want to Go to Prison! 1999), for instance, is a simple working-class Zaporozhets-driving Russian man, but not a typical *muzhik;* he uses his formidable technical skills to soup up the much maligned car to such a degree that he leaves any Mercedes in the dust. His victory in an impromptu road rally[44] impresses the defeated New Russian, who offers our hero a job that turns out to be illegal, forcing him to flee (in his Zaporozhets, naturally) to the Netherlands. He eventually drives triumphantly back to Russia and his simple, noble life, the lowly car's reliability and stamina a contrast to the flashy, ephemeral speed of the Mercedes.

Another film, Petr Lutsik's dark comedy *Okraina* (Borderlands, 1998), depicts a different sort of lower-class victory over New Russians; the finale features three peasants from the Ural Mountains murdering a sinister Moscow oil executive in his office and then leaving the high-rise building—and all of Moscow—in flames. A third film, Stanislav Govorukhin's *Voroshilovskii strelok* (Sharpshooter of the Voroshilov Regiment, 1998), depicts redemptive, righteous violence toward New Russians in a much less stylized way: the hero, a World War II veteran, creatively emasculates his granddaughter's unrepentant rapists one by one with his sharpshooter's rifle. Such motifs hark back to traditional folk *anekdoty* that depict clashes between the peasant and the landowner, priest, or other representative of the elite. The jokeloric conflict between the New Russian and the *muzhik* is also in the Russian literary tradition of the "little man" and his encounters with representatives of power.

Another recent impulse has drawn on public nostalgia. Several recent films and television productions have depicted victories over modern Russia's greed, cynicism, and violence of characters played by film icons of the 1960s and 1970s, including Mikhail Ul'ianov (who played Lenin six times and Marshal Zhukov twelve times), Nonna Mordiukova, Viacheslav Tikhonov (who played the immortal Shtirlits), Liudmila Gurchenko, Liia Akhedzhakova, and Oleg Efremov.[45] Television's "Russian project" series of public-service announcements is also in this vein, featuring many of the same actors in roles as average Russians doing culturally specific everyday things and concluding with such encouraging slogans as "Everything's going to be OK," "This is my city," and—in an implicit challenge to the New Russians— "I live in Russia, too."

CONCLUSION

The rapid decline of the *anekdot* in the late 1980s and 1990s was partly due to the explosion of available genres—humor delivery systems—that began with the literal explosion at Chernobyl's reactor # 4 in April 1986. The softening of irony as a mode of representation and the move from sharp satire to a lighter form of irony and to nostalgia were also indicative of the overall *anekdot* crisis. The marketing of Soviet nostalgia in contemporary Russia curiously suggests a view of nostalgia as something edible or potable; several Moscow restaurants and bars have names or themes taken from Soviet-era culture, especially popular films of the Stagnation period: *Beloe solntse pustyni, Mesto vstrechi, Kavkazskaia plennitsa, Garazh.*[46] There is also Café Petrovich (a Stagnation-themed restaurant owned by cartoonist Andrei Bil'zho) and Café Anekdot. Kitsch, that satisfying blend of nostalgia and irony, informs other products, as well, including a brand of condoms called "Van'ka-vstan'-ka" (literally "Get up, Ivan!" and also the name of a toy). A more collective national nostalgia for different Russian pasts is evident in such brand names as Imperial Bank, the New Russians' favorite newspaper *Kommersant"* (written in pre-Soviet orthography), the Revolutionary Vodka Bar, and Emel'ian Pugachev mustard. A cynic might say that those who do not understand the past are doomed to eat it. But the trend to consumable nostalgia can be contextualized in that same renaissance of material life as a cultural category, and it also testifies to a shift in prevailing domestic popular views of Russo-Soviet culture itself.

A similar reclamation project had to be undertaken in the verbal realm. The post-socialist-realist dilemma of representation grew out of the fact that so many words and other signs had for decades been so compromised by their ideological encoding that all signifying activity was suspect. As I have tried to demonstrate, the *anekdot* was a marker of a lack—the severe paucity of ingenuous public discourse in Soviet culture—as well as an "object of special devotion" (to use Ray Browne's elegant definition of a fetish[47]) for millions. As a fetish-genre, the Russo-Soviet *anekdot*, like the unearthed fetish objects of extinct civilizations,[48] has become something of a museum piece in the absence of the cultural context that engendered and empowered it.

From the present vantage point, however, the *anekdot* corpus represents one of the most distilled yet multifarious documents of that context. It was substantially the genre's variegated provenance and multifunctionality over the previous centuries that made its twentieth-century instantiation a form of expression supremely adaptable to the changing sociopolitical contexts and symbolic regimes in which it circulated. Simultaneously independent from and parasitically attached to mass cultural production and other authoritative discourse, the *anekdot* served as a template for a collective satirical voice-over narration of the Soviet century.

Notes

INTRODUCTION

First epigraph is from Leonid Il'ich Brezhnev, *Malaia zemlia* (Moscow: Izdatel'stvo Politicheskoi literatury, 1979), 22.

Second epigraph is from Mary Douglas, "Jokes," in *Rethinking Popular Culture: Contemporary Perspectives in Cultural Studies,* ed. Chandra Mukerji and Michael Schudson (Berkeley: University of California Press, 1991), 293.

1. In what follows, I use the transliterated Russian word *"anekdot"* in most cases, although for stylistic reasons I often substitute "Russian joke" or "Soviet joke," or simply "joke" when the context makes it clear that I am referring to the Russo-Soviet genre. When discussing the connotations of the etymological ancestors and counterparts of the word *"anekdot"* in classical and Western European culture, or in a general international context, I use the English "anecdote."

2. All translations from Russian-language sources, including *anekdoty,* are mine.

3. The corpus on which this study is based (numbering between two and three thousand *anekdoty*) includes (1) *anekdoty* collected orally by me in Moscow and St. Petersburg and among native Russians in the United States between 1992 and 2008; (2) *anekdoty* published in book collections, periodicals, or on the Internet; and (3) *anekdoty* collected by other scholars who have either published them or shared them with me. *Anekdoty* from published sources are so indicated by endnote citations.

4. Douglas, "Jokes," 291.

5. The scholar of the *anekdot* faces a problem shared by all analysts of contemporary urban folklore: the integrity of the material. From a scholarly perspective, many published Russian jokes are suspect, as they are undated, often taken (without attribution) from other sources, and sometimes composed from scratch by the joke-book "compiler." Although I am not a folklorist, I am certainly aware of the need for authenticity and credibility in source texts, so in my choice of published *anekdoty* I have favored those found in multiple sources, in sources dating from the period I am discussing, or that I recall hearing orally but did not transcribe.

6. On the Rzhevskii cycle, see Federica Visani, "Poruchik Rzhevskii: Rozhdenie prototeksta kak aktualizatsiia starogo siuzheta" (unpublished article, 2002).

7. On the Chukchi cycle, see Emil Draitser, *Taking Penguins to the Movies: Ethnic Humor in Russia* (Detroit, Mich.: Wayne State University Press, 1998), 75–100.

8. On the Shtirlits cycle, see: A. F. Belousov, "Anekdoty o Shtirlitse," *Zhivaia starina* 1 (1995): 16–18; and Mark Lipovetskii, "Prezident Shtirlits," *Iskusstvo kino* 11 (2000): 73–76.

9. On Vinni-Pukh jokes, see Aleksandra Arkhipova, "'Rolevaia struktura' detskikh tsiklov anekdotov (na materiale anekdotov o Vinni-Pukhe i Piatachke, o Cheburashke i Krokodile Gene)" (B.A. thesis, Rossiiskii gosudarstvennyi gumanitarnyi universitet, 1999).

10. On the notion of a parallel culture in the Soviet Union, see Aleksei Dmitrievich Yurchak, "The Cynical Reason of Late Socialism: Power, Pretense and the *Anekdot*," *Public Culture* 9 (1997): 161–88; and Boris Briker and Anatolii Vishevskii, "Iumor v populiarnoi kul'ture sovetskogo intelligenta 60-x–70-x godov," *Wiener Slawistischer Almanach* 24 (1989): 147–70.

11. Among the most comprehensive examinations of the genre are Elena Shmeleva and Aleksei Shmelev, *Russkii anekdot: Tekst i rechevoi zhanr* (Moscow: Iazyki slavianskoi kul'tury, 2002); Ol'ga Chirkova, *Poetika sovremennogo narodnogo anekdota* (Ph.D. dissertation, Volgograd University, 1997); and Viktor Khrul', *Anekdot kak forma massovoi kommunikatsii* (Ph.D. dissertation, Moscow State University, 1993).

12. Ol'ga Smolitskaia, "'Anekdoty o frantsuzakh': K probleme sistematizatsii i strukturno-tipologicheskogo izucheniia anekdota," *Novoe literaturnoe obozrenie* 22 (1996): 386.

13. George Orwell, "Funny, But Not Vulgar," in *As I Please: 1943–1945*, vol. 3 of *The Collected Essays, Journalism and Letters of George Orwell*, ed. Sonia Orwell and Ian Angus, 4 vols. (New York: Harcourt Brace Jovanovich, 1968), 284. Orwell's comment recalls the central premise of relief theories of humor, the best-known proponent of which is Sigmund Freud. See also Bruce Adams, *Tiny Revolutions in Russia: Twentieth-Century Soviet and Russian History in Anecdotes* (New York: Routledge Curzon, 2005).

14. Arthur Asa Berger, "The Politics of Laughter," in *The Social Faces of Humour: Practices and Issues*, ed. George E. C. Paton, Chris Powell, and Stephen Wagg (Aldershot, England, and Brookfield, Vt.: Arena/Ashgate, 1996), 27.

15. Zara Abdullaeva, "Popular Culture," trans. Sergei Volynets and Dmitri N. Shalin, in *Russian Culture at the Crossroads: Paradoxes of Postcommunist Consciousness*, ed. Dmitri N. Shalin (Boulder, Colo.: Westview, 1996), 235.

16. Iurii Sokolov, "Vernyi anekdot," *Zhurnalist* 4 (1991): 94–95. In the original Russian, Sokolov's comment rhymes: "pro Emmu" . . . "pro Sistemu."

17. L. I. Abramenko, ed., *Sovetskii anekdot: Antologiia* (Moscow: Data-Strom, 1991), 3.

18. Smolitskaia, "'Anekdoty o frantsuzakh,'" 391.

19. V. Bakhtin, "Anekdoty nas spasali vsegda," in *Samizdat veka,* comp. Anatolii Strelianyi, Genrikh Sapgir, Vladimir Bakhtin, and Nikita Ordynskii (Minsk/Moscow: Polifakt, 1997), 799. The year 1983 also saw two prominent prosecutions of members of the creative intelligentsia: poet Irina Ratushinskaia (sentenced to seven years) and writer Leonid Borodin (ten years added to a previous sentence). See Catriona Kelly, "The Retreat from Dogmatism: Populism Under Khrushchev and Brezhnev," in *Russian Cultural Studies: An Introduction,* ed. Catriona Kelly and David Shepherd (New York: Oxford University Press, 1998), 251.

20. The proverb lent itself especially well to mobilization by the state culture industry. In addition to its didactic potential, the genre's incapacity for reflexivity, writes Susan Stewart, is a major reason for its attractiveness to those aspiring to discursive hegemony: "In the space which the literature of play allows to be marked only with difference, the proverb chisels its univocal meaning. In this is the politics of the proverb, and the politics of any evaluation which cannot move back on itself." (Susan Stewart, "Some Riddles and Proverbs of Textuality: An Essay in Literary Value and Evaluation," *Criticism* 21.2 [Spring 1979]: 105). See chapters 4 and 5 of this book for my interpretation of reflexivity in the *anekdot.*

21. See M. G. Krivoshlyk, *Istoricheskie anekdoty iz zhizni russkikh zamechatel'nykh liudei (S portretami i kratkimi biografiami),* 2nd ed. (St. Petersburg, 1897; Moscow: ANS-Print, 1991). The best-known publication of transcribed folk *anekdoty* is to be found in Aleksandr Nikolaevich Afanas'ev, *Narodnye russkie skazki A. N. Afanas'eva v trekh tomakh,* ed. L. G. Barag and N. G. Novikov (Moscow: Nauka, 1984–85). I cite several of the *anekdoty* therein in chapter 1.

22. Zhanna Dolgopolova writes that only "Persian, Turkish, Arabic, and Latvian" *anekdoty* were published in the USSR (Zhanna Dolgopolova, "The Contrary World of the Anecdote," *Melbourne Slavonic Studies* 15 [1981]: 2). The best-known of these were the anecdotal exploits of the legendary Central Asian trickster Khodzha Nasreddin. Abramenko reports that authentic contemporary *anekdot* motifs did occasionally find their way into print during the Soviet period, but that Soviet characters in them were typically renamed as foreigners— "Jeans, Pauls, and Smiths"—thus transforming domestic social satire into barbs directed at the capitalist West (Dolgopolova, 4).

23. For a historical and "mythopoetic" analysis of the comic stage tradition among Russo-Soviet students, see Milikhat Vafaevich Iunisov, *Mifopoetika studencheskogo smekha (STEM i KVN)* (Moscow: Gosudarstvennyi institut iskusstvoznaniia, 1999).

24. The legendary clown and comedian Iurii Nikulin, while serving as director of the Moscow Circus in the early 1980s, conducted a contest in which people would send in "quips for clowns." Rumor has it that Nikulin later published many of the entries (which were in fact *anekdoty*) in his well-known perestroika-era column in the magazine *Ogonek* (Little Fire) and in a popular collection based on the column, *Anekdoty ot Nikulina* (Aleksandr Belousov, personal communication).

25. This item on the list may appear anomalous, since queues are not private, but it was mentioned by several informants as a typical setting for *anekdot* telling during Stagnation. The telling of *anekdoty* in such a setting indicates the sociopolitical differences between that period and the Stalin period, with its famous kitchen culture, and the extent to which an ironic, satirical worldview characterized public opinion during Stagnation. Note also that food lines are analogous to the traditional marketplace, which Mikhail Bakhtin identifies as a key site for popular use of the "carnival idiom" (Mikhail Bakhtin, *Rabelais and His World,* trans. Hélène Iswolsky [Bloomington: Indiana University Press, 1984], 17).

26. Collections of ideologically irreverent *chastushki* are plentiful. See, for example, A. D. Volkov, comp., *Zavetnye chastushki v dvukh tomakh iz sobraniia A. D. Volkova,* ed. A. V. Kulagina (Moscow: Ladomir, 1999).

27. Anatolii Lunacharskii, "O smekhe," *Literaturnyi kritik* 4 (1935): 9.

28. Maksim Gor'kii, *Sobranie sochinenii,* 27 (Moscow: Golitizdat, 1953), 503, cited in V. M. Sidel'nikov, "Ideino-khudozhestvennaia spetsifika russkogo narodnogo anekdota," *Voprosy literaturovedeniia* 1 (Moscow: Universitet druzhby narodov im. P. Lamumby, 1964), 22.

29. M. Bakhtin, *Rabelais,* 12.

30. V. Azov, "Satira pod spudom," *Poslednie novosti,* May 14, 1932: 2, cited in Rashit Iangirov, "Anekdoty 's borodoi': Materialy k istorii nepodtsenzurnogo sovetskogo fol'klora," *Novoe literaturnoe obozrenie* 31 (1998): 156.

31. Egon Larsen, *Wit as a Weapon: The Political Joke in History* (London: Frederick Muller, 1980), 81.

32. V. Nerush and M. Pavlov, "Shepotom iz-za ugla," *Komsomol'skaia Pravda,* Oct. 15, 1982: 4.

33. Enrid Alaev, *Mir anekdota. Anekdoty nashikh chitatelei* (Moscow: Anons, 1995), 52.

34. V. Pertsov, "Anekdot (Opyt sotsiologicheskogo analiza)," *Novyi Lef* 2 (1927): 41.

35. Lunacharskii, "O smekhe," 6.

36. Dmitrii Moldavskii, *Tovarishch Smekh* (Leningrad: Lenizdat, 1981), 7.

37. In a 1927 article, V. Pertsov had described the *anekdot* in terms that closely resemble the scene from *Volga-Volga:* "A gust of wind, the seeds are spread like dandelion fluff, and the *anekdot* is instantly planted in tens of thousands of heads at once" (Pertsov, "Anekdot," 41). There are apocryphal reports

of targeted, strategic joke propagation by the Soviet security agencies. The enormous cycle about Russian Civil War hero Vasilii Chapaev, for example, by some accounts was created in the bowels of the Lubianka in the late 1960s as a means of drawing satirical attention away from Lenin as his 1970 centennial approached.

38. S. S. Averintsev, "Bakhtin i russkoe otnoshenie k smekhu," in *Ot mifa k literature: Sbornik v chest' semidesiatipiatiletiia Eleazara Moiseevicha Meletinskogo*, comp. S. Iu. Nekliudov and E. S. Novik (Moscow: Rossiiskii universitet, 1993), 342.

39. M. Bakhtin, *Rabelais,* 6.

40. Maksim Krongauz, "Sovetskii antisovetskii iumor: O Dovlatove," *Moskovskii lingvisticheskii zhurnal* 2 (1996): 227. This anecdote, and the title of Krongauz's article, bring to mind Vladimir Voinovich's *Antisovetskii Sovetskii Soiuz: Dokumental'naia fantasmagoriia v 4-kh chastiakh* (Moscow: Materik, 2002).

41. Lev Barskii and I. Pis'mennyi, "Vlast' smekha: Kratkii kurs istorii SSSR v anekdotakh, karikaturakh i postanovleniiakh TsK," *Ogonek* 13 (Mar. 30, 1998): 46.

42. Bakhtin identifies two similar currents in modern humor: "purely negative satire" and "recreational drollery deprived of philosophical content" (M. Bakhtin, *Rabelais,* 12).

43. I am certainly not suggesting that dissidents did not tell *anekdoty,* just that there are essential strategic and tactical differences between dissident textual production and the discursive impulses reflected in *anekdoty.*

44. Mikhail Bakhtin, "The Problem of Speech Genres," in *Speech Genres and Other Late Essays,* trans. Vern W. McGee, ed. Caryl Emerson and Michael Holquist (Austin: University of Texas Press, 1986), 68.

45. Richard Bauman, "Performance," in *Folklore, Cultural Performances, and Popular Entertainments: A Communications-Centered Handbook,* ed. Bauman (New York: Oxford University Press, 1992), 47.

46. Henri Bergson, *Laughter: An Essay on the Meaning of the Comic,* trans. Cloudesley Brereton and Fred Rothwell (London: MacMillan and Co., 1911; Copenhagen: Green Integer, 1999), 39.

47. On the reception of Soviet political discourse as popular entertainment, see Tat'iana Cherednichenko, *Tipologiia sovetskoi massovoi kul'tury: Mezhdu 'Brezhnevym' i 'Pugachevoi'* (Moscow: RIK Kul'tura, 1993).

48. Linda Hutcheon, *Irony's Edge: The Theory and Politics of Irony* (London: Routledge, 1994), 13.

49. Several historical surveys of humor theory use the "three theories" approach. Two of the clearest and most concise are to be found in John Morreall, *The Philosophy of Laughter and Humor* (Albany: State University of New York Press, 1987; and Susan C. Vogel, *Humor: A Semiogenetic Approach* (Bochum, West Germany: Studienverlag Brockmeyer, 1989), 5–17.

50. Vogel, *Humor,* 6.

51. Nikolai Chernyshevskii, "Vozvyshennoe i komicheskoe," in *Izbrannye filosofskie sochineniia* 1 (Leningrad: Gospolitizdat, 1950), 293.

52. Ibid., 286.

53. Viktor Shklovskii, "K teorii komicheskogo," *Epopeia: Literaturnyi ezhemesiachnik pod redaktsiei Andreia Belogo* 3 (1922): 62.

54. M. Bakhtin, *Rabelais*, 10.

55. Bergson, *Laughter,* 14.

56. Barbara A. Babcock, "Arrange Me into Disorder: Fragments and Reflections on Ritual Clowning," in *Rite, Drama, Festival, Spectacle: Rehearsals Toward a Theory of Cultural Performance,* ed. John J. MacAloon (Philadelphia: Institute for the Study of Human Issues, 1984), 103.

57. M. Bakhtin, *Rabelais,* 10.

58. Ibid., 6.

59. In her foreword to the English translation of Bakhtin's *Rabelais*, Krystyna Pomorska notes this connection (xi).

60. M. Bakhtin, *Rabelais,* 18 and passim.

61. Cited in Chirkova, *Poetika,* 6–7.

62. The entry for *"anekdot"* in the second edition of the *Encyclopedia* (1950) does in fact mention "sharp political content" as a generic feature, but only in reference to its Western European Renaissance-era form (*Bol'shaia sovetskaia entsiklopediia,* 2nd ed., 439).

63. Alaev, *Mir anekdota,* 52.

64. See, for example, Sidel'nikov, "Ideino-khudozhestvennaia spetsifika"; A. A. Ivanov, "K zhanrovoi spetsifike narodnogo anekdota (na primere analiza kompozitsii siuzhetov o durakakh)," in *Analiz khudozhestvennogo teksta: Problemy i perspektivy. Mezhvuzovskii sbornik* (Ioshkar-Ola: Miriiskii gosudarstvennyi universitet, 1991), 13–19; and Zhanna Dolgopolova, "Ispol'zovanie stilisticheskoi kontaminatsii kak sredstvo komicheskogo," in *XXII Gertsenovskie chteniia. Filologicheskie nauki. Programma i kratkoe soderzhanie dokladov. 15 apr.–10 maia 1969 goda* (Leningrad: Leningradskii pedagogicheskii institut im. A. I. Gertsena, 1969), 49–51. Iu. M. Sokolov's seminal 1938 textbook of Russian folklore contains a nine-page discussion of the *anekdot* (Iu. M. Sokolov, *Russian Folklore,* trans. Catherine Ruth Smith, introduction by Felix J. Oinas. [Detroit: Folklore Associates, 1971], 442–50) in the first part of the book, on pre-Revolutionary folklore, but the word is mentioned only a handful of times in passing in the second part, which deals with Soviet folklore.

65. The first scholarly examination of the native contemporary *anekdot* was published in 1989 in a compilation of the proceedings of a conference devoted to the genre (Aleksandr Belousov, comp., *Uchebnyi material po teorii literatury: Zhanry slovesnogo teksta. Anekdot* [Tallinn: Tallinskii pedagogicheskii institut, 1989]). Since then, there have been three dissertations, several monographs, and dozens of articles (adding to work done in the West, primarily by émigrés

such as Zhanna Dolgopolova, Andrei Siniavskii, and Emil Draitser). The most concentrated and extensive scholarly treatments of the contemporary *anekdot* to date are the monograph by linguists Elena Shmeleva and Aleksei Shmelev (*Russkii anekdot*) and dissertations by Viktor Khrul' (*Anekdot kak forma massovoi kommunikatsii*), Ol'ga Chirkova (*Poetika sovremennogo narodnogo anekdota*), and Endre Lendvai (*Pragmalingvisticheskie mekhanizmy sovremennogo russkogo anekdota* [Ph.D. Diss., Gosudarstvennyi institut russkogo iazyka im. A. S. Pushkina, 2001]). Efim Kurganov has published several book-length works on the *anekdot* from a wide-angle diachronic perspective that does not sharply distinguish the contemporary genre from its eighteenth- and nineteenth-century forebear: *Anekdot kak zhanr* (St. Petersburg: Gumanitarnoe agenstvo "Akademicheckii proekt," 1997); *Literaturnyi anekdot pushkinskoi epokhi* (Ph.D. dissertation, University of Helsinki, 1995); and *Pokhval'noe slovo anekdotu* (St. Petersburg: Izdatel'stvo zhurnala "Zvezda," 2001). Emil Draitser's books on ethnic humor (*Taking Penguins to the Movies*) and sexual humor (*Making War, Not Love: Gender and Sexuality in Russian Humor* [New York: St. Martin's, 1999]) in contemporary Russia provide a wealth of information and insight (and are unique in Anglophone publishing). All other notable analyses of the *anekdot* are articles or chapters. Among the more interpretive treatments of the genre are three concentrated essays by Zara Abdullaeva on the significance of the *anekdot* in Soviet social and intellectual life: "Anekdot," *Iskusstvo kino* 9 (2000): 66–67; "Ob anekdote," *Iskusstvo kino* 2 (1993): 82–86; and "Vse my vyshli iz anekdota," *Znanie—sila* 2 (1993): 113–20. Aleksei Yurchak examined the socioanthropological significance of the *anekdot* in the era of "late socialism" ("The Cynical Reason"). Andrei Siniavskii (writing as Abram Terts) wrote the rich and compelling article "Anekdot v anekdote," *Sintaksis* 1 (1978): 77–95.

66. See M. Bakhtin, *Rabelais.*

67. Gregor Benton wrote that "the gap between self and society, the widespread tension between two codes of meaning and behavior, those of private and public life—these are the ingredients for an excellent humor" (Gregor Benton, "The Origins of the Political Joke," *Humour in Society: Resistance and Control,* ed. Chris Powell and George Paton [New York: St. Martin's, 1988], 36).

68. Douglas, "Jokes," 295.

69. William F. Hanks, "Discourse Genres in a Theory of Practice," *American Ethnologist* 14.4 (Nov. 1987): 668.

70. On the evolution of the tale from folklore to literature in European culture, see Jack Zipes, *Fairy Tale as Myth/Myth as Fairy Tale* (Lexington: University Press of Kentucky, 1994), especially 1–48.

71. Many people, of course, did maintain secret written archives of *anekdoty,* some of which were published after the collectors emigrated. See, for example, Emil Draitser, ed. and comp., *Forbidden Laughter (Soviet Underground Jokes),* trans. Jon Pariser (Los Angeles: Almanac, 1978); Dora Shturman and

Sergei Tiktin, eds., *Sovetskii soiuz v zerkale politicheskogo anekdota* (London: Overseas Publications Interchange, 1985); Iulis Telesin, ed., *1001 izbrannyi sovetskii politicheskii anekdot* (Tenafly, N.J.: Ermitazh, 1986); and Zhanna Dolgopolova, ed., *Russia Dies Laughing: Jokes from Soviet Russia* (London: André Deutsch, 1982). Other formerly secret collections were published in the USSR beginning in the perestroika period. See especially Iurii Borev, *Staliniada* (Riga: Kursiv, 1990) and *Fariseia: Poslestalinskaia epokha v predaniiakh i anekdotakh* (Moscow: Nezavisimyi al'manakh "Konets veka," 1992).

72. Sally Kux, *On the Boundary of Life and Literature: The Anecdote in Early Nineteenth-Century Russia* (Ph.D. diss., Stanford University, 1994), 36.

CHAPTER ONE

Epigraph for chapter is from a citation in L. L. Khvalin-Gor'kii, comp., *Anekdoty s gosudareva dvora, ili 150 istoricheskikh anekdotov iz zhizni russkikh gosudarei XVII–XIX vekov* (Nizhnii Novgorod: Pegas, 1990), 3.

1. Kurganov, *Anekdot kak zhanr,* 7. One prominent example of classical joke books is the fifth-century collection by Hierocles the Grammarian, *The Philogelos or Laughter-Lover,* trans. and ed. Barry Baldwin (Amsterdam: J. C. Gieben, 1983).

2. Voltaire, it is worth noting, published his own collection of anecdotes about Peter the Great, *Anecdotes sur le czar Pierre le Grand* (1748; Oxford: Voltaire Foundation, 1999).

3. *An-,* not + *ek-,* out + *didonai,* to give. An older, obsolete meaning of the Greek word is "unmarried (for a woman)" (P. Ia. Chernykh, *Istoriko-etimologicheskii slovar' sovremennogo russkogo iazyka* [Moscow: Russkii iazyk, 1993], 44).

4. Procopius, *The Secret History,* trans. G. A. Williamson (Baltimore, Md.: Penguin, 1966). Although Procopius's book was the first known work to be called *anekdota,* the true generic ancestor of the contemporary *anekdot* (and the joke)—the short, punch-lined narrative—is older (Kurganov, *Anekdot kak zhanr,* 7). The following texts from Hierocles's *Philogelos,* for instance, are strikingly similar to contemporary *anekdoty* and jokes: "An alcoholic was drinking in a bar when someone came up to him and said, 'Your wife is dead.' 'Bartender, some dark wine please!'" (43); "A young man with two horny old women on his hands said to his slaves, 'Give one of them a drink, and screw the other!' The women replied in unison, 'We aren't thirsty!'" (47).

5. The gist of Procopius's exposé is that Justinian was a demon in human guise, Theodora a depraved prostitute, and war hero Belisarius an incompetent henpecked coward.

6. G. A. Williamson, introduction to Procopius, *The Secret History,* 7. *The Secret History* also sparked controversy due to its ambivalent implications for

Catholic Church authority. Recognizing the work as authentic was desirable for the Vatican, on the one hand, since the man Procopius had discredited was an emperor of Byzantium and therefore an enemy of Rome. On the other hand, warned jurists, validating a villainous portrait of a ruler whose civil law code was still widely respected and cited might undermine judicial authority (A. A. Chekalova, notes to Prokopii kesariiskii, *Voina s persami. Voina s vandalami. Tainaia istoriia*, trans. and ed. Chekalova [Moscow: Nauka, 1993], 446).

7. Iurii Borev, *Estetika* (Moscow: Politizdat, 1969).

8. This information is from Vladimir Bakhtin, who chose the quotation for the title of his article, "Anekdoty nas spasali vsegda."

9. Procopius, *The Secret History,* 38–39.

10. V. I. Tiupa, "Novella i apolog," in *Russkaia novella: Problemy teorii i istorii,* ed. V. M. Markovich and V. Shmid (St. Petersburg: Izdatel'stvo Sanktpeterburgskogo universiteta, 1993), 15.

11. Russian folklore study began in the 1860s with the work of Aleksandr Afanas'ev and Fedor Buslaev, proponents of the so-called Mythological School. Collection of Russian folk texts had been sporadic and unsystematic until the early nineteenth century, when the Russian Romantic movement sparked an interest in native folk culture. On the history of folklore study in Russia and the Soviet Union see Felix J. Oinas and Stephen Soudakoff, ed., *The Study of Russian Folklore* (The Hague: Mouton, 1975); and Dana Prescott Howell, *The Development of Soviet Folkloristics* (New York: Garland, 1992).

12. Many folklorists of the twentieth century also refused to grant the *anekdot* complete generic sovereignty, most notably Propp (see Vladimir Iakovlevich Propp, *Problemy komizma i smekha,* 2nd ed. [St. Petersburg: Aleteiia, 1997]).

13. A. I. Nikiforov, "Skazka, ee bytovanie i nositeli," in *Russkaia fol'kloristika: Khrestomatiia dlia vuzov* (Moscow: Vysshaia shkola, 1965), 351.

14. Iu. I. Iudin, *Russkaia narodnaia bytovaia skazka* (Moscow: Academia, 1998), 27. Iudin sees a causative link between the "formative era of class relations" and the emergence of the *bytovaia skazka,* which he describes as a "reworking of ancestral mythological stories" (5).

15. A. P. Pel'ttser, "Proiskhozhdenie anekdotov v russkoi narodnoi slovesnosti," in *Sbornik khar'kovskogo istoriko-filologicheskogo obshchestva* 11 (Khar'kov, 1897), 61.

16. E. M. Meletinskii, "Skazka-anekdot v sisteme fol'klornykh zhanrov," in Belousov, ed., *Uchebnyi material,* 59.

17. Zipes, *Fairy Tale as Myth,* 3.

18. Ibid. Zipes's view partially conflicts with that of Mikhail Bakhtin, whose concept of carnival reads such "individual," oppositional symbolic activity as an integral, very much "authorized" element of the exercise of authority itself (M. Bakhtin, *Rabelais,* passim).

19. Meletinskii, "Skazka-anekdot," 59.

20. Pel'ttser, "Proiskhozhdenie," 62.

21. The account of the evolution of folkloric forms given here is closest to the theory put forth by Vladimir Propp, which, it should be noted, is far from universally accepted and is by no means the only such theory.

22. Meletinskii, "Skazka-anekdot," 73.

23. N. P. Andreev, *Ukazatel' skazochnykh siuzhetov po sisteme Aarne* (Leningrad: Izdanie Gosudarstvennogo Russkogo Geograficheskogo Obshchestvo, 1929), 97.

24. Meletinskii, "Skazka-anekdot," 71.

25. E. M. Meletinskii, *Geroi volshebnoi skazki. Proiskhozhdenie obraza* (Moscow: Vostochnaia literatura, 1958), 239, cited in Iudin, *Russkaia narodnaia bytovaia skazka*, 10.

26. Vasilii Berezaiskii, for example, compiler of a 1798 collection of *anekdoty* about the residents of the legendary Russian "fooltown" Poshekhon'e, was an avid debunker of superstitions, one of the most prominent of which, in his opinion, was belief in wonder tales (Dmitrii Moldavskii, "Vasilii Berezaiskii i ego 'Anekdoty drevnykh poshekhontsev,'" in *Russkaia satiricheskaia skazka v zapisiakh serediny XIX–nachala XX veka,* ed. and comp. Moldavskii [Moscow: AN SSSR, 1955], 243).

27. I. A. Chudinova quotes an unnamed nineteenth-century cultural historian to illustrate how Peter used popular cultural forms (e.g., raucous public festivals and parades with garish costumes and loud instruments) to emphasize the novelty of his reformed Russia and to distract people from the authority of the Orthodox Church: "The yelps and thunder of the monstrous orchestra as it moved through the city was meant to underscore the governmental import of the event and to . . . destroy the people's anticipation of the installation of a new patriarch" ("Shutki i potekhi Petra Velikogo," 881, cited in I. A. Chudinova, "Smekh, vesel'e, shabash: Traditsii skomoroshestva v period petrovskikh reform," in *Skomorokhi: Problemy i perspectivy izucheniia (K 140-letiiu so dnia vykhoda pervoi raboty of skomorokhakh),* ed. V. V. Koshelev [St. Petersburg: Rossiiskii institut istorii iskusstv, 1994], 155).

28. Jack V. Haney, *An Introduction to the Russian Folktale* (Armonk, N.Y.: M. E. Sharpe, 1999), 109.

29. Andreev's index is a translation and expansion (to include Russian texts) of the standard index of European folktales, Antti Aarne, *The Types of the Folktale: A Classification and Bibliography,* trans. Stith Thompson (Helsinki, Finland: Academia Scientarum Fennica, 1961).

30. N. P. Andreev, *Ukazatel' skazochnykh siuzhetov po sisteme Aarne* (Leningrad: Izdanie Gosudarstvennogo Russkogo Geograficheskogo Obshchestvo, 1929), 119–20. It should be noted that Andreev's statistics date from the 1920s and that many blanks in the taxonomy of Russian tales have been filled in since.

31. Sokolov, *Russian Folklore,* 439.

32. O. K. Gerlovan, "Poniatie o skazke v Rossii XVIII–nachala XIX v.," *Filologicheskie nauki* 1 (1996): 95.

33. Roman Jakobson, "On Russian Fairy Tales," in *Russian Fairy Tales Collected by Aleksandr Afanas'ev*, trans. Norbert Guterman (New York: Pantheon, 1973), 633.

34. Gerlovan, "Poniatie," 98–99.

35. Kurganov, *Literaturnyi anekdot*, 44.

36. Gerlovan, "Poniatie," 99.

37. William E. Harkins, "Folktales," in *Handbook of Russian Literature*, ed. Victor Terras (New Haven, Conn.: Yale University Press, 1985), 148.

38. Pel'ttser, "Proiskhozhdenie," 65; Harkins, "Folktales," 148.

39. Pel'ttser, "Proiskhozhdenie," 65.

40. Meletinskii, "Skazka-anekdot," 61.

41. Kurganov, *Anekdot kak zhanr*, 13. In chapter 2 I discuss the influence on folk texts of the mass urbanization of the Russian peasantry that began with the emancipation of the serfs in 1861.

42. Haney, *Introduction*, 8.

43. From the beginning of folktale compilation, collections of "secret" or "indecent" tales have existed parallel to the canonical corpus. Afanas'ev's *Zavetnye skazki* was first published during his lifetime in Geneva and has been republished several times since, most recently in 1998 (Aleksandr Afanas'ev, *Narodnye russkie skazki ne dlia pechati, zavetnye poslovitsy i pogovorki, sobrannye i obrabotannye A. N. Afanas'evym. 1857–1862*, ed. O. B. Alekseeva, et al. [Moscow: Ladomir, 1998]). On the publication history of the tales, see Jack V. Haney, "Mr. Afanasiev's Naughty Little Secrets: 'Russkie zavetnye skazki,'" *SEEFA Journal* 3.2 (Fall 1998), accessed Jan. 3, 2002, <http://www.virginia.edu/slavic/seefa/ZAVETNYE.HTM>.

44. A. I. Nikiforov, "Erotika v velikorusskoi narodnoi skazke," *Khudozhestvennyi fol'klor* 4–5 (1929): 122.

45. I. N. Raikova, "Problema klassifikatsii neskazochnoi prozy v istorii nauki," in *Nauka o fol'klore segodnia: Mezhdistsiplinarnye vzaimodeistviia k 70-letnemu iubileiu Fedora Martynovicha Selivanova. Mezhdunarodnaia nauchnaia konferentsiia (Moskva 29–31 oktiabria 1997 goda)* (Moscow: Dialog MGU, 1998), 210. The first known recorded Russian folktale, about a peasant's encounter with a bear while stuck inside a honey tree, was reportedly told to Pope Clement VII by the Russian ambassador to the Vatican in 1525 and written down in Latin by a historian. The ambassador prefaced the tale as a real-life event that had happened to a "certain villager who lived not far from him" (Haney, *Introduction*, 3).

46. Chirkova, *Poetika*, 3–4.

47. Kurganov, *Anekdot kak zhanr*, 10.

48. Pel'ttser, "Proiskhozhdenie," 59–60.

49. The use of a toponym was often a marker of *anekdoty* about "fooltowns"; that is, a protagonist's connection to a certain place might signal that he is about to enact a codified quality (e.g., stupidity, stinginess) associated with the inhabitants of that place. On this, see Iudin, *Russkaia narodnaia bytovaia skazka,* 27.

50. Ibid.

51. In addition to their "conscious emphasis on verisimilitude," writes Raikova, nonfolktale prose genres are characterized by "extra-aesthetic functions (informative, didactic, etiological, mnemonic, utilitarian, etc.), . . . an absence of compositional and stylistic canons, and a close connection between the oral text and the situational speech context" (Raikova, "Problema," 210).

52. Afanas'ev, *Narodnye russkie skazki A. N. Afanas'eva,* vol. 3, 196. The punch line of this text ("If you drown, don't bother") entered the language as an idiom still in use today (Valery Belyanin, personal communication, July 2002).

53. Afanas'ev, *Narodnye russkie skazki A. N. Afanas'eva,* vol. 3, 196.

54. Ibid.

55. Afanas'ev, *Narodnye russkie skazki ne dlia pechati,* 463.

56. Valentina Kharitonova, "Anekdoty (stat'ia o podlinnykh anekdotakh so mnozhestvom primerov)," *Istoki: Al'manakh* 21 (1990): 184.

57. The etymology of the Russian word "*skomorokh*" is unclear, but despite the fact that the *skomorokhi* were not only comedians but musicians, actors, acrobats, and animal trainers, most of the suggested origins of the word have to do with humor: the Arabic *maskhara* [laughter, mockery] (Pel'ttser, "Proiskhozhdenie," 79); the ancient Greek *skommarxos* [joke, prank]; the Italian *scaramuccia* [jester] (Max Vasmer, *Etimologicheskii slovar' russkogo iazyka,* trans. O. N. Trubacheva, ed. B. A. Larina [Moscow: Progress, 1964], 648).

58. I follow Galina Patterson in translating the Russian word "*shut*" as "buffoon" (Galina Patterson, *The Buffoon in Nineteenth and Twentieth Century Russian Literature: The Literary Model and Its Cultural Roots* [Ph.D. dissertation, University of Wisconsin–Madison, 1998]).

59. For the same reason, and also due to the Russian Orthodox Church's six-century monopoly on written culture, there are no known transcripts of Russian folklore before the seventeenth century (Jakobson, "On Russian Fairy Tales," 632), the 1525 Latin tale cited here being an anomalous exception.

60. Russell Zguta, *Russian Minstrels: A History of the* Skomorokhi (Philadelphia: University of Pennsylvania Press, 1978), 15. The church also disapproved of the *skomorokhi* because their performances typically ended in villagewide drinking binges. Also, the *skomorokhi* sometimes conned, robbed, or otherwise fleeced their audiences (Pel'ttser, "Proiskhozhdenie," 82), suggesting that their actions might have given real-life impetus to traditional trickster narratives.

61. Cited in Zguta, *Russian Minstrels,* 3.

62. Ibid., 23–24.

63. Ibid., 81. Harkins wrote that the *skomorokh* repertoire and style was also likely influenced by "foreign itinerant entertainers, including the German *Spielmänner,* who visited Russia in the medieval period, and perhaps by Byzantine mime entertainers, who are depicted in early frescoes on the walls of the Cathedral of St. Sophia in Kiev" (Harkins, "Skomorokhi," in *Handbook of Russian Literature,* 422).

64. Zguta, *Russian Minstrels,* 89.

65. Z. I. Vlasova, "Skomorokhi i fol'klor," *Etnograficheskie istoki fol'klornykh iavlenii. Russkii fol'klor* 24 (Leningrad: Nauka, 1987), 50.

66. Ibid., 59.

67. Ibid., 52.

68. Ibid., 59.

69. Ibid., 60.

70. Ivan employed *bakhari* (blind storytellers) to help put him to sleep at night. The tsar also reportedly liked to put on masks and frolic with the *skomorokhi* (Pel'ttser, "Proiskhozhdenie," 80).

71. Zguta, *Russian Minstrels,* 97.

72. Ibid., 89.

73. Vlasova, "Skomorokhi," 54.

74. Zguta, *Russian Minstrels,* xi. The notion of the popular entertainer as a spokesman would find resonance in Soviet culture in such figures as Mikhail Zhvanetskii (see chapter 3).

75. Vadim Rudnev, *Slovar' kul'tury XX veka* (Moscow: Agraf, 1997), 28.

76. This comment is in a letter from P. A. Demidov to G. F. Miller (cited in Zguta, *Russian Minstrels,* 65).

77. Ibid., 97.

78. A. V. Kokorev, "Russkie stikhotvornye fatsetsii XVIII v.," in *Starinnaia russkaia povest': Stat'i i issledovaniia,* ed. N. K. Gudzii (Moscow: AN SSSR, 1941), 220.

79. Pel'ttser, "Proiskhozhdenie," 77.

80. Ibid., 76.

81. *Anekdoty o shute Balakireve: Prodelki i shutki, ostroumnye otvety i blagie sovety slavnogo Balakireva, pridvornogo shuta imperatora Petra Velikog,* 4th ed. (St. Petersburg: Izdanie knigoprodavtsa A. A. Kholmushina, 1899), 33, cited in B. N. Putilov, ed. and comp., *Petr Velikii v predaniiakh, legendakh, anekdotakh, skazkakh, pesniakh* (Akademicheskii proekt, 2000), 152.

82. One nineteenth-century anthology collected *anekdoty* about three other renowned jesters in addition to Balakirev: Ian D'Acosta, a Portuguese émigré who came to Russia during the reign of Peter the Great; Antonio Pedrillo, an Italian initially invited to Russia as a court violinist; and a certain Kul'kovskii, about whom biographical data are scarce. For more information and dozens of *anekdoty* from this and similar collections see Kurganov, *Anekdot kak zhanr.*

83. *Anekdoty o shute Balakireve,* 4.

84. Ibid., 5.

85. Ibid., 6.

86. Krivoshlyk, *Istoricheskie anekdoty,* 21. Peter himself used the jesters' customary license to speak frankly to promote his reforms, urging the jesters "to make a game of the old-fashioned prejudices and customs so firmly rooted in society. . . . Under cover of a jester, [Peter] conveyed many a plain truth to the nobles. When the latter used to complain to him of the too unceremonious behavior of the jesters, he would answer, 'What can I do with them? They are fools, you know'" (Sergy N. Shoubinsky, "Court Jesters and Their Weddings in the Reigns of Peter the Great and Anna Ivanovna," in H. D. Romanoff, *Historical Narratives from the Russian* (London: Rivingtons, 1871), 4–5.

87. Adam Olearius, *The Travels of Olearius in Seventeenth-Century Russia,* trans. and ed. Samuel H. Baron (Stanford, Calif.: Stanford University Press, 1967), 142.

88. Kurganov, *Literaturnyi anekdot,* 36.

89. Ibid.

90. I. E. Andreevskii, "Anekdoty," in *Entsiklopedicheskii slovar',* ed. Andreevskii (St. Petersburg: Brokgauz and Efron, 1890), 776.

91. Kokorev, "Russkie stikhotvornye fatsetsii," 217.

92. Ibid., 218–19.

93. On the place of *lubochnaia literatura* in Russian popular culture see Neia Zorkaia, *Fol'klor, Lubok, Ekran* (Moscow: Iskusstvo, 1994); and Farrell, "Medieval Popular Humor."

94. Khrul', *Anekdot kak forma,* 31.

95. Pel'ttser, "Proiskhozhdenie," 76.

96. Leonid Grossman, "Iskusstvo anekdota u Pushkina," in *Sobranie sochinenii v chetyrekh tomakh. Tom pervyi: Pushkin: Issledovaniia i stat'i* (Moscow: Sovremennye problemy, 1928), 45.

97. Pel'ttser, "Proiskhozhdenie," 57.

98. Ibid., 58.

99. A. E. Chekunova, "Poiavlenie istoricheskogo anekdota v Rossii," *Voprosy istorii* 2 (1997): 131; Kurganov, *Anekdot kak zhanr,* 7.

100. Chekunova, "Poiavlenie," 133.

101. Kux, *On the Boundary,* 10–11. The expanded social range of the categories of protagonists listed in the title indicates the changes already under way in the historical *anekdot* by the beginning of the nineteenth century.

102. V. A. Nevskaia, "'. . . Dnei minuvshikh anekdoty,'" *Russkaia rech'* 5 (1992): 79.

103. Krivoshlyk, *Istoricheskie anekdoty,* 9–10.

104. Kurganov and Okhotin, *Russkii literaturnyi anekdot,* 9.

105. More than two centuries after Peter's death, another leader would also be the subject of sanctioned narratives that highlighted his kindness and mercy. Joseph Stalin's image in the *anekdot* tradition, of course, ridicules his official image but, interestingly, does not deprive him of the pleasure of exercising his power over life and death in just as whimsical a manner as Peter (see the sneezing joke in chapter 2).

106. Krivoshlyk, *Istoricheskie anekdoty,* 29.

107. Nevskaia, "'. . . Dnei,'" 79.

108. Kux, *On the Boundary,* 42.

109. Ibid., 7–8.

110. Sidel'nikov, "Ideino-khudozhestvennaia spetsifika," 30.

111. Pel'ttser, "Proiskhozhdenie," 59.

112. Petr Bogatyrev and Roman Jakobson, "Folklore as a Special Form of Creativity," trans. Manfred Jacobson, in *The Prague School: Selected Writings, 1929–1946,* ed. Peter Steiner (Austin: University of Texas Press, 1982), 37.

113. Pel'ttser, "Proiskhozhdenie," 57.

114. Aleksandr Belousov, "Ot sostavitelia," in Belousov, comp., *Uchebnyi material,* 5.

115. Nikolai Mikhailovich Karamzin, "Otchego v Rossii malo avtorskikh talantov," in Karamzin, *Izbrannye sochineniia v dvukh tomakh,* vol. 2 (Moscow: Khudozhestvennaia literatura, 1964), 183–87. Cited in Kux, *On the Boundary,* 22.

116. Cited in Chekunova, "Poiavlenie," 143. Gerlovan writes that Russian authors of tales took on a similar project: "Seeing the resemblance of translated tales and novels to Russian folk compositions, [Russian writers] set themselves the task of creating 'Slavic,' 'Russian' tales in order to expose the reader to a familiar and at the same time unfamiliar world" (Gerlovan, "Poniatie," 100).

117. Belousov, "Ot sostavitelia," 7.

118. Kux, *On the Boundary,* 2.

119. Aleksandr Pushkin, "Table-Talk," in *Polnoe sobranie sochinenii v dvadtsati tomakh* 12 (St. Petersburg: Nauka, 1999), 95.

120. Kurganov, *Literaturnyi anekdot,* 36.

121. Catherine composed two tales—"The Tale of Tsarevich Khlor" and "The Tale of Tsarevich Fevei"—in addition to her numerous plays.

122. Kux writes that folk elements were sometimes "superficially and/or consciously included to lend a pseudo-folk flavor" to literary compositions (Kux, *On the Boundary,* 6).

123. Grossman, "Iskusstvo anekdota," 46.

124. Efim Kurganov, "'U nas byla i est' ustnaia literature . . .'" in *Russkii literaturnyi anekdot kontsa XVIII–nachala XIX veka,* comp. Kurganov and N. Okhotin (Moscow: Khudozhestvennaia literatura, 1990), 3.

125. Jakobson, "On Russian Fairy Tales," 647.

126. Kux, *On the Boundary,* 41. Grossman points out the intriguing fact

that Karl Marx's first political article was published in a Zurich philosophical anthology called *Anecdota* (Grossman, "Iskusstvo anekdota," 46).

127. Iurii Borev, *XX vek v predaniiakh i anekdotakh: v 6-ti knigakh,* vol. 1 (Rostov-na-Donu: Feniks, 1996), 3.

128. Kurganov, "U nas," 3.

129. Ibid.

130. Kux, *On the Boundary,* 3.

131. Kurganov, "U nas," 4.

132. Bergson, *Laughter,* 24.

133. Cited in Kurganov, *Literaturnyi anekdot,* 199.

134. Kurganov and Okhotin, comps., *Russkii literaturnyi anekdot,* 206.

135. Dolgopolova, "The Contrary World," 1.

136. Nikolai Gogol, *Letters of Nikolai Gogol,* ed. Carl Proffer, trans. Carl Proffer and Vera Krivoshein (Ann Arbor: University of Michigan Press, 1967), 52.

137. Kux, *On the Boundary,* 12.

CHAPTER TWO

First chapter epigraph is from Gilbert Morris Cuthbertson, *Political Myth and Epic* (Ann Arbor: Michigan State University Press, 1975), xxi.

Second chapter epigraph is from I. Shaitanov, "Mezhdu eposom i anekdotom," *Literaturnoe obozrenie* 1 (1995): 19. A. F. Sedov has made a similar observation: "The more an issue is inflated by Officialdom, the more probable the appearance of anekdoty about it" (A. F. Sedov, *Politicheskii anekdot kak iavlenie kul'tury: Populiarnyi ocherk. Vesy* 11 [Balashov: Balashovskii filial Saratovskogo gosudarstvennogo universiteta, 1999], 5).

1. Richard Stites, *Russian Popular Culture: Entertainment and Society Since 1900* (Cambridge: Cambridge University Press, 1992), 4.

2. Anatolii Vishnevskii, *Serp i rubl': Konservativnaia modernizatsiia v SSSR* (Moscow: O. G. I., 1998), 83. For their part, Soviet ethnographers rejected the distinction between rural and urban as late as 1984, objecting that such a dichotomy "presupposes the dismemberment of what is the genetically singular culture of an ethnos" (O. R. Budina and N. N. Shmeleva, "Tradition in the Development of the Culture of Everyday Life in a Modern Russian City," *Soviet Anthropology and Archeology* 22.4 [Spring 1984]: 73). Downplaying or denying the rural-urban social divide was an important element of the official view of the Soviet Union as a worker-peasant state.

3. Jeffrey Brooks, *When Russia Learned to Read: Literacy and Popular Literature 1861–1917* (Princeton, N.J.: Princeton University Press, 2000), xiii, 32.

4. Sergei Iur'evich Nekliudov, "Posle fol'klora," *Zhivaia starina* 1 (1995): 2.

5. Kurganov, *Literaturnyi anekdot,* 44.

6. One indication of official hostility toward the *anekdot* was the reluctance of Soviet folklorists to grant the folk *anekdot* full genre status. It was consistently (though not exclusively—see Sidel'nikov, "Ideino-khudozhestvennaia spetsifika," for example) classified as a subgenre of the everyday tale.

7. Kurganov, *Anekdot kak zhanr,* 13.

8. Although it is much shorter than the folktale, the *anekdot*—in the form of long, open-ended sessions in which they are told en masse in an associative chain—has served a similar function, especially during Stagnation, when marathon *anekdot* telling was a common pastime in the insular collectives that characterized the period.

9. Pel'ttser, "Proiskhozhdenie," 63.

10. Meletinskii, *Geroi volshebnoi skazki,* 239, cited in Iudin, *Russkaia narodnaia bytovaia skazka,* 10. Meletinskii's use of the word "moribund" recalls Bergson's characterization of laughter as a means of purging, through "corrective" laughter, organic formations, institutions, and phenomena that have been overlaid with inflexible, nonlifelike attributes or accoutrements (Bergson, *Laughter,* 82).

11. Katerina Clark (*The Soviet Novel: History as Ritual,* 3rd ed. [Bloomington: Indiana University Press, 2000]) wrote that the Russian revolutionaries' use of traditional forms began in the second half of the nineteenth century, when authors of propagandistic tracts "imitated genres they believed would appeal to the masses: folktales, folk epics [*byliny*], short stories narrated as if told by a peasant or worker, and religious writings" (48–49). Such "fakeloric" texts did not provoke a counterimpulse in oral culture until they became institutionalized in mass culture following the Revolution.

12. Julia Latynina, "New Folklore and Newspeak," in *Re-entering the Sign: Articulating New Russian Culture,* ed. Ellen E. Berry and Anesa Miller-Pogacar (Ann Arbor: University of Michigan Press, 1995), 79.

13. Ibid., 80–83.

14. Ibid., 83. Writing from a more Sovietological than folkloristic perspective, Christie Davies nevertheless identified a similar "fundamental contradiction" in socialist societies "between the rational outlook engendered by modern processes of production, administration and scientific enquiry, and the irrational, arbitrary, muddled and obstructive exercise of power that emerges from their political system" (Christie Davies, "Stupidity and Rationality: Jokes from the Iron Cage," in *Humour in Society: Resistance and Control,* ed. Chris Powell and George E. C. Paton [New York: St. Martin's, 1988], 21).

15. Chirkova, *Poetika,* 25.

16. There were certainly pre-Revolutionary *anekdoty* about Russian royalty and other public figures, but they are mostly in the mold of the historical *anekdot,* i.e., based on purported actual moments from the subjects' lives.

17. Chirkova, *Poetika,* 3–4.

157

18. Sergei Romanov, *Usypal'nitsa: Biografiia sovetskikh 'tsarei' v anekdot-akh* (Moscow: IRLE, 1994), 7. Upon his return to Russia from exile in 1917, Lenin gave a speech at the Finland Station in Petrograd while standing atop an armored train car. The event—at which Lenin articulated the formative Bolshe-vik slogans that would be canonized as the April Theses—became a seminal epi-sode in the Soviet state's creation mythology.

19. *Anekdoty o politikakh—Epokha zastoia (1953–1985)*, accessed Mar. 23, 2003, http://rels.obninsk.com/Rels/Lg/anecdote/zastoi.htm.

20. Susan Stewart wrote that verbal genres tend to fall into categories according to their relationship to the ideological or intellectual status quo: "Prov-erbs and the novels of realism are seen as standing in a metonymic relation-ship to common sense, while riddles and nonsense literature are seen as stand-ing in a paradoxical and metaphorical relation to common sense" (*Nonsense,* ix). On a Russian brand of nonsense, the so-called abstract or absurd *anekdot,* see chapter 4.

21. Meletinskii, "Skazka-anekdot," 59.

22. Bronislaw Malinowski, "Myth in Primitive Psychology," in *Magic, Science, and Religion and Other Essays* (Boston: Beacon, 1948), 84, cited in Gil-bert Morris Cuthbertson, *Political Myth and Epic* (Ann Arbor: Michigan State University Press, 1975), 3.

23. Zipes, *Fairy Tale as Myth,* 1.

24. Douglas implied that such a maneuver is essential to the joke genre. She described her "formula for identifying jokes": "A joke is a play upon form. It brings into relation disparate elements in such a way that one accepted pattern is challenged by the appearance of another which in some way was hidden in the first" (Douglas, "Jokes," 296).

25. An *anekdot* from the era of Vladimir Putin has a premise very similar to that of the Soviet Chukchi joke I cite here (http://www.anekdot .ru/an/an0006/000627.html#1): "Putin's reform program: 1. Make people rich and happy. Appendix 1: list of aforementioned people."

26. Salvatore Attardo and Jean-Charles Chabanne, "Jokes as a Text Type," *Humor* 5.1–2 (1992): 170.

27. Viktor Shklovskii, "K teorii komicheskogo," *Epopeia: Literaturnyi ezhem-esiachnik pod redaktsiei Andreia Belogo* 3 (1922): 63.

28. Stites, *Russian Popular Culture,* 9.

29. Sergei Karachevtsev, *"Dlia nekuriashchikh": Anekdoty* (Riga: Mir, n.d.), 20. The German has confused the Russian *otdokhnut'* [relax] or *vzdokhnut'* [in-hale] with *sdokhnut'* [croak, as in "to die").

30. Shklovskii, "K teorii," 60.

31. M. A. Krongauz, "Bessilie iazyka v epokhu zrelogo sotsializma," in *Znak: Sbornik statei po lingvistike, semiotike i poetike pamiati A. N. Zhurinskogo* (Moscow: Russkii uchebnyi tsentr MS, 1994), 236.

32. Zoshchenko's stories were sometimes excoriated in the press for being too "anecdotal" (Shaitanov, "Mezhdu eposom," 18).

33. "Piter" is a nickname for St. Petersburg, which was, of course, renamed Leningrad after Lenin's death. In English translation, this joke has an ethnic connotation ("JuLenin" sounds like "JewLenin") that is not present in the original.

34. On this subgenre, see N. A. Kupina, *Totalitarnyi iazyk: Slovar' i rechevye reaktsii* (Ekaterinburg: Izdatel'stvo Ural'skogo universiteta, 1995), 100–102.

35. Evgenii Andreevich, *Kreml' i narod: Politicheskie anekdoty* (Munich: 1951), 15.

36. This is a pun on the word "*selo*," which is indeed the past-tense form of "to set" but also means "to go to prison." The same play on words was no doubt used in Russia long before the Soviet period, but it took on new significance then.

37. Shklovskii, "K teorii," 62.

38. Iangirov, "Anekdoty 's borodoi'," 172.

39. There is a similar *anekdot* involving a donkey and a rabbit.

40. Sergei Nekliudov, "Posle fol'klora," *Zhivaia starina* 1 (1995): 3. On the capacity of the *anekdot* for satirizing state "ceremonies," see Krongauz, "Bessilie," and chapter 3 of this book.

41. Latynina, "New Folklore," 85.

42. Averintsev, "Bakhtin i russkoe," 342.

43. Iangirov, "Anekdoty 's borodoi'," 166. In other variants of this *anekdot,* the resident is relieved to discover that the commotion is only the result of a fire in the building.

44. Stalin reportedly enjoyed *anekdoty,* and even listened to émigré comedy records (Mikhail Korshunov and Viktoriia Terekhova, "Nas bylo chetvero . . . ," *Detskaia Literatura* 3 [1994]: 27). Medvedev reports that NKVD chief Beria regularly told Stalin the latest jokes about him. Stalin in anecdotes (in the Western sense of the word; informal accounts of the real person of Stalin) used dark humor in a kind of doubly ironic, reflexive move: I know I am a dangerous tyrant, but officially I am not, so joking about, for instance, having the transportation minister shot if trains do not run on time (in the minister's presence, of course) is ironic vis-à-vis that official truth, while demonstrating a sense of humor affirms the leader's positive image.

45. Thurston's article argues this point throughout.

46. Andreevich, *Kreml',* 10.

47. Ibid., 21–22.

48. Barskii and Pis'mennyi, "Vlast' smekha," 46.

49. Gregor Benton (p. 37) compares Khrushchev to another Communist leader, Deng Xiaoping, who was also an "earthy man" who himself used humor and succeeded a humorless despot.

50. Vadim Rudnev writes that Khrushchev inspired many more *anekdoty* than Stalin because the former was an "intermediary" figure (Rudnev, *Slovar'*, 28), reminiscent of the archetype of the trickster, "a mythological character who unsuccessfully imitates high-status heroes" (M. Iu. Timofeev, "Rzhevskii, Chapaev, Shtirlits: Natsional'nye i gendernye kharakteristiki voennykh v sovetskikh anekdotakh," in *Doklady Pervoi Mezhdunarodnoi konferentsii "Gender: Iazyk, kul'tura, kommunikatsiia," 25–26 noiabria 1999 goda* [Moscow: Moskovskii gosudarstvennyi linguisticheskii universitet, 2001], 324).

51. Khrushchev's door reads *treplo kukuruznoe,* a reference to Khrushchev's legendary obsession—inspired by a trip to the United States, where he was impressed by Iowa cornfields—with introducing corn to Soviet agriculture.

52. This is a play on Stalin and Khrushchev's names. On the Radio Armenia cycle, a mass-media-age successor to a much older tradition of Armenian riddles, see George Kalbouss, "On 'Armenian Riddles' and Their Offspring 'Radio Erevan,'" *Slavic and East European Journal* 21.3 (1977): 447–49; Elena Hellberg-Hirn, "The Other Way Round: The Jokelore of Radio Yerevan," *Arv: Scandinavian Yearbook of Folklore* 41 (1985): 89–104; and Elena Iakovlevna Shmeleva, "Anekdoty ob armianskom radio: struktura i iazykovye osobennosti," *Fol'klor i postfol'klor: struktura, tipologiia, semiotika,* accessed Nov. 29, 2002 (http://www.ruthenia.ru/folklore/shmeleva1.htm).

53. Lenin and Brezhnev had the same patronymic, Il'ich (son of Il'ia).

54. Adding the two dots changes the word to "Lënin," that is, "Leonid's."

55. Iurii Borev, "Intelligentskii fol'klor," in *Istoriia gosudarstva sovetskogo v predaniiakh i anekdotakh* (Moscow: Ripol, 1995), 3.

56. The more prosaic folk genres that the state did end up embracing—the tale, the *chastushka,* the folk song, and so on—were used in such nonironic didactic ways that the response was similar to that of schoolchildren to the saccharine propaganda of elementary curricula. There are in fact crucial parallels between school folklore and the Soviet *anekdot,* both of which thrived and continue to thrive in "totalitarian systems." Russian scholars have done extensive work on children's humor. See, for example, Aleksandra Arkhipova, "'Rolevaia struktura' detskikh tsiklov anekdotov (na materiale anekdotov o Vinni-Pukhe i Piatachke, o Cheburashke i Krokodile Gene)," B.A. thesis, Moscow, Rossiiskii gosudarstvennyi Gumanitarnyi universitet, 1999; Aleksandr Fedorovich Belousov, "Anekdoticheskii tsikl o krokodile Gene i Cheburashke," in *Problemy poetiki iazyka i literatury. Materialy mezhvuzovskoi nauchnoi konferentsii, 22–24 maia 1996 goda* (Petrozavodsk: Izdatel'stvo karel'skogo gosudarstvennogo pedagogicheskogo universiteta, 1996), 3–20; and S. V. Moshkin and V. N. Rudenko, "Children's Political Jokes," *Russian Education and Society* 38.9 (Sept. 1996): 69–79.

57. Abram Terts (p. 81) writes something similar about literal question-and-answer *anekdoty,* such as the Radio Armenia cycle, which pose questions that it was forbidden to answer.

58. Walter J. Ong, *Orality and Literacy: The Technologizing of the Word* (London: Routledge, 1982), 38.

59. Pertsov, "Anekdot," 41. Several observers have referred to the genre as a form of epic, including Siniavskii/Terts ("Anekdot v anecdote," 77) and Kurganov (*Anekdot kak zhanr*, 56).

60. I. Shaitanov, "Mezhdu eposom," 20.

61. Leonid Stolovich, "Anekdot kak zerkalo nashei evoliutsii," *Izvestiia* 20 Mar. 1993: 10.

62. *Bol'shaia sovetskaia entsiklopediia*, 1st ed. (Moscow: Sovetskaia entsiklopediia, 1926, 1947).

63. Benton points out the elite class origins of the political joke, which, he says, was not a genre of the masses because they had no contact with larger political structures, and insufficient distance from local politics to engage it satirically. The mass culture and centralization in the Soviet Union blurred differences between the national and the local, or rather inserted national political issues into local spheres of perception and discourse.

64. E. Kuskova, "Vospominanie," *Sovremennye zapiski* 12 (1922): 147. I use a literal translation of the Russian version of the first line of the "Internationale" here, because the joke does not work otherwise. The standard English version of the line is "Arise, ye prisoners of starvation."

65. One of the only explicit statements of the official Soviet position on the *anekdot*, in fact, is the article-length response to a reader's question published in *Komsomol'skaia Pravda* that I cite in the Introduction. Among the most notorious examples of an official text that uses state-popular dialogue as a device (again, in question-and-answer format) is Joseph Stalin's 1950 pamphlet, *Concerning Marxism in Linguistics* (London: Soviet News, 1950).

66. Alaev, *Mir anekdota*, 12.

67. Siniavskii/Terts, "Anekdot v anecdote," 92.

68. Shturman and Tiktin, *Sovetskii soiuz*, 10.

69. Caroline Humphrey, *Karl Marx Collective: Economy, Society and Religion in a Siberian Collective Farm* (Cambridge: Cambridge University Press, 1983), 7.

70. Alexander Zinoviev, *The Reality of Communism*, trans. Charles Janson (New York: Schocken Books, 1984), 9.

71. The Third Party Program was a long time coming: the First and Second Party Programs were adopted in 1903 and 1919, respectively.

72. *Program of the Communist Party of the Soviet Union [Draft]* (New York: Crosscurrents Press, 1961), 123.

73. Tat'iana Cherednichenko, *Tipologiia sovetskoi massovoi kul'tury: Mezhdu "Brezhnevym" i "Pugachevoi"* (Moscow: RIK Kul'tura, 1993), 10.

74. This is a parody of the Leninist slogan, "Lenin is dead, but his cause [*delo*] lives on."

75. John Beverley, "The Margins at the Center: On *Testimonio* (Testimonial Narrative)," in *The Real Thing: Testimonial Discourse and Latin America*, ed. Georg M. Gugelberger (Durham, N.C.: Duke University Press, 1996), 24.

CHAPTER THREE

Epigraph for chapter is from *Nonsense,* 52.

1. Dmitrii Makarov, "Natsii v zerkale anekdota," *Argumenty i fakty* 4.953 (Jan. 1999): 15. There are other such legendary accounts of targeted strategic joke propagation by the Soviet security agencies. The Chapaev cycle, for example, by some accounts was created in the bowels of the Lubianka prison in the late 1960s as a means of drawing satirical attention away from Lenin as his 1970 centennial approached.

2. The term "era of Stagnation" [*epokha "zastoi"*] was initially used in the 1980s in reference to the stagnant economy during the second half of Leonid Il'ich Brezhnev's eighteen-year rule (1964–82) plus the brief tenures of his immediate successors, Iurii Andropov (1982–83) and Konstantin Chernenko (1983–85). Cultural scholars have used the term in a different way, to delineate the period of state retrenchment between the reform-oriented Thaw (1953–64) and perestroika (1985–91) periods.

3. Miron Petrovskii, "Novyi anekdot znaesh'?" *Filosofskaia i sotsiologicheskaia mysl'* 5 (1990): 47.

4. Alaev, *Mir anekdota,* 20. The deputy's astute linkage of alcohol and *anekdoty* as phenomena of a similar order touches on an issue with which I deal in chapters 5 and 6.

5. V. Bakhtin, "Anekdoty," 799.

6. The *anekdot* was featured prominently, for instance, in many well-known *samizdat* and *tamizdat* novels. Two such works—Vladimir Voinovich's *Zhizn' i neobyknovennye prikliucheniia soldata Ivana Chonkina* (The Life and Extraordinary Adventures of Private Ivan Chonkin, 1980) and Venedikt Erofeev's *Moskva-Petushki* (Moscow-Petushki, 1969)—are in fact subtitled *roman-anekdot* (novel-*anekdot*). Aleksandr Zinov'ev's satirical novels, especially his mammoth *Ziiaiushchie vysoty* (The Yawning Heights, 1976), are peppered with *anekdoty* told by characters.

7. Kurganov, *Anekdot kak zhanr,* 7.

8. The role to which Kurganov referred, let us recall, is a traditional one for the genre and its ancestors: literary anecdotes in the nineteenth century often served as "seeds" for larger genres.

9. Terts traced the process back much farther than Soviet history: "At one time it was the historical song and the legend that were composed on the heels of current events. In a different period, the *chastushka* fulfilled that role. Now the mission has been completely assigned to the *anekdot*" (90–91).

10. Catriona Kelly and David Shepherd, eds., *Russian Cultural Studies: An Introduction* (New York: Oxford University Press, 1998), 12.

11. The Brezhnevian retrenchment was a policy shift exemplified most dramatically by the 1968 suppression of the Prague Spring but that was nascent in cultural politics years before, the widely publicized persecution of Iosif Brodskii in 1964 and Andrei Siniavskii and Iulii Daniel' in 1965–66 being the best-known examples. There were spasms of reactionism even during the Khrushchev years, of course (the 1956 intervention in Hungary and the 1957 persecution of Pasternak, for example), but with Brezhnev's ascent to power the conservatism became sustained and systemic.

12. Petr Vail' and Aleksandr Genis, *60-e. Mir sovetskogo cheloveka* (Moscow: Novoe literaturnoe obozrenie, 1998), 142–52.

13. Ibid., 142.

14. Lev Anninskii, *Shestidesiatniki i my. Kinematograf, stavshii i ne stavshii istoriei* (Moscow: Kinotsentr, 1991), 6. The notion of "secret freedom" is certainly not new in Russian thought. Recall the nineteenth-century writer Konstantin Aksakov's opinion that Russians' tolerance for authoritarian government is a result of their capacity to find a measure of "inner, communal" freedom (cited in Daniel Rancour-Laferriere, *The Slave Soul of Russia: Moral Masochism and the Cult of Suffering* [New York: New York University Press, 1995], 37–38).

15. The lack of attention to Stagnation culture stands in particular contrast to the wealth of scholarship on Stalinist culture published over the past decade or so.

16. Krongauz used the term *"epokha zrelogo sotsializma"* (the era of mature socialism), which, though encountered more rarely in official discourse than "the era of developed [*razvitogo*] socialism," he considered more descriptive of the nature of the social system as it had congealed by the Brezhnev period ("Bessilie," 234). The term also helpfully evokes the extreme "maturity" of Brezhnev himself, as well as that of his epigones, Andropov and Chernenko.

17. After Brezhnev, of course, subsequent leaders were added to the *anekdot*: "Gorbachev: Vyiti vsem iz vagonov I krichat':—U nas net rel'sov, net dazhe shpag! Vperedi propasti!" ("Gorbachev: Everyone get out of the train and shout, "We have no rails! We don't even have crossties! We're heading toward a cliff!""). The version included here is a composite of texts found in Lev Abramovich Barskii, *Eto prosto smeshno* (Moscow: Kh.G.S., 1992), 58, and V. Bakhtin ("Anekdoty," 809).

18. Mikhail Epstein, "The Origins and Meaning of Russian Postmodernism," in *Re-entering the Sign*, 26.

19. Anatoly Vishevsky, *Soviet Literary Culture in the 1970s: The Politics of Irony* (Gainesville: University Press of Florida, 1993), 4.

20. Andrei Nemzer, "Desiat' bukv po vertikali," introduction to *Anketa*, by Aleksei Slapovskii (St. Petersburg: Kurs, 1997), 3.

21. Yurchak, "Cynical Reason," 174.

22. I am not suggesting here that the *anekdot* was dormant in the summer; on the contrary, it was a staple of dacha life.

23. A distinctive though undoubtedly rare aspect of joke telling in totalitarian societies was the use of a "provocation *anekdot*" by a secret informer to elicit in response incriminating statements (i.e., *anekdoty*) or actions (i.e., failure to report the *anekdot* teller to the authorities). This practice is alluded to in *anekdoty* themselves, for example: "A conversation in the gulag: 'What are you in for?' 'Laziness. My friend and I were swapping *anekdoty* and I thought, "I'll turn him in tomorrow." But in the morning they were already coming for *me.*'"

24. Yurchak, "Cynical Reason," 175.

25. Krongauz, "Bessilie," 234.

26. On the topic of Soviet ritual see Andrei Chernyshov, *Sovremennaia sovetskaia Mifologiia* (Tver', 1992) and V. V. Glebkin, *Ritual v Sovetskoi Kul'ture* (Moscow: Ianus-K, 1998).

27. Nekliudov's point about these two concepts is valid mainly in regard to their scholarly usage, and only in Russian (*ritual* versus *tseremoniia*). The denotational distinction between them that he points out does not inform the English concepts of "ritual" and "ceremony," at least in everyday parlance.

28. On television in the late Soviet period, see Ellen Mickiewicz, *Split Signals: Television and Politics in the Soviet Union* (New York: Oxford University Press, 1988) and Elena Prokhorova, *Fragmented Mythologies: Soviet Adventure Mini-Series of the 1970s* (Diss., Pittsburgh, Pa., University of Pittsburgh, 2003).

29. The Stalin era produced its own "telegraphic" *anekdoty*, which reflected that epoch's notion of common experience (Barskii, *Eto prosto smeshno* 295): "Allo, pozovite, pozhaluista, Abramovicha." "Ego net." "On na rabote?" "Net." "On v komandirovke?" "Net." "On v otpuske?" "Net." "Ia vas pravil'no ponial?" "Da." ("Hello, may I speak to Abramovich?" "He's not here." "Is he at work?" "No." "Is he away on business?" "No." "Is he on vacation?" "No." "Do I understand you correctly?" "Yes"]. I have heard this joke characterized both as a product of the Stalin era and of the late 1970s, the period of third-wave (primarily Jewish) emigration.

30. K. N. Rogov, "O proekte 'Rossiia/Russia'—1970-e gody," in *Semidesiatye kak predmet istorii russkoi kul'ture. Rossiia/Russia* 1(9), ed. Rogov (Moscow: Ob"edinennoe Gumanitarnoe Izdatel'stvo, 1998), 9.

31. Ibid.

32. One scholar of the *anekdot* characterizes the difference between the two periods in familiar metaphors: "If (under Stalin) the country resembled something between a military barracks and a gigantic concentration camp, now it looked like an equally enormous insane asylum, the residents of which recognized more and more the absurdity of their own existence. . . . Fear had given

way to laughter" (Konstantin Fedorovich Sedov, *Osnovy psikhalingvistiki v anekdotakh* [Moscow: Labirint, 1998], 10–11).

33. I do not mean to dismiss the arrests, exiles, forced hospitalizations, and other types of political persecution that took place in the 1960s through the 1980s, only to draw a contrast with the pre-1953 environment.

34. Recall Louis Althusser's distinction between "ideological state apparatuses" and the "repressive state apparatus" (Louis Althusser, "Ideology and Ideological State Apparatuses [Notes Toward an Investigation]," in *Lenin and Philosophy and Other Essays*, trans. Ben Brewster [New York: Monthly Review Press, 1971], 144).

35. K. B. Sokolov, "Gorodskoi fol'klor protiv ofitsial'noi kartiny mira," in *Khudozhestvennaia zhizn' Rossii 1970-kh godov kak sistemnoe tseloe*, ed. Neia Zorkaia, et al. (St. Petersburg: Aleteiia, 2001), 229. Again, the Party's renewed publicly announced interest in the ideological content of cultural texts can actually be dated to the beginning of the 1960s, specifically to the Third Party Program of 1961.

36. Krongauz, "Bessilie," 236.

37. Ibid., 235.

38. On the general atmosphere of irony during Stagnation, see Vishevsky, *Soviet Literary Culture*.

39. M. Bakhtin, *Rabelais*, 7.

40. Borev, "Intelligentskii fol'klor," 3.

41. Ibid.

42. Dolgopolova, "The Contrary World," 1.

43. Abdullaeva, "Vse my vyshli," 116.

44. Kolobok is the Russian analogue to the nursery-rhyme Gingerbread Man. Kolobok consists only of a head, however, which is the premise of this *anekdot*.

45. David Navon, "The Seemingly Appropriate but Virtually Inappropriate: Notes on Characteristics of Jokes," *Poetics* 17.3 (June 1988): 211.

46. John Beverley mentioned Solzhenitsyn's *The Gulag Archipelago* as a Russian example of the Latin American genre known as *testimonio* ("Margins at the Center," 36).

47. Katerina Clark, *The Soviet Novel: History as Ritual*, 3rd ed. (Bloomington: Indiana University Press, 2000), 9.

48. Shmeleva and Shmelev, *Russkii anekdot*, 24.

49. James von Geldern and Richard Stites, eds., *Mass Culture in Soviet Russia: Tales, Poems, Songs, Movies, Plays, and Folklore, 1917–1953* (Bloomington: Indiana University Press, 1995), 118–19.

50. Ol'ga Smolitskaia, "Performans: Kak Zhanroobrazuiushchii element sovetskogo anekdota," *Fol'klor i postfol'klor: struktura, tipologiia, semiotika*, accessed Dec. 1, 2002, http://www.ruthenia.ru/folklore/smolitskaya1.htm.

51. Ibid.

52. Yurchak, "Cynical Reason," 161.

53. Douglas, "Jokes," 305.

54. An important exception is the excellent article by Briker and Vishevskii, "Iumor v populiarnoi kul'ture sovetskogo intelligenta 60-x–70-x godov."

55. Ibid., 151.

56. A four-volume collection of Zhvanetskii's works (*Sobranie proizvedenii*) was published in 2001. The majority of the stories and monologues included in the anthology had never been published before.

57. Iunisov, *Mifopoetika*, 12.

58. Zhvanetskii's unadorned comic performances are reminiscent of a telling scene from Riazanov's 1956 film *Karnaval'naia noch'* (Carnival Night), in which a retrograde bureaucrat and ideologue "edits" a clown act until the two performers are in suits and ties performing the lines deadpan.

59. Another cultural image along these lines is the hapless protagonist of Aleksandr Galich's song "Kak vystupil Klim Petrovich na sobranii v zashchitu mira" (How Klim Petrovich Gave a Speech at a Meeting in Defense of Peace), who finds himself reading from a page a speech clearly written for a woman, but he is caught up in the momentum of the ceremony and is unable to stop (see Krongauz's analysis of the song in "Bessilie").

60. There is a rhythm to his readings that is not merely audible, but visible, as one can see when one of his videotaped monologues is fast-forwarded.

61. Vishevsky, *Soviet Literary Culture*, 142.

62. Since so many monologues by Zhvanetskii remained unpublished until very recently, many are datable only in terms of the decade they were composed. His recent collection, *Sobranie proizvedenii,* is in four volumes, each of which contains material from a different decade (1960s–1990s).

63. Andrei Bitov, "Pod kupolom Glasnosti," introduction to *God za dva,* by Mikhail Zhvanetskii (Leningrad: Leningradskii komitet literatorov, 1991),9–10.

64. Vishevsky, *Soviet Literary Culture*, 59.

65. Petrovskii, "Novyi anekdot znaesh'?" 46.

66. von Geldern and Stites, *Mass Culture,* 118–19.

67. During perestroika, some enterprising raconteurs earned rubles as *anekdot* buskers on the Arbat and other pedestrian thoroughfares in Moscow (Valery Belyanin, personal communication, July 2002).

68. Briker and Vishevskii, "Iumor," 150. Stites (p. 5) referred to a similar phenomenon when he wrote of the existence of "themes, conventions, and commonplaces" that run across Russian popular-culture genres and constitute a "cultural code [. . .], the secondary language that connects the artists and entertainers with their audiences and reveals certain values, characteristics, and aspirations of Russian people not easily discernible in ideology or constitutions."

69. Vishevsky, *Soviet Literary Culture*, 60.

70. Briker and Vishevskii, "Iumor," 150.

CHAPTER FOUR

1. Siniavskii/Terts, "Anekdot v anecdote," 358.

2. Meta-folklore was rare but not unknown in the pre-Soviet Russian tradition. In the mid-nineteenth century, Afanas'ev collected several folktales in which tale-telling itself constitutes part or even most of the narrative. In "How a Husband Weaned His Wife from Fairy Tales," for example, an innkeeper beats his wife for refusing to take in lodgers who do not tell tales well (Aleksandr Afanas'ev, *Russian Fairy Tales Collected by Aleksandr Afanas'ev*, trans. Norbert Guterman, folkloristic commentary by Roman Jakobson [New York: Pantheon, 1973], 308). In "The Armless Maiden" the titular heroine tries to communicate with her brother and her husband in various ways that are thwarted by her evil sister-in-law and, after suffering a series of misfortunes—including, as the title suggests, amputation of her arms—finally resorts to the tale as a means of conveying the truth and defeating her enemy (ibid., 294–99).

3. Chirkova, *Poetika*, 8.

4. M. Bakhtin, "The Problem of Speech Genres," 68. Bakhtin calls the utterance "the *real unit* of speech communication," a discrete speech act by an individual "speech subject" (ibid., 71; emphasis in original). An utterance may be written or oral, premeditated or extemporaneous, as short as a single word in an informal conversation or as long as "a multi-volume novel" (ibid., 60). Bakhtin's broadly inclusive definition of the speech genre, while problematic, is a useful tool in dealing with the issue of the so-called "hybrid generic nature" of the *anekdot* as both a form of artistic [*khudozhestvennyi*] composition and extemporaneous conversational [*razgovornyi* or *rechevoi*] expression. Bakhtin's theory is also relevant to discussions of the oral *anekdot* versus the printed *anekdot*.

5. Bauman, "Performance," 47. Bauman, citing Barbara Babcock's ideas about the reflexivity of performance, wrote that performance as a cultural practice is "signification about signification" that "calls attention to and involves self-conscious manipulation of the formal features of the communicative system, . . . making one at least conscious of its devices" (ibid.).

6. Ibid.

7. Meletinskii, "Skazka-anekdot," 319.

8. Susan Stewart, "Some Riddles and Proverbs of Textuality: An Essay in Literary Value and Evaluation," *Criticism* 21.2 (Spring 1979): 101.

9. See Banc and Dundes's collection of translated (mostly Romanian) jokes titled *First Prize Fifteen Years*.

10. As I mentioned in the Introduction, although arrests for *anekdot* telling

were a feature most characteristic of Stalinist culture, there were isolated episodes during subsequent periods.

11. V. Bakhtin, "Anekdoty," 799.

12. On the cultural significance of narrating one's own mischief-making activities (specifically among Russian males), see Nancy Ries, *Russian Talk: Culture and Conversation During Perestroika* (Ithaca, N.Y.: Cornell University Press, 1997), 65–68.

13. Alan Dundes gives an example of a meta-generic American joke: "It was a dark and stormy night and this guy goes up to this old farmhouse. He's a salesman and he says to the farmer, "I'm a salesman, my car broke down, and I need a place to stay." And the farmer says, "That's all right, but there's just one thing, we have no extra rooms to spare so you'll have to sleep with my son." And the salesman says, "Oh my God, I must be in the wrong joke" (Alan Dundes, "Metafolklore and Oral Literary Criticism," *The Monist* 50 [1966]: 509–10).

14. Colonel Isaev is Shtirlits's actual identity in the film. Viacheslav Tikhonov is the actor who played Shtirlits.

15. This text refers to the wave of stupidity jokes about Soviet generals and their wives in the 1950s.

16. Although abstract *anekdoty* resemble the Anglophone shaggy-dog story in some respects, they differ from that genre in their brevity; shaggy-dog stories amount to practical jokes on the listener, who is tricked into paying attention to a drawn-out narrative under the pretense that the reward will be a humorous punch line.

17. The abstract *anekdot* was not, incidentally, the only form of contemporary folklore to use the absurd to do violence to its own fundamental genetic code. Consider the *chastushka-neskladukha* [misfit *chastushka*], for example: "Po stene polzet kirpich, / Volosatyi kak benzin. / Eta pesnia pro liubov.' / Krasnoi Armii—'Ura!'" (Vladimir Bakhtin, "Po stene polzet kirpich, ili Kak podvodnaia lodka v stepiakh Ukrainy pogibla v zhestokom vozdushnom boiu," interview with Mikhail Grigor'ev, *Trud*, April 21, 1995, 9) (A brick crawls up the wall, / Hairy as gasoline. / This is a song of love. / Hooray for the Red Army!).

18. Pavel Borodin, "Abstraktnyi anekdot kak sotsiokul'turnyi fenomen," in *Material mezhdunarodnoi konferentsii 'Fol'klor i sovremennost',' posviashchennoi pamiati professora N. I. Savushkinoi (20–22 oktiabria 1994 goda)* (Moscow: Moskovskii gorodskoi dvorets tvorchestva, 1995), 87–88.

19. Babcock, "Arrange Me into Disorder," 103.

20. Borodin, "Abstraktnyi anekdot," 89.

21. Suzanne Fleischman (*Tense and Narrativity: From Medieval Performance to Modern Fiction* [Austin: University of Texas Press, 1990], 3) opines that the perception of meaning in texts depends on "culture-specific 'frames' . . . , clusters of interrelated expectations associated with prototypical experiences or situation contexts," and that these frames can refer to "real-world situa-

tions" and/or "textual worlds, which also fall into recognizable types—genres—to which similar sets of expectations attach."

22. Briker and Vishevskii, "Iumor," 148.

23. Gertrude Jaeger and Philip Selznick, "A Normative Theory of Culture," *American Sociological Review* 29.5 (1964): 663, cited in Asa Briggs, "Culture," in *Folklore, Cultural Performances, and Popular Entertainments: A Communications-Centered Handbook,* ed. Richard Bauman (New York: Oxford University Press, 1992), 10.

24. Vladimir Elistratov, "Argo i kul'tura," *Slovar' moskovskogo argo: Materialy 1980–1994 gg.* (Moscow: Russkie slovari, 1994), 600.

25. M. A. K. Halliday, "Anti-Languages," *American Anthropologist* 78 (1976): 570–84.

26. See also Wierzbicka, who writes that "official totalitarian language usually generates its own opposite—an underground antitotalitarian language" (Anna Wierzbicka, "Antitotalitarian Language in Poland: Some Mechanisms of Linguistic Self-Defense," *Language in Society* 19.1 [1990]: 2).

27. Later, Rzhevskii was often depicted in encounters with another fictional character, Natasha Rostova from Tolstoi's *War and Peace*, Sergei Bondarchuk's famous screen adaptation of which appeared in 1966–67. On the Rzhevskii cycle, see Visani, "Poruchik Rzhevskii."

28. Ong, *Orality*, 3.

29. Robert W. Thurston, "Social Dimensions of Stalinist Rule: Humor and Terror in the USSR, 1935–1941," *Journal of Social History* 24.3 (Spring 1991): 550.

30. Arkhipova points out that *Nu, pogodi!* did not inspire an *anekdot* cycle also because its protagonists, a wolf and a hare, do not speak. On *Nu, pogodi!* see also D. Zabolotskikh, "Skazka sovetskogo vremeni," *Iskusstvo kino* 10 (1998), 82–86.

31. See chapter 5 on the significance of Russian protagonists in Russian jokes.

32. This is another untranslatable *anekdot*. Brezhnev says during a speech "Our country is going to shit . . . to shit . . . to shit . . ." [in Russian, *na govno . . . na govno . . . na govno . . .*], but when he finishes the sentence, it turns out he is saying that "our country is going in step [*noga v nogu*] with all the civilized countries of the world."

33. Krongauz, "Bessilie," 241.

34. Cherednichenko, *Tipologiia*, 10. A variant of this joke that privileges dissident, rather than pop, culture substitutes Andrei Sakharov for Pugacheva.

35. Ibid.

36. Richard Schechner, "Collective Reflexivity: Restoration of Behavior," in *A Crack in the Mirror: Reflexive Perspectives in Anthropology*, ed. Jay Ruby (Philadelphia: University of Pennsylvania Press, 1982), 39.

37. Stewart, "Some Riddles," 99.

38. Schechner, "Collective Reflexivity," 39.

39. Natal'ia Sokolova, "Iz starykh tetradei 1935–1937," *Voprosy literatury* 2 (1997): 364.

40. Bauman, "Performance," 47.

CHAPTER FIVE

First chapter epigraph is from *Program of the Communist Party of the Soviet Union,* 107.

Second chapter epigraph is from Algis Ruksenas, *Is That You Laughing, Comrade? The World's Best Russian (Underground) Jokes,* ill. George Kocar (Secaucus, N.J.: Citadel, 1986), 23. I cite this *anekdot* in English, as Ruksenas does in his collection of translated *anekdoty,* because I was unable to find the Russian original.

1. As an imperfect hermeneutic compromise, I use "Russians" to refer to the strategically ill-defined Soviet identity, historically dominated by the Russian ethnicity.

2. Christie Davies, *The Mirth of Nations* (New Brunswick, N.J.: Transaction, 2002), 1.

3. See especially Khrul', *Anekdot kak forma,* 54–99.

4. Such jokes did of course circulate in the non-Russian republics of the Soviet Union and in Eastern-bloc countries, but in the multiethnic *anekdoty* of urban Russia, which are my focus, the Russian is almost always joined by representatives of nationalities outside the Soviet sphere of influence, most commonly Americans, French, and English. There are, however, many *anekdoty* that compare and contrast a Jewish character and a Russian character (often along with representatives of other ethnicities, as well). Such *anekdoty* are a different animal, one that does not figure in my project, especially here, where my focus is Russian reflexive humor.

5. Davies, *Mirth,* 12.

6. According to a study conducted by I. M. Kobozeva ("Nemets, anglichanin, frantsuzi russkii: Vyiavlenie natsional'nykh kharakterov chevez analiz konnotatsii etnonimov," *Vestnik Moskovskogo universiteta. Seriia 9. Filologiaa.* 3 [1995]), the typical Russian traits listed by Russians themselves include recklessness, generosity, laziness, simplicity, denseness, disorganization, unceremoniousness, superficiality, lack of curiosity, and a love of drink (cited in Timofeev, "Rzhevskii, Chapaev, Shtirlits," 326).

7. Iulis Telesin, *1001,* 147. Aleksandr Vertinskii (1889–1957) indeed returned home in 1943 after having emigrated in 1919 (so the claim of this *anekdot* that he left "under the tsar" is slightly inaccurate).

8. Alaev, *Mir anekdota,* 80–81.

9. Alexander Zinoviev wrote that such an anthropomorphic view of the collective was characteristic of the citizenry as well, that the "intimate life" and "personal relations and activities" of the Soviet collective "bind [it] into something bigger than a family, that is into a sort of single personality: the super-personality of Communist society; into the kind of 'we' that has the right to regard itself as an 'I'" (*Reality*, 122). Elsewhere he was even more explicit: "The behaviour of the Soviet Union on the world stage as a collective individual is a classic example of immoral behaviour" (*Reality*, 238).

10. M. Bakhtin, *Rabelais*, 12.

11. The self-image of intellectuals was certainly affected by the state's inversion of the traditional labor hierarchy to reflect the worker state, an inversion reflected in the following *anekdot* (Barskii, *Eto prosto smeshno*, 33): "Doctor, I was visiting my relative in your psychiatric hospital, and a patient came up to us. He was a perfectly normal, rational man. He works as a butcher in a store." "Oh, that one. He has delusions of grandeur. He's really just an ordinary professor."

12. See Rancour-Laferriere on "masochistic tendencies among the Russian intelligentsia" (*Slave Soul*, 42–50). On the *anekdot* as a form of intellectual folklore, see Borev, *Istoriia*, 3. On the self-deprecatory nature of Jewish humor, see Sigmund Freud, *Jokes and Their Relation to the Unconscious*, trans. James Strachey (New York: W. W. Norton, 1960), 133–37; Elliott Oring, *Engaging Humor* (Urbana: University of Illinois Press, 2003), 116–28; and Davies, *Mirth*, 51–75, and "Exploring the Thesis of the Self-Deprecating Jewish Sense of Humor."

13. Stites (p. 1) mentioned a common distinction between "folk culture" (rural) and "popular culture" (urban).

14. Kelly and Shepherd, *Russian Cultural Studies*, 9.

15. Nerush and Pavlov, "Shepotom," 4.

16. See Daniel Rancour-Laferriere's book-length study of Russian "moral masochism," *The Slave Soul of Russia*.

17. Zinoviev, *Reality*, 237. Boris Miasoedov similarly reads Russian boorish behavior as a symptom of the sociopolitical environment (Boris Miasoedov, *O khamstve i stervoznosti v russkoi zhizni* [Moscow: Russkaia entsiklopediia, 1998], 4).

18. Zinoviev, *Reality*, 123.

19. Lev Barskii reports that this is (legendary film-satire) director El'dar Riazanov's favorite *anekdot* (Lev Barskii, *Eto prosto smeshno* [Moscow: Kh. G. S., 1992], 12–13).

20. I. G. Iakovenko, "Nenormativnyi anekdot kak modeliruiushchaia sistema: Opyt kul'turologicheskogo analiza," *Novoe literaturnoe obozrenie* 43 (2000): 336. This rather untranslatable *anekdot* depicts an entity identified as "Pizdets Vsemu" (roughly, Fuck Everything, though with a female connotation due to the word "*pizdets*," derived from the word "*pizda*," "cunt") that flies over villages and destroys them (each time with the comment "Fuck That Village!")

until it encounters in one village a house that will not be razed. Fuck Everything goes into the house and discovers that it is occupied by another entity (the immovable object to Fuck Everything's irresistible force), which identifies itself as "Pokhui Vse" (even more roughly, Doesn't Give a Shit About Anything, and this time associated with the male organ: the word *"pokhui"* is derived from *khui*, "prick").

21. Ries, *Russian Talk*, 78–79.

22. Barskii, *Eto prosto smeshno*, 101.

23. Stewart, "Some Riddles," 100.

24. Arthur Koestler, *The Act of Creation* (London: Arkana, 1989), 31.

25. As I discuss in the final chapter, the sudden appearance of such forces in the post-Soviet period would help hamstring the *anekdot*.

26. Dundes calls the phenomenon of multiethnic jokes "international slurs" (Alan Dundes, "Slurs International: Folk Comparisons of Ethnicity and National Character," *Southern Folklore Quarterly* 39 (1975): 15–38, reprinted in *Wise Words: Essays on the Proverb*, ed. Wolfgang Mieder [New York: Garland, 1994], 197). Khrul' calls the Russian variant of this type of joke the "Russian and Others" [*Russkii i drugie*] cycle (*Anekdot kak forma*, 54 and passim). Shmeleva and Shmelev call them "multi-national" jokes (*Russkii anekdot*, 75).

27. To wit (some of the humor of this *anekdot* relies on the fact that the nationalities are listed in rhymed pairs): "Chem zhenshchiny rzlichnykh stran uderzhivaiut svoikh muzhei: amerikanka—delom, frantsuzhenka—telom, pol'ka—skikom, evreika—krikom, anglichanka—vospitaniem, nemka—pitaniem, shvedka— zdorov'em, finka—khladnokroviem, mad'iarka—umeniem, indianka—terpeniem, meksikanka—mest'iu, kitaianka—lest'iu, iaponka—gratsiei, russkaia—partorganizatsiei" (Khrul', *Anekdot kak forma*, 186) ("How do women of various countries hold on to their men? American [women]: with business. French: with their bodies. Polish: with cleverness. Jewish: with shouts. English: with breeding. German: with food. Swedish: with health. Finnish: with sang-froid. Hungarian: with know-how. Indian: with patience. Mexican: with vengeance. Chinese: with flattery. Japanese: with grace. Russian: with the Party Organization").

Karachevtsev (*"Dlia nekuriashchikh"* 88) includes a similar but apolitical (and nonrhyming) *anekdot* in his collection from the 1930s: "Why do women love? Italian (women)—due to temperament. Spanish—for pleasure. German—out of sensitivity. Turkish—out of habit. Austrian—out of a love for art. Dutch—out of obligation. English—for health. Creole—out of instinct. American—for profit. French—out of curiosity. Hungarian—by vocation. Jewish—out of passion. Swedish—out of boredom. Japanese—out of hospitality. Russian—for all of these reasons combined."

28. Siniavskii/Terts, "Anekdot v anekdote," 90.

29. Chapaev was reportedly legendary even before his death (L. Muratov, "Uroki legendarnogo filma," *Neva* 12 [1984], 169).

30. Podolsk.ru, accessed Apr. 12, 2000, http://www.podolsk.ru/newsf.php3?detail=n985061017.news.

31. The codirectors, Georgii Vasil'ev and Sergei Vasil'ev, listed on the credits as the Vasil'ev Brothers [Brat'ia Vasil'evy], were not really brothers; they merely had the same last name.

32. "Chapaeva posmotrit vsia strana," *Pravda*, Nov. 21, 1934: 1, cited in *The Film Factory: Russian and Soviet Cinema in Documents*, trans. Richard Taylor, ed. Richard Taylor and Ian Christie (Cambridge, Mass.: Harvard University Press, 1988), 334.

33. Osip Mandel'shtam, "Den' stoial o piati golovakh . . . ," in *Sochineniia v dvukh tomakh. Tom 1: Stikhotvoreniia, perevody* (Tula: Filin, 1994), 164.

34. A. I. Kozhevnikov, *Bol'shoi slovar': Krylatye frazy otechestvennogo kino* (St. Petersburg: Neva, 2001), 376–77.

35. The raven in the song is a symbol of battlefield death; the bird picks at the corpse of the dead soldier.

36. Barskii relates a most intriguing legend regarding the genesis of the Chapaev cycle: in the months leading up to the one-hundredth anniversary of Lenin's birth in 1970, the story goes, the Soviet government nervously (and correctly) anticipated a deluge of jokes at the expense of poor Il'ich. To counter this, the KGB was enlisted to compose and propagate a corpus of Chapaev *anekdoty* that would divert satirical attention away from Lenin. It was said that new Chapaev jokes were appearing so quickly that the poor general was spinning in his grave fast enough to be used as an electric fan in hell (*Eto prosto smeshno*, 14).

37. Dmitrii Sevriukov, "Interesnoe kino: Etot neotrazimyi Chapaev!" *Speed-Info*, Sept. 1998: 2.

38. The novel was translated as *The Buddha's Little Finger* by Andrew Bromfield in 2000.

39. Vadim Lur'e cites similar Elvis-like rumors about cosmonaut Iurii Gagarin, who was killed in a training accident several years after his famous 1961 spaceflight (Vadim Lur'e, "Zhizn,' smert' i bessmertie Vasiliia Chapaeva," *Nezavisimaia gazeta*, Feb. 9, 1991: 8). Somehow Chapaev's reputation lent itself to bizarre stories even outside the USSR, including an entry for Joseph Stalin in the 1942 edition of the American periodical *Current Biography* that amazingly informs us that "[Stalin's] first wife, Catherine, by whom he had one son, Chapaev, died in 1917" and that "Chapaev, a captain of the Artillery, received the Order of Lenin" for his service in World War II ("Joseph Stalin," *Current Biography*, 1942, 796).

40. See, for example, Paimen's 1938 collection of folk texts about "Chapai" (V. Paimen, comp., *Chapai: Sbornik narodnykh pesen, skazok, rasskazov i vospominanii o legendarnom geroe grazhdanskoi voiny V. I. Chapaeve* [Moscow: Sovetskii pisatel', 1938]).

41. V. M. Sidel'nikov, *Krasnoarmeiskii fol'klor* (Moscow: Sovetskii pisatel', 1938), 99.

42. L. Muratov, "Uroki legendarnogo fil'ma," *Neva* 12 (1984): 175.

43. All three of these protagonists share a "volume" of the ambitiously titled *Polnoe sobranie anekdotov* (Complete Collection of Anekdoty) under the rubric *Anekdoty o narodnykh geroiakh* (*Anekdoty* About Folk Heroes), a triumvirate whose juxtaposition helped inspire the cycles I examine in this chapter. V. Smetanin and K. Donskaia, comps. and eds., *Anekdoty o narodnykh geroev (Chapaev, Shtirlits, Chukcha), Polnoe sobranie anekdotov* 8 (Moscow: DataStrom, 1994).

44. The Russian for "urinalysis"—*analiz mochi*—indeed sounds Italian, due mainly to the ending.

45. This joke plays on the name of Spanish-born Communist Dolores Ibarruri, which sounds like the Russian word *ebat'*, "to fuck," and also on one of the slogans of the Spanish Civil War, "It's better to die on your feet than to live on your knees."

46. See Aleksandr Prokhorov, "'I Need Some Life-Assertive Character' or How to Die in the Most Inspiring Pose: Bodies in the Stalinist Museum of *Hammer and Sickle*," *Studies in Slavic Cultures* 1 (2000): 28–46.

47. "Chapaeva posmotrit," cited in Taylor and Christie, *Film Factory*, 334.

48. Siniavskii/Terts, "Anekdot v anekdote," 89.

49. Ries, *Russian Talk*, 81.

50. Timofeev, "Rzhevskii, Chapaev, Shtirlits," 322.

51. Ibid., 328.

52. In the post-Soviet period, the New Russian would fulfill this ambassadorial role in the *anekdot*.

53. See Mark Endlin, *Chapaev v Amerike I dr* (n.p.: Smeshanin, 1980).

54. Barskii, *Eto prosto smeshno*, 195.

55. Draitser, *Taking Penguins*, 36.

56. I have only found one *anekdot* that even hints at this warrior spirit (*Evrei-olenovod* [Minsk: Literatura, 1997], 297): "A Chinese envoy comes to the Chukchi: 'We're declaring war on you. How many of you are there?' 'About five hundred. And you?' 'One billion.' 'Tsk-tsk-tsk, where will we bury you all?'"].

57. Draitser, *Taking Penguins*, 98.

58. Ibid.

59. The typical speech marker of the Chukchi in *anekdoty* is the word "*odnako*" (however), which he uses liberally, indiscriminately, and ungrammatically. The origin of this detail of the cycle is unknown.

60. Draitser takes the title of his book on Russian ethnic humor, *Taking Penguins to the Movies*, from one of these jokes.

61. Galya Diment and Yuri Slezkine, introduction to *Between Heaven and*

Hell: The Myth of Siberia in Russian Culture, ed. Diment and Slezkine (New York: St. Martin's, 1993), 5.

62. See, for example, Aleksandr Mironov, "Strana golubykh prostorov (Vmesto predisloviia)," in *Chukotskie novelly*, 2nd ed. (Arkhangel'sk: Severnoe izdatel'stvo, 1937), 3–6.

63. Draitser, *Taking Penguins*, 82; Belousov, personal communication, March 20, 1999.

64. The singular in Russian is *chukcha*.

65. Belousov, personal communication, March 20, 1999; Draitser, *Taking Penguins*, 82.

66. This is an international phenomenon, incidentally, which may account for the prevalence of chickens and ducks in American jokes, and the frequency of speech impediments such as lisps in comedic performance.

67. The popular American series of how-to books, *For Dummies*, is translated into Russian as *dlia chainikov* (for *chainiks*).

68. Draitser, *Taking Penguins*, 114.

69. See Draitser, *Taking Penguins*, 82–83, on further linguistic associations of the word "Chukchi" in Russian.

70. Also worth mentioning in this regard is Stalin's 1934 establishment of the Jewish Autonomous Region of Birobidzhan in remote Siberia and the election of the oligarch Roman Abramovich as governor of Chukotka in 2000.

71. *Evrei-olenovod*, 2.

72. Draitser, *Taking Penguins*, 88.

73. A much earlier film that depicts Chukchi life is Sergei Gerasimov's *Semero smelykh* (The Bold Seven, 1936), about a group of Communist Youth League members on a mission in Chukotka. The film has few images of the native population of Chukotka, but they are characteristic of Soviet representations of Chukchi: a large clan living in a dark, smoke-filled igloo (Chukchi actually traditionally lived in hide tents called *iarangi*), waiting for a plane to appear and bring the Soviet doctor to save a dying man.

74. An intriguing connotational association of the term *"nachal'nik Chukotki"*—though possibly a red herring—is reported in a 1901 ethnographic description of the Chukchi: "Sometimes there is a northwesterly wind that locals call *nachal'nik* . . . it blows with terrifying force, destroying everything in its path and freezing the blood in one's veins with its icy breath" (Ian'shinova, 3).

75. Bil'dy was in fact not a Chukchi, but a Nanai, another ethnic group of arctic Siberia. On Bil'dy and his hit, see Leonid Parfenov, *Namedni-72*, television series, NTV, 1998.

76. E. Rabinovich posited this textbook as *the* source of the joke cycle, a bold yet doubtful assertion.

77. See Draitser, *Taking Penguins*, 94–97; and Barskii, *Eto prosto smeshno*,

195, where he wrote: "*Anekdoty* about Chukchi do not have an ethnic character, [. . .]. Rather, they present an image of a stupefied, beaten-down people. You know which one."

78. Draitser pointed out this ratio (*Taking Penguins*, 96).

79. Christie Davies, *Jokes and Their Relation to Society* (Berlin: Mouton de Gruyer, 1998), 12.

80. Ibid., 1.

CHAPTER SIX

Chapter epigraph is from Abram Terts (Andrei Siniavskii), "Anekdot v anecdote," 77–95.

1. Sigmund Freud, *Jokes and Their Relation to the Unconscious*, trans. James Strachey (New York: W. W. Norton, 1960), 123.

2. Krongauz, "Sovetskii antisovetskii iumor," 228.

3. This phenomenon was, however, taken to its logical extreme in the jokelore ("Anekdoty v nomer," 1): "Where do you work?" "I wash corpses in the morgue." "Does it pay well?" "Not bad: for every seven I wash, I get to keep the eighth." The macabre nature of such humor is part of a larger cultural trend that I discuss later in this chapter.

4. Despite its continued presence in bookstalls, however, the *anekdot* collection has not enjoyed a wide readership for several years now. In a 1997 survey of reading habits among various Russian demographic groups, the *anekdot* was listed as a favorite genre (in third place, after crime novels and science fiction) only among sixteen- to thirty-nine-year-olds with no higher education (Natal'ia Zorkaia, "Knizhnoe chtenie v postperestroiku: Popytka diagnoza," *Pushkin* 1 [Oct. 1997]: 35).

5. A. V. Voznesenskii, "O sovremennom anekdotopechatanii," *Novoe literaturnoe obozrenie* 22 (1996): 393.

6. *Studencheskii meridian* publishes the *anekdoty* it receives from readers as a separate series of paperbacks under the title *Anekdoty nashikh chitatelei* (*Our Readers' Anekdoty*).

7. See especially Borev, *Staliniada* and *Fariseia*.

8. The joke has recently been challenged as the chief Russian (nonpornographic) cybergenre by the animated series *Masiania* (see http://www.mult.ru), which began as a web cartoon but made the jump to television in 2002.

9. There were also, predictably, several jokes linking the two-headed eagle, symbol of the Russian empire, to the radioactive events of Chernobyl.

10. I have also heard a variant of this *anekdot* in which the democrats' banner reads "Yeltsin's Still Alive" [*El'tsin eshche zhivoi*].

11. Vovochka is analogous to Dirty Ernie or Little Herbie in Anglophone jokes, as well as to similar characters in folk humor traditions around the world.

Reasons for the comparison to Putin include the president's somewhat impish appearance (short stature, protruding ears, beady eyes) and past connections between Vovochka and another Kremlin occupant, Lenin (also a Vladimir). On the Vovochka cycle, see Aleksandr Fedorovich Belousov, "Vovochka," in Antimir russkoi kul'tury: Iazyk. Fol'klor. Literatura, comp. N. Bogomolov (Moscow: Ladomir, 1996), 165–86.

12. See Lipovetskii, "Prezident Shtirlits."

13. Putin often prefaces speeches and other public comments with these words.

14. Among the most intriguing statements of support for the Putin government to date is Mikhail Zhvanetskii's September 2000 newspaper article "Pishushchemu i pokazyvaiushchemu" (Moskovskie novosti, Sept. 18–25, 2000, 1). Zhvanetskii lambasted the liberal journalists at the television channel NTV—which was on the verge of being taken over by pro-Kremlin interests—for what he considered sensationalistically violent and obscene reporting. He also accused them of gross exaggeration in their criticism of the Kremlin, citing the absence of Putin jokes among the Russian populace as evidence of the president's competence.

15. Yeltsin announced his resignation and appointment of Putin as his successor in a televised speech on New Year's Eve, 1999.

16. Dmitry Mozheitov, "New Russians at Large," Russia Journal 30.73, Aug. 5, 2000, accessed Sept. 29, 2001, <http://www.russiajournal.com/ls/article.shtml?ad=992>.

17. Dmitry Mozheitov, the author of the article, is more skeptical than Aslamova: "It is unclear, however, how these skills are associated with the intellect and wit allegedly present among New Russians of the twenty-first century." The rest of the article is worth quoting in full: "Supporting the event was a selection of show-biz celebrities: Belarus composer Eduard Khanok, who at one time wrote music for pop prima donna Alla Pugachyova; television hosts Lidia Ivanova and Ivan Kononov; Russia's number-one feminist, Maria Arbatova; and poet Viktor Pelenyagre. Public relations agency representative Kazbek was initially named "The New Russian—2000," but was forced to leave the casino for being drunk and could not claim his prize. Casino chips worth $1,000 and a private dance with striptease girls went instead to a representative of the Yerevan Cognac Factory known only as "Sedrak."

18. Aleksei Levinson, "Chego starye intelligenty ne dali 'New Russians,'" Iskusstvo kino 1 (1995): 28. Levinson's article is one of several about the New Russians published together in Iskusstvo kino 1 (1995). Aleksei Yurchak also discusses the role of business publications in shaping the New Russians' public image and lifestyle (Aleksei Yurchak, "Russian Neoliberal: The Entrepreneurial Ethic and the Spirit of 'True Careerism,'" Russian Review 62 [Jan. 2003]: 72–90).

19. Levinson briefly discussed the connection between the NEPmen and the New Russians in another article: Alekse Levinson, "'Novye russkie' i ikh sosedi po anekdoticheskim kontekstom (vmesto poslesloviia k publikatsii)," *Novoe literaturnoe obozrenie* 22 (1996): 383–85.

20. Levinson, "Chego," 29. Levinson even credits *Kommersant"* with originating the term *"novye russkie,"* a translation of the English term coined by Hedrick Smith in the title of his book *The New Russians* (New York: Random House, 1990), a moniker subsequently picked up by the U.S. media.

21. Levinson, "Chego," 28.

22. A small and rarely encountered generic subspecies that spun off from the New Russian cycle is the *anekdot o starykh russkikh* ("Old Russian" joke), which focuses on the hapless, unreconstructed Soviet-era everyman, the New Russian's perennial victim in New Russian jokes.

23. Draitser, *Taking Penguins*, 154.

24. See Levinson, "Chego," 29, on the New Russians' role as patrons of the arts.

25. Ibid.

26. Bergson, *Laughter.*

27. Ol'ga Bukharkova, "Krysha: Proshchai, epokha otmorozkov," *Ogonek* 7 (Feb. 2000): 28. Daniil Dondurei lists similar influences in describing the provenance of the New Russians: "[It is a] bourgeoisie that emerged simultaneously from the Party *nomenklatura,* anti-Soviet, pro-Western, and Slavophile circles, the criminal realm, and from people who have never heard of the Komsomol" (Daniil Dondurei, "Novye russkie" idut!" *Iskusstvo kino* 1 [1995]: 1). It should be noted that most of the commentators cited here, who discussed the New Russians as a discrete demographic group exhibiting a discernible measure of uniformity, qualified their "ethnographic" analyses by acknowledging the social, educational, ethnic, and professional diversity among the new capitalists. For my part, I consciously privilege the popular-culture representations of the New Russians, leaving the problematic issue of actual human beings to the social scientists.

28. The reflux influence of the cycle on actual real-life behavior is perhaps best exemplified by an incident reported in the online newspaper www. lenta.ru in March 2000: a fifty-year-old Novosibirsk resident locked himself in his apartment and threatened to shoot himself with a rifle after having been in a fender bender with the driver of an expensive foreign car, who demanded money from the man ("Posle stolknoveniia s 'krutoi' inomarkoi voditel'reshil zastrelit'sia," *Lenta.ru,* accessed Mar. 8, 2000, http://www.lenta.ru/Russia/2000/ 03/808/dtp).

29. The Moscow English-language satirical weekly *The eXile* coined the term "flatheads" to describe young, thuggish New Russians.

30. The French rendering of the term "New Russian"—*nouveau russe*—is

a play on *nouveau riche.* The Russian transliteration of the French—*nuvorish*— was used before "New Russian" came into common usage.

31. Levinson, "Novye russkie," 385.

32. The simplistic, crude image of the New Russian extorting or physically stealing money from innocent Russians is in contrast to the white-collar crime that affected many more people: Sergei Mavrodi's mass pyramid scheme, MMM. There were occasional jokes about Mavrodi: ("Judge: "How could you trick people who trusted you?" Mavrodi: "That's a strange question, your honor. How could I have tricked people who *didn't* trust me?"). There were also jokes based on the aggressive and highly successful advertising campaign waged by MMM, further testifying to the role of the mass media, especially television, in generating folkloric material. On the MMM episode and its relevance in Russian culture, see Eliot Borenstein, "Public Offerings: MMM and the Marketing of Melodrama," in *Consuming Russia: Popular Culture, Sex, and Society Since Gorbachev,* ed. Adele Barker (Durham, N.C.: Duke University Press, 1999), 49–75.

33. Draitser did not, however, view the cycle as an ironic version of the old racist ethnic jokes, interpreting it instead as a welcome medium for introspection on the part of ethnic Russians: "The emerging and widely popular 'New Russians' jokelore can be interpreted as a sign of a healthy tendency on the part of the Russian group, of a strengthening of the sense of identity by Russians who have begun to look for culprits within their own group, not outside of it [. . .] [T]hey now ridicule the stupidity, low culture, criminality, and extravagance of a subset of their own group [. . .]. Thus, today it is no longer only 'the other' who is at fault for the substandard level of living, but also Russians themselves" (*Taking Penguins*, 159).

34. Levinson, "Novye russkie," 383; Draitser, *Taking Penguins,* 36.

35. Draitser, *Taking Penguins,* 55.

36. Semen Faibisovich, "'Novye russkie'—snaruzhi i iznutri," *Iskusstvo kino* 1 (1995): 34.

37. A well-known monologue by Zhvanetskii, "Klub kinoputeshestvie" ("TV Travel Club," 1970s), satirizes 1970s Soviet television's lame attempt to compensate for the lack of travel opportunities by taking viewers on virtual vacations abroad via their television screens.

38. There are, however, *anekdoty* (both original and translated) about Bill Gates. In their book-in-progress on the New Russians, Helena Goscilo and Nadezhda Azhgikhina underscore the distinction between the New Russians and the so-called oligarchs.

39. The two cycles intersect in the following *anekdot* from *Anekdoty nashikh chitatelei* (Alaev, *Mir anekdota*): "In Chukotka there are now 'New Chukchi.' They differ from the old Chukchi in that they have crimson snowshoes and 600 reindeer."

40. On the New Russian as trickster, see Mark Lipovetsky, "New Russians as a Cultural Myth," *Russian Review* 62.1 (Jan. 2003), 54–71. On the trickster persona and its place in *anekdot* culture in general, see Vadim Petrovich Rudnev, "Pragmatika anekdota," *Daugava* 6 (1990): 99–102.

41. Ries, *Russian Talk*, 65–71.

42. Lipovetsky, "New Russians," 56.

43. See Daniil Dondurei, "Kinematografisty o 'novykh russkikh,'" *Iskusstvo kino* 1 (1995): 1, for a discussion of New Russians within the creative intelligentsia.

44. In the summer of 2001, *The eXile* organized a cross-country Zaporozhets rally modeled on the Paris-Dakar rally.

45. Ul'ianov starred in the previously mentioned *Voroshilovskii strelok* and (with Efremov and Tikhonov) in Sergei Ursuliak's *Sochinenie ko dniu pobedy* (A Fantasy for Victory Day, 1997). Mordiukova played the title role in Denis Evstigneev's *Mama* (1999). Gurchenko and Akhedzhakova starred in El'dar Riazanov's *Starye kliachi* (Old Jades, 2000).

46. The names are taken from the following films: *Beloe solntse pustyni* (White Sun of the Desert, 1969, by Vladimir Motyl'), Stanislav Govorukhin's *Mesto vstrechi izmenit' nel'zia* (The Meeting Place Cannot Be Changed, 1979), Leonid Gaidai's *Kavkazskaia plennitsa* (Prisoner of the Caucasus, 1966), and Riazanov's *Garazh* (Garage, 1979).

47. Ray Browne, ed., *Objects of Special Devotion: Fetishism in Popular Culture* (Bowling Green, Ohio: Bowling Green University Popular Press, 1982).

48. Freud, it is worth noting, was an avid collector of such objects, which he called "my old and dirty gods." See the Sigmund Freud Museum Vienna web site, accessed Sept. 14, 2001, http://www.freud-museum.at/e/inhalt/museum ausstellungenGoetter.htm.

Bibliography

Aarne, Antti. *The Types of the Folktale: A Classification and Bibliography.* Trans. Stith Thompson. Helsinki, Finland: Academia Scientarum Fennica, 1961.

Abdullaeva, Zara. "Anekdot." *Iskusstvo kino* 9 (2000): 66–67.

———. "Ob anekdote." *Iskusstvo kino* 2 (1993): 82–86.

———. "Popular Culture." Trans. Sergei Volynets and Dmitri N. Shalin. In *Russian Culture at the Crossroads: Paradoxes of Postcommunist Consciousness.* Ed. Dmitri N. Shalin. Boulder, Colo.: Westview, 1996, 209–38.

———. "Vse my vyshli iz anekdota." *Znanie—sila* 2 (1993): 113–20.

Abramenko, L. I., ed. *Sovetskii anekdot: Antologiia.* Moscow: DataStrom, 1991.

Adams, Bruce. *Tiny Revolutions in Russia: Twentieth-Century Soviet and Russian History in Anecdotes.* New York: Routledge Curzon, 2005.

Afanas'ev, Aleksandr Nikolaevich. *Narodnye russkie skazki A. N. Afanas'eva v trekh tomakh.* Ed. L. G. Barag and N. G. Novikov. 3 vols. Moscow: Nauka, 1984–85.

———. *Narodnye russkie skazki ne dlia pechati, zavetnye poslovitsy i pogovorki, sobrannye i obrabotannye A. N. Afanas'evym. 1857–1862.* Ed. O. B. Alekseeva, V. I. Eremina, E. A. Kostiukhin, and L. V. Bessmertnykh. Moscow: Ladomir, 1998.

———. *Russian Fairy Tales Collected by Aleksandr Afanas'ev.* Trans. Norbert Guterman. Folkloristic commentary by Roman Jakobson. New York: Pantheon, 1973.

Afanas'eva, E. S., V. Iu. Afiani, L. A. Velichanskaia, Z. K. Vodop'ianova, and E. V. Kochubei, comps. *Ideologicheskie komissii TsK KPSS. 1958–1964: Dokumenty.* Moscow: Rossiiskaia politicheskaia entsiklopediia, 1998.

Afiani, V. Iu. "Ideologicheskie komissii TsK KPSS (1958–1964 gg.) v mekhanizme upravleniia kul'turoi." In Afanas'eva et al., 23–28.

Aimermakher, Karl. "Partiinoe upravlenie kul'turoi i formy ee samoorganizatsii (1953–1964/67)." In Afanas'eva et al., 5–22.

Aksenova, A. "Metafizika anekdota, ili Semantika lzhi." *Literaturnoe obozrenie* 11–12 (1994): 52–61.

Alaev, Enrid. *Mir anekdota. Anekdoty nashikh chitatelei.* Moscow: *Anons* magazine, 1995.

Althusser, Louis. "Ideology and Ideological State Apparatuses (Notes Toward an Investigation)." In *Lenin and Philosophy and Other Essays,* trans. Ben Brewster. New York: Monthly Review Press, 1971, 127–86.

Andreev, N. P. *Ukazatel' skazochnykh siuzhetov po sisteme Aarne.* Leningrad: Izdanie Gosudarstvennogo Russkogo Geograficheskogo Obshchestvo, 1929.

Andreevich, Evgenii. *Kreml' i narod: Politicheskie anekdoty.* Munich: 1951.

Andreevskii, I. E. "Anekdoty." In *Entsiklopedicheskii slovar',* ed. I. E. Andreevskii. Vol. 1. St. Petersburg: Brokgauz and Efron, 1890, 776.

Anekdoty iz kollektsii Zhirinovskogo. St. Petersburg: Simpleks, 1994.

Anekdoty o politikakh—Epokha zastoia (1953–1985), accessed Mar. 23, 2003. http://rels.obninsk.com/Rels/Lg/anecdote/zastoi.htm.

Anekdoty o shute Balakireve: Prodelki i shutki, ostroumnye otvety i blagie sovety slavnogo Balakireva, pridvornogo shuta imperatora Petra Velikogo. 4th ed. St. Petersburg: Izdanie knigoprodavtsa A. A. Kholmushina, 1899.

Anekdoty pro tsaria Nikolaia dikaria na zlobu dnia. Petrograd: 1918.

Anekdoty ruskie, ili velikie dostopamiatnye deianiia i dobrodetel'nye primery slavnykh muzhei, polkovodtsov, grazhdanskikh chinovnikov, kupechestva i drugikh osob vsiakogo zvaniia, otlichivshikhsia geroicheskoiu tverdostiiu, neustrashimostiiu dukha, userdiem, blagotvoritel'nostiiu, istinnoiu pravotoiu del svoikh i drugimi mnogimi primerami nepokolebimoi preverzhennosti k vere, gosudariu i liubvi k otechestvu. St. Petersburg: 1809.

"Anekdoty v nomer." *Komsomol'skaia Pravda,* Mar. 31, 1999: 1.

Anninskii, Lev. *Shestidesiatniki i my. Kinematograf, stavshii i ne stavshii istoriei.* Moscow: Kinotsentr, 1991.

———. "Svetlaia tainopis' chumnogo baraka." In Strelianyi et al., 5–10.

Antisovetskie anekdoty: Bor'ba narodnoi propagandy s bol'shevistkoi. Buenos Aires: n.d.

Apte, Mahadev L. "Humor." In Bauman, *Folklore,* 67–75.

Arias-King, Fredo. "Is It Power or Principle? A Footnote on Clinton's Russia Policy." Nov. 13, 1998. Johnson's Russia List, accessed Sept. 12, 2003. http://www.cdi.org/russia/johnson/2475.html##6.

Aristotle. *Aristotle's Poetics.* Trans. George Whalley. Ed. John Baxter and Patrick Atherton. Montreal: McGill–Queen's University Press, 1997.

Arkhipova, Aleksandra. "'Rolevaia struktura' detskikh tsiklov anekdotov (na materiale anekdotov o Vinni-Pukhe i Piatachke, o Cheburashke i Krokodile Gene)." B.A. thesis, Moscow, Rossiiskii gosudarstvennyi Gumanitarnyi universitet, 1999.

Arnason, Johann P. "Communism and Modernity." *Daedalus* 129.1 (Winter 2000): 61–90.

Arnau, Frank. *Witze in Braun und Rot: Eine Anthologie.* Freiburg, West Germany: Hyperion, 1969.

Attardo, Salvatore, and Jean-Charles Chabanne. "Jokes as a Text Type." *Humor* 5.1–2 (1992): 165–76.

Averchenko, Arkadii. *Arkadii Averchenko v "Novom Satirikone," 1917 g.– 1918 g.: rasskazy i fel'etony.* Comp. and ed. N. K. Goleizovskii. Moscow: Krug, 1994.

Averintsev, S. S. "Bakhtin i russkoe otnoshenie k smekhu." In *Ot mifa k literature: Sbornik v chest' semidesiatipiatiletiia Eleazara Moiseevicha Meletinskogo.* Comp. S. Iu. Nekliudov and E. S. Novik. Moscow: Rossiiskii universitet, 1993, 341–45.

Azov, V. "Satira pod spudom." *Poslednie novosti,* May 14, 1932: 2.

Babcock, Barbara A. "Arrange Me into Disorder: Fragments and Reflections on Ritual Clowning." In *Rite, Drama, Festival, Spectacle: Rehearsals Toward a Theory of Cultural Performance,* ed. John J. MacAloon. Philadelphia: Institute for the Study of Human Issues, 1984, 102–28.

———, ed. *Signs About Signs: The Semiotics of Self-Reference.* Special issue of *Semiotica* 30.1–2 (1980).

Bakhtin, Mikhail. "The Problem of Speech Genres." In *Speech Genres and Other Late Essays,* trans. Vern W. McGee, ed. Caryl Emerson and Michael Holquist. Austin: University of Texas Press, 1986, 60–102.

———. *Rabelais and His World.* Trans. Hélène Iswolsky. Bloomington: Indiana University Press, 1984.

Bakhtin, Vladimir. "Anekdoty nas spasali vsegda." In Strelianyi et al., 799–818.

———. "Narodnoe mnenie." *Neva* 6 (1989): 193–96.

———. "Po stene polzet kirpich, ili Kak podvodnaia lodka v stepiakh Ukrainy pogibla v zhestokom vozdushnom boiu." Interview with Mikhail Grigor'ev. *Trud,* Apr. 21, 1995: 9.

———. "Rasskazhu vam anekdot." Interview. *Pravda,* June 18, 1989: 4.

———. "Vchera mne rasskazali anekdot . . ." Interview with I. Foniakov. *Literaturnaia gazeta,* May 17, 1989: 16.

Banc, C., and Alan Dundes. *First Prize Fifteen Years: An Annotated Collection of Romanian Political Jokes.* Rutherford, N.J.: Farleigh Dickinson University Press, 1986.

Bantysh-Kamenskii, D. N. *Slovar' dostopamiatnykh liudei russkoi zemli.* Part 3. St. Petersburg: 1847.

Barker, Adele, ed. *Consuming Russia: Popular Culture, Sex, and Society Since Gorbachev.* Durham, N.C.: Duke University Press, 1999.

Barskii, Lev Abramovich. *Chelovek! Eto zvuchit gor'ko. Eto prosto smeshno. V pervom chtenii. Anekdoty.* Moscow: Kh. G. S., 1994.

———. *Eto prosto smeshno.* Moscow: Kh. G. S., 1992.

Barskii, Lev Abramovich, and I. Pis'mennyi, comps. "Vlast' smekha: Kratkii kurs istorii SSSR v anekdotakh, karikaturakh i postanovleniiakh TsK." *Ogonek* 13 (Mar. 30, 1998): 40–48.

Bauman, Richard, ed. *Folklore, Cultural Performances, and Popular Entertainments: A Communications-Centered Handbook.* New York: Oxford University Press, 1992.

———. "Genre." In Bauman, *Folklore,* 53–59.

———. "Introduction." In Bauman, *Folklore,* xiii–xxi.

———. "Performance." In Bauman, *Folklore,* 41–49.

———. *Verbal Art as Performance.* Rowley, Mass.: Newbury House, 1977.

Beckmann, P. *Hammer and Tickle: Clandestine Laughter in the Soviet Empire.* Boulder, Colo.: Golem, 1980.

Belousov, Aleksandr Fedorovich. "Anekdoticheskii tsikl o krokodile Gene i Cheburashke." In *Problemy poetiki iazyka i literatury. Materialy mezhvuzovskoi nauchnoi konferentsii, 22–24 maia 1996 goda.* Petrozavodsk: Izdatel'stvo Karel'skogo gosudarstvennogo pedagogicheskogo universiteta, 1996, 3–20.

———. "Anekdoty o Shtirlitse." *Zhivaia starina* 1 (1995): 16–18.

———. *Gorodskoi fol'klor.* Tallinn: 1987.

———. "Mnimyi Shtirlits." In Belousov, *Uchebnyi material,* 104–17.

———. "Ot sostavitelia." In Belousov, *Uchebnyi material,* 3–10.

———. "Sovremennyi anekdot." Unpublished article. 1999.

———, comp. *Uchebnyi material po teorii literatury: Zhanry slovesnogo teksta. Anekdot.* Tallinn: Tallinskii pedagogicheskii institut, 1989.

———. "Vovochka." In Bogomolov, 165–86.

Benton, Gregor. "The Origins of the Political Joke." In *Humour in Society: Resistance and Control,* ed. Chris Powell and George Paton. New York: St. Martin's, 1988, 33–55.

Berezaiskii, Vasilii, comp. *Anekdoty drevnykh poshekhontsev.* St. Petersburg: 1798.

Berger, Arthur Asa. *An Anatomy of Humor.* New Brunswick, N.J.: Transaction, 1993.

———. "The Politics of Laughter." In Paton et al., 15–28.

———. "What's in a Joke? A Micro-Analysis." *Elementa* 1 (1994): 321–30.

Bergson, Henri. *Laughter: An Essay on the Meaning of the Comic.* Trans. Cloudesley Brereton and Fred Rothwell. London: MacMillan and Co., 1911. Copenhagen: Green Integer, 1999.

Berry, Ellen E., and Anesa Miller-Pogacar, eds. *Re-entering the Sign: Articulating New Russian Culture.* Ann Arbor: University of Michigan Press, 1995.

Beverley, John. "The Margins at the Center: On *Testimonio* (Testimonial Narrative)." In *The Real Thing: Testimonial Discourse and Latin America,* ed. Georg M. Gugelberger. Durham, N.C.: Duke University Press, 1996, 23–41.

Bitov, Andrei. "Pod kupolom Glasnosti." Introduction. In Zhvanetskii, *God za dva,* 4–13.

Blazhes, V. V. "Sovremennye ustnye iumoristicheskie rasskazy v ikh sviazi s narodno-poeticheskoi traditsiei." In *Fol'klor Urala: Sovremennyi russkii fol'klor promyshlennogo regiona: Sbornik nauchnykh trudov,* ed. V. P. Krugliashova. Sverdlovsk: Ural'skii gosudarstvennyi universitet, 1989, 38–47.

Blazhes, V. V., and A. V. Matveev. "Sovremennye ustnye iumoristicheskie rasskazy v ikh sviazi s fol'klornoi traditsiei." In *Fol'klor narodov RSFSR: Sovremennoe sosoianie fol'klornykh traditsii i ikh vzaimodeistvie: Mezhvuzovskii nauchnyi sbornik,* ed. L. G. Barag. Ufa: Izdatel'stvo Bashkirskogo universiteta, 1989, 58–64.

Bogatyrev, Petr, and Roman Jakobson. "Folklore as a Special Form of Creativity." Trans. Manfred Jacobson. In *The Prague School: Selected Writings, 1929–1946,* ed. Peter Steiner. Austin: University of Texas Press, 1982, 32–46.

Bogomolov, N., comp. *Anti-mir russkoi kul'tury: Iazyk. Fol'klor. Literatura.* Moscow: Ladomir, 1996.

Bol'shaia sovetskaia entsiklopediia. 1st ed. Moscow: Sovetskaia entsiklopediia, 1926, 1947.

Bol'shaia sovetskaia entsiklopediia. 2nd ed. Moscow: Bol'shaia sovetskaia entsiklopediia, 1949–1958.

Bol'shoi entsiklopedicheskii slovar'. Ed. A. M. Prokhorov. 2nd ed., 2 vols. Moscow: Bol'shaia rossiiskaia entsiklopediia, 1997.

Borenstein, Eliot. "Public Offerings: MMM and the Marketing of Melodrama." In Barker, 49–75.

Borev, Iurii Borisovich. *Estetika.* Moscow: Politizdat, 1969.

———. *Fariseia: Poslestalinskaia epokha v predaniiakh i anekdotakh.* Moscow: Nezavisimyi al'manakh "Konets veka," 1992.

———. "Intelligentskii fol'klor." In Borev, *Istoriia,* 3.

———. *Istoriia gosudarstva sovetskogo v predaniiakh i anekdotakh.* Moscow: Ripol, 1995.

———. *Iz zhizni zvezd i meteoritov.* Moscow: Ripol, 1996.

———. *Komicheskoe, ili o tom, kak smekh kaznit nesovershenstvo mira, ochishchaet i obnovliaet cheloveka i utverzhdaet radost' bytiia.* Moscow: Iskusstvo, 1970.

———. *Staliniada.* Riga: Kursiv, 1990.

———. *Vvedenie v estetiku.* Moscow: Sovetskii khudozhnik, 1965.

———. *XX vek v predaniiakh i anekdotakh: v 6-ti knigakh.* Rostov-na-Donu: Feniks, 1996.

Borisov, S. B. "Estetika 'chernogo iumora' v rossiiskoi traditsii." In *Iz istorii russkoi esteticheskoi mysli: Mezhvuzovskii sbornik nauchnykh trudov,* ed. A. P. Valitskaia et al. St. Petersburg: Obrazovanie, 1993, 139–53.

Borodin, Pavel. "Abstraktnyi anekdot kak sotsiokul'turnyi fenomen." In *Material mezhdunarodnoi konferentsii "Fol'klor i sovremennost'," posviashchennoi pamiati professora N. I. Savushkinoi (20–22 oktiabria 1994 goda).* Moscow: Moskovskii gorodskoi dvorets tvorchestva, 1995, 86–91.

———. "Anekdoticheskii tsikl: Osobennosti stroeniia." Dec. 12, 2001. http://www.karabistr.ru/ pamoney/anecdot/cykl.html.

———. "Dramaturgiia anekdota." Dec. 12, 2001. http://www.karabistr.ru/pamoney/anecdot/drama.html.

———. "K probleme genezisa anekdota." Dec. 12, 2001. http://www.karabistr.ru/pamoney/anecdot/genesis.html.

———. "O vzaimodeistvii anekdota i paremii." Dec. 12, 2001. http://www.karabistr.ru/pamoney/anecdot/paremii.html.

Boskin, Joseph. *Rebellious Laughter: People's Humor in American Culture.* Syracuse, N.Y.: Syracuse University Press, 1997.

Bracciolini, Poggio, Gian Francesco, and Giovanni Geivano Pontano. *The Facetiae of Poggio and Other Medieval Story-Tellers.* Trans. and ed. Edward Storer. London: George Routledge and Sons, 1928.

Brezhnev, Leonid Il'ich. *Malaia zemlia.* Moscow: Izdatel'stvo Politicheskoi literatury, 1979.

Briggs, Asa. "Culture." In Bauman, *Folklore,* 3–11.

Briker, Boris, and Anatolii Vishevskii. "Iumor v populiarnoi kul'ture sovetskogo intelligenta 60-x–70-x godov." *Wiener Slawistischer Almanach* 24 (1989): 147–70.

Britsyna, Olesya. "Anecdotes, Jokes and Jests in Everyday Communication: Folklore Texts Under Observation and Experimental Study." *Fabula* 40.1–2 (1999): 26–32.

Brooks, Jeffrey. *Thank You, Comrade Stalin! Soviet Public Culture from Revolution to Cold War.* Princeton, N.J.: Princeton University Press, 2000.

———. *When Russia Learned to Read: Literacy and Popular Literature 1861–1917.* Princeton, N.J.: Princeton University Press, 1985.

Brooks, Peter. *The Melodramatic Imagination: Balzac, Henry James, Melodrama, and the Mode of Excess.* New Haven, Conn.: Yale University Press, 1976.

Browne, Ray, ed. *Objects of Special Devotion: Fetishism in Popular Culture.* Bowling Green, Ohio: Bowling Green University Popular Press, 1982.

Budina, O. R., and N. N. Shmeleva. "Tradition in the Development of the Culture of Everyday Life in a Modern Russian City." *Soviet Anthropology and Archeology* 22.4 (Spring 1984): 72–97.

Bukharkova, Ol'ga. "Krysha: Proshchai, epokha otmorozkov." *Ogonek* 7 (Feb. 2000): 28.

Bulgakov, Mikhail. *Zoikina kvartira: Okonchatel'nyi tekst.* Ann Arbor, Mich.: Ardis, 1971.

Buslaev, Fedor Ivanovich. *Istoricheskie ocherki russkoi narodnoi slovesnosti i iskusstva.* St. Petersburg: Obshchestvennaia Pol'za, 1861. The Hague: Mouton, 1969.

Butenko, I. A. "Iumor kak predmet sotsiologii?" *Sotsiologicheskie issledovaniia* 5 (1997): 135–40.

Capek, Karel. "O prirode anekdota." 1925. Trans. V. Kamenskaia. *Voprosy literatury* 11 (1975): 302–8.

"*Chapaeva* posmotrit vsia strana." *Pravda,* Nov. 21, 1934: 1.

Chekunova, A. E. "Poiavlenie istoricheskogo anekdota v Rossii." *Voprosy istorii* 2 (1997): 131–40.

———. "Rossiiskii istoricheskii anekdot ekaterininskoi pory." *Voprosy istorii* 4 (1998): 138–45.

Cherednichenko, Tat'iana. *Tipologiia sovetskoi massovoi kul'tury: Mezhdu "Brezhnevym" i "Pugachevoi."* Moscow: RIK Kul'tura, 1993.

Chernykh, P. Ia. *Istoriko-etimologicheskii slovar' sovremennogo russkogo iazyka.* Moscow: Russkii iazyk, 1993.

Chernyshev, Sergei. "Russkoe samoopredelenie." *Russkii zhurnal,* Sept. 6, 1997. http://www.russ.ru/journal/odna_8/97-09-06/chern.htm. Jan. 2, 2001.

Chernyshevskii, Nikolai G. "Vozvyshennoe i komicheskoe." In Nikolai G. Chernyshevskii, *Izbrannye filosofskie sochineniia.* Vol. 1. Leningrad: Gospolitizdat, 1950, 252–99.

Chernyshov, Andrei. *Sovremennaia sovetskaia mifologiia.* Tver': 1992.

Chirkova, Ol'ga. "Personazhi ukhodiat iz basen: Istoki sovremennogo anekdota." *Russkaia rech'* 4 (1997): 102–7.

———. "Poetika komicheskogo v sovremennom narodnom anekdote." *Filologicheskie nauki* 5–6 (1998): 30–38.

———. *Poetika sovremennogo narodnogo anekdota.* Ph.D. diss., Volgograd University, 1997.

Chistov, K. V. "Prozaicheskie zhanry v sisteme fol'klora." *Prozaicheskie zhanry fol'klora narodov SSSR: Tezisy dokladov na Vsesoiuznoi nauchnoi konferentsii. 21–23 maia 1974. Gor. Minsk.* Minsk: Akademiia nauk Soiuza sovetskikh sotsialisticheskikh respublik, 1974, 6–31.

Chudinova, I. A. "Smekh, vesel'e, shabash: Traditsii skomoroshestva v period petrovskikh reform." In *Skomorokhi: Problemy i perspectivy izucheniia (K 140-letiiu so dnia vykhoda pervoi raboty of skomorokhakh),* ed. V. V. Koshelev. St. Petersburg: Rossiiskii institut istorii iskusstv, 1994, 149–59.

Chulkov, M. D. *Peresmeshnik, ili Slavenskie skazki.* 4 parts. 1766–68.

Clark, Katerina. *The Soviet Novel: History as Ritual.* 3rd ed. Bloomington: Indiana University Press, 2000.

Cochran, Robert. "'What Courage!': Romanian 'Our Leader' Jokes." *Journal of American Folklore* 102.405 (1989): 259–74.

Cohen, Ted. *Jokes: Philosophical Thoughts on Joking Matters.* Chicago: University of Chicago Press, 1999.

Colombo, John Robert. *Iron Curtains: Humour of the Soviet Union.* Toronto: Colombo, 1996.

Condee, Nancy. "Introduction." In *Soviet Hieroglyphics,* vii–xxiii.

————, ed. *Soviet Hieroglyphics: Visual Culture in Late Twentieth-Century Russia.* Bloomington: Indiana University Press. London: British Film Institute, 1995.

Condee, Nancy, and Vladimir Padunov. "The ABC of Russian Consumer Culture: Readings, Ratings and Real Estate." In *Soviet Hieroglyphics*, 130–72.

————. "The Cultural Combat Zone: Where Is the DMZ?" *Soviet Union/Union Soviétique* 15.2–3 (1988): 167–85.

————. "Makulakul'tura: Reprocessing Culture." *Russian Culture in Transition: Selected Papers of the Working Group for the Study of Contemporary Russian Culture, 1990–91. Stanford Slavic Studies 7.* Ed. Gregory Freidin. Stanford, Calif.: Stanford University Department of Slavic Languages and Literatures, 1993, 53–80.

————. "The Outposts of Official Art: Recharting Soviet Cultural History." *Framework* 34 (1987): 59–106.

————. "Pair-a-Dice Lost: The Socialist Gamble, Market Determinism, and Compulsory Postmodernism." *New Formations* 22 (1994): 72–94.

————. "Perestroika Suicide: Not by *Bred* Alone." *New Left Review* 189 (Sept.–Oct. 1991): 67–89.

Cottom, Daniel. *Text and Culture: The Politics of Interpretation.* Minneapolis: University of Minnesota Press, 1989.

Cuthbertson, Gilbert Morris. *Political Myth and Epic.* Ann Arbor: Michigan State University Press, 1975.

Danilov, Oleg. *My idem smotret' 'Chapaeva'!* Moscow Art Theater, Moscow. Nov. 4, 1998.

Davies, Christie. "The Collapse of the World's Best Political Jokes." *National Review* 42.15 (Aug. 6, 1990): 32.

————. *Ethnic Humor Around the World: A Comparative Analysis.* Bloomington: Indiana University Press, 1990.

————. "Exploring the Thesis of the Self-Deprecating Jewish Sense of Humor." In Ziv and Zajdman, 29–46.

————. *Jokes and Their Relation to Society.* Berlin: Mouton de Gruyer, 1998.

————. *The Mirth of Nations.* New Brunswick, N.J.: Transaction, 2002.

————. "Stupidity and Rationality: Jokes from the Iron Cage." In Powell and Paton, 1–32.

Descartes, Rene. *Les passions de l'âime.* Paris: 1649.

Diment, Galya, and Yuri Slezkine, eds. *Between Heaven and Hell: The Myth of Siberia in Russian Culture.* New York: St. Martin's, 1993.

Dmitriev, Anatolii. "Iu. Borev i intelligentskii fol'klor." *Sotsiologicheskie issledovaniia* 7 (1995): 138–41.

————. "Iuridicheskii anekdot kak reaktsiia obshchestva." *Gosudarstvo i pravo* 8/9 (1994): 172–80.

————. *Sotsiologiia iumora: Ocherki.* Moscow: Rossiiskaia Akademiia Nauk, 1996.

———. *Sotsiologiia politicheskogo iumora*. Moscow: Rossiiskaia politicheskaia entsiklopediia, 1998.

Dolgopolova, Zhanna. "The Contrary World of the Anecdote." *Melbourne Slavonic Studies* 15 (1981): 1–12.

———. "Ispol'zovanie stilisticheskoi kontaminatsii kak sredstvo komicheskogo." *XXII Gertsenovskie chteniia. Filologicheskie nauki. Programma i kratkoe soderzhanie dokladov. 15 apr.–10 maia 1969 goda*. Leningrad: Leningradskii pedagogicheskii institut im. A. I. Gertsena, 1969, 49–51.

———, ed. *Russia Dies Laughing: Jokes from Soviet Russia*. London: André Deutsch, 1982.

Domanovskii, L. V., and N. V. Novikov. *Russkoe narodno-poeticheskoe tvorchestvo protiv tserkvi i religii*. Leningrad: Izdatel'stvo Akademiia nauk Soiuza sovetskikh sotsialisticheskikh respublik, 1961.

Dondurei, Daniil. "Kinematografisty o 'novykh russkikh.'" *Iskusstvo kino* 1 (1995): 25–27.

———. "'Novye russkie' idut!" *Iskusstvo kino* 1 (1995): 1.

Douglas, Mary. "Jokes." In *Rethinking Popular Culture: Contemporary Perspectives in Cultural Studies*, ed. Chandra Mukerji and Michael Schudson. Berkeley: University of California Press, 1991, 291–310.

Draitser, Emil. "The Art of Storytelling in Contemporary Russian Satirical Folklore." *Slavic and East European Journal* 26.2 (1982): 233–38.

———. "Comparative Analysis of Russian and American Humor." *META: Journal des Traducteurs* 34.1 (1989): 88–90.

———, ed. and comp. *Forbidden Laughter (Soviet Underground Jokes)*. Trans. Jon Pariser. Los Angeles: Almanac, 1978.

———. *Making War, Not Love: Gender and Sexuality in Russian Humor*. New York: St. Martin's, 1999.

———. "Smekh i politika." *Novoe Russkoe Slovo*, Oct. 5, 1987: 4.

———. "Sociological Aspects of the Russian Jewish Jokes of the Exodus." *Humor* 7.3 (1994): 245–67.

———. "Soviet Underground Jokes as a Means of Popular Entertainment." *Journal of Popular Culture* 23.1 (Summer 1989): 117–25.

———. *Taking Penguins to the Movies: Ethnic Humor in Russia*. Detroit, Mich.: Wayne State University Press, 1998.

Dundes, Alan. "Metafolklore and Oral Literary Criticism." *The Monist* 50 (1966): 505–16.

———. "Slurs International: Folk Comparisons of Ethnicity and National Character." *Southern Folklore Quarterly* 39 (1975): 15–38. Reprinted in *Wise Words: Essays on the Proverb*. Ed. Wolfgang Mieder. New York: Garland, 1994, 183–209.

Efimova, Alla. *Communist Nostalgia: On Soviet and Post-Soviet Memory*. Ph.D. diss., Rochester, N.Y.: University of Rochester, 1997.

Eliade, Mircea. *Myth and Reality*. Trans. Willard R. Trask. New York: Harper and Row, 1963.

Elistratov, Vladimir. "Argo i kul'tura." In Vladimir Elistratov, *Slovar' moskovskogo argo: Materialy 1980–1994 gg*. Moscow: Russkie slovari, 1994, 592–699.

Endlin, Mark. *Chapaev v Amerike i dr.* N.p.: Smeshanin, 1980.

Epstein, Mikhail. "The Origins and Meaning of Russian Postmodernism." In Berry and Miller-Pogacar, 25–47.

———. *Relativistic Patterns in Totalitarian Thinking: An Inquiry into the Language of Soviet Ideology*. Kennan Institute Occasional Papers, 243. Washington, D.C.: Kennan Institute for Advanced Russian Studies, 1991.

Erofeev, Venedikt. *Moskva-Petushki i pr.: Roman-anekdot*. Petrozavodsk: Kareko, 1995.

Erokaev, S. *Anekdoty i baiki pro novykh russkikh: Sbornik tematicheskikh anekdotov*. St. Petersburg: Totem, 1997.

Erokhin, Aleksei. "Abzats." *Ogonek* 14 (Apr. 1995): 43.

———. "Smert' anekdota." *Moskovskie novosti* 22 (May 31, 1992): 22–23.

Eroshkin, S., et al., comps. *Anekdoty pro novykh russkikh. Malinovye parusa*. St. Petersburg: DiK, 1997.

Evrei-olenovod. Minsk: Literatura, 1997.

Faibisovich, Semen. "'Novye russkie'—snaruzhi i iznutri." *Iskusstvo kino* 1 (1995): 34–38.

Fairclough, Norman. *Critical Discourse Analysis: The Critical Study of Language*. London: Longman, 1995.

Famintsyn, A. S. *Skomorokhi na Rusi*. 1889. St. Petersburg: Aleteiia, 1995.

Faraday, George Wheeldon. *The Cult of Artistic Autonomy and the Crisis of the Post-Soviet Film Industry*. Ph.D. Diss., Raleigh, N.C.: Duke University, 1997.

Farrell, Dianne Ecklund. "Medieval Popular Humor in Russian Eighteenth Century *Lubki*." *Slavic Review* 50.3 (Fall 1991): 551–65.

Farrer, Dean. "The Soviet Folktale as an Ideological Strategy for Survival in International Business Relations." *Studies in Soviet Thought* 13.1 (1973): 55–75.

Feokistov, Ivan. *Anekdoty i predaniia o Petre Velikom po Golikovu i dr.* St. Petersburg: 1896.

Fialkova, Larisa. "Chornobyl's Folklore: Vernacular Commentary on Nuclear Disaster." *Journal of Folklore Research* 38.3 (2001): 181–204.

Filippov, Boris. "Nesmeshnoe o smeshnom." In *Iumor i satira poslerevoliutsionnoi Rossii: Antologiia v dvukh tomakh*, comp. Boris Fillipov and Vadim Medish. Vol. 1. 2 vols. London: Overseas Publications Interchange, 1983, 7–18.

Fleischman, Suzanne. *Tense and Narrativity: From Medieval Performance to Modern Fiction*. Austin: University of Texas Press, 1990.

Forrai, George, ed. *Russian Express: Don't Leave Home! Jokes from Behind the Iron Curtain.* Hong Kong: WMA, 1988.

Freidin, Gregory, ed. *Russian Culture in Transition: Selected Papers of the Working Group for the Study of Contemporary Russian Culture, 1990–1991. Stanford Slavic Studies 7.* Stanford, Calif.: Stanford University Department of Slavic Languages and Literatures, 1993.

Freud, Sigmund. *Jokes and Their Relation to the Unconscious.* Trans. James Strachey. New York: W. W. Norton, 1960.

Furmanov, Dmitrii. *Chapaev. Krasnyi desant. Miatezh.* Leningrad: Lenizdat, 1967.

Gaidar, Arkadii. *Chuk i gek.* Moscow: Gosudarstvennoe izdatel'stvo detskoi literatury, 1948.

Galich, Aleksandr. "O tom, kak Klim Petrovich vystupal na mitinge v zashchitu mira." In Aleksandr Galich, *General'naia repetitsiia.* Moscow: Sovetskii pisatel', 1991, 52–54.

Geertz, Clifford. *The Interpretation of Cultures: Selected Essays.* New York: Basic Books, 1973.

Gerlovan, O. K. "Poniatie o skazke v Rossii XVIII–nachala XIX v." *Filologicheskie nauki* 1 (1996): 95–103.

Gessen, Masha. *Dead Again: The Russian Intelligentsia After Communism.* London: Verso, 1997.

Gifford, D. J. "Iconographical Notes Towards a Definition of the Medieval Fool." In *Studies in Honour of Enid Welsford,* ed. Paul V. A. Williams. Cambridge, England: D. S. Brewer, 1979.

Glebkin, V. V. *Ritual v sovetskoi kul'ture.* Moscow: Ianus-K, 1998.

Glinka, Sergei. *Russkie anekdoty voennye, grazhdanskie i istoricheskie, izobrazhaiushchie svoistvo i t.d.* Moscow: 1811.

Gogol, Nikolai. *Letters of Nikolai Gogol.* Ed. Carl Proffer. Trans. Carl Proffer and Vera Krivoshein. Ann Arbor: University of Michigan Press, 1967.

Goncharenko, Nadiia. "Anekdot." *Suchasnist'* 6 (1998): 116–25.

Gopman, V., and V. Mil'china, comps. "Anekdoty o novykh russkikh." *Novoe literaturnoe obozrenie* 22 (1996): 380–82.

Gor'kii, Maksim. *Sobranie sochinenii.* Vol. 27. Moscow: Golitizdat, 1953.

Grossman, Leonid. "Iskusstvo anekdota u Pushkina." In Leonid Grossman, *Sobranie sochinenii v chetyrekh tomakh. Tom pervyi: Pushkin: Issledovaniia i stat'i.* Vol. 1. 4 vols. Moscow: Sovremennye problemy, 1928, 45–79.

Halliday, M. A. K. "Anti-Languages." *American Anthropologist* 78 (1976): 570–84.

Haney, Jack V. *An Introduction to the Russian Folktale.* Vol. 1 of *The Complete Russian Folktale.* Armonk, N.Y.: M. E. Sharpe, 1999.

———. "Mr. Afanasiev's Naughty Little Secrets: 'Russkie zavetnye skazki.'" *SEEFA Journal* 3.2 (Fall 1998). Jan. 3, 2002. http://www.virginia.edu/slavic/seefa/ZAVETNYE.htm.

——, ed. and trans. *Russian Animal Tales.* Vol. 2 of *The Complete Russian Folktale.* Armonk, N.Y.: M. E. Sharpe, 1999.

Hanks, William F. "Discourse Genres in a Theory of Practice." *American Ethnologist* 14.4 (Nov. 1987): 668–92.

Harkins, William E. "Folktales." In Terras, 147–48.

——. *"Skomorokhi."* In Terras 422.

Harris, David A., and Izrail Rabinovich. *The Jokes of Oppression: The Humor of Soviet Jews.* Northvale, N.J.: J. Aronson, 1988.

——, comps. *On a Lighter Note? Soviet Jewish Humor.* New York: American Jewish Committee, Institute of Human Relations, 1986.

Hayden, Robert M. "Imagined Communities and Real Victims: Self-determination and Ethnic Cleansing in Yugoslavia." *American Ethnologist* 23.4 (Nov. 1996): 783–801.

Hellberg-Hirn, Elena. "The Other Way Round: The Jokelore of Radio Yerevan." *Arv: Scandinavian Yearbook of Folklore* 41 (1985): 89–104.

——. "Zapretnye temy i ustnoe slovo." *Studia Slavica Finlandensia* 11 (1994): 77–83.

Hierocles the Grammarian. *The Philogelos or Laughter-Lover.* Trans. and ed. Barry Baldwin. Amsterdam: J. C. Gieben, 1983.

Hobbes, Thomas. *Leviathan.* 1651. Oxford: Clarendon, 1909.

Horkheimer, Max, and Theodor W. Adorno. *Dialectic of Enlightenment.* Trans. John Cumming. New York: Continuum, 1972.

Horton, Andrew. "Introduction." In *Comedy/Cinema/Theory*, ed. Andrew Horton. Berkeley: University of California Press, 1991, 1–21.

Horvath, Agnes. *The Political Psychology of Trickster-Clown: An Analytical Experiment Around Communism as Myth.* EUI Working Paper SPS 97/5. Badia Fiesolana, Italy: European University Institute, 1997.

Howell, Dana Prescott. *The Development of Soviet Folkloristics.* New York: Garland, 1992.

Huizinga, Johan. *Homo Ludens: A Study of the Play Element in Culture.* Boston: Beacon, 1955.

Humphrey, Caroline. *Karl Marx Collective: Economy, Society and Religion in a Siberian Collective Farm.* Cambridge: Cambridge University Press, 1983.

Hutcheon, Linda. *Irony's Edge: The Theory and Politics of Irony.* London: Routledge, 1994.

Hutton, Jan. "Some Aspects of Contemporary Soviet Folktales." *Journal of Russian Studies* 55 (1989): 30–40.

Hyers, M. Conrad. *Zen and the Comic Spirit.* Philadelphia: Westminster, 1973.

Iakovenko, I. G. "Nenormativnyi anekdot kak modeliruiushchaia sistema: Opyt kul'turologicheskogo analiza." *Novoe literaturnoe obozrenie* 43 (2000): 335–46.

Iangirov, Rashit. "Anekdoty 's borodoi': Materialy k istorii nepodtsenzurnogo sovetskogo fol'klora." *Novoe literaturnoe obozrenie* 31 (1998): 155–74.

Ian'shinova, N. I., comp. *Chukchi.* Moscow: S. Kudrin, 1901.

Irten'ev, Igor', and Andrei Bil'zho. *Imperiia dobra.* N.p.: S. Nitochkin, 1994.

Istoricheskie anekdoty. Mar. 20, 2003. http://www.mandat.ru/history_anekdot .shtml.

Iudin, Iu. I. *Russkaia narodnaia bytovaia skazka.* Moscow: Academia, 1998.

Iunisov, Milikhat Vafaevich. *Mifopoetika studencheskogo smekha (STEM i KVN).* Moscow: Gosudarstvennyi institut iskusstvoznaniia, 1999.

Ivanits, Linda J. *Russian Folk Belief.* Armonk, N.Y.: M. E. Sharpe, 1989.

Ivanov, A. A. "Fol'kor v nashi dni (voprosy bytovaniia i metodiki sobiraniia)." In *Material mezhdunarodnoi konferentsii 'Fol'klor i sovremennost,'" posviash-chennoi pamiati professora N. I. Savushkinoi (20–22 oktiabria 1994 goda).* Moscow: Moskovskii gorodskoi dvorets tvorchestva, 1995, 7–10.

———. "K zhanrovoi spetsifike narodnogo anekdota (na primere analiza kompozitsii siuzhetov o durakakh)." In *Analiz khudozhestvennogo teksta: Problemy i perspektivy. Mezhvuzovskii sbornik.* Ioshkar-Ola: Miriiskii gosudarstvennyi universitet, 1991, 13–19.

Ivanova, T. "Sovetskii anekdot v SShA." *Zhivaia starina* 1 (1995): 57.

Ivanova, T. G. "Bylichki i 'anekdoty' v Shenkurskom raione Arkhangel'skoi oblasti." *Russkii fol'klor* 23 (1985): 26–32.

Jaeger, Gertrude, and Philip Selznick. "A Normative Theory of Culture." *American Sociological Review* 29.5 (1964): 653–69.

Jakobson, Roman. "On Russian Fairy Tales." In Afanas'ev, *Russian Fairy Tales,* 631–56.

Jakobson, Roman, and Petr Bogatyrev. "On the Boundary Between Studies of Folklore and Literature." In *Readings in Russian Poetics: Formalist and Structuralist Views,* ed. Ladislav Matejka and Krystyna Pomorska. Ann Arbor: Michigan Slavic Publications, 1978, 91–93.

Johnson, Priscilla, and Leopold Labedz, eds. *Khrushchev and the Arts: The Politics of Soviet Culture, 1962–1964.* Cambridge, Mass.: MIT Press, 1965.

Johnson, Ragnar. "Jokes, Theories, Anthropology." *Semiotica* 22.3–4 (1978): 309–34.

"Joseph Stalin." *Current Biography* 1942: 796.

Kalbouss, George. "On 'Armenian Riddles' and Their Offspring 'Radio Erevan.'" *Slavic and East European Journal* 21.3 (1977): 447–49.

Kant, Immanuel. *Kritik der Urteiskraft.* 1790. *Critique of Judgement.* Trans. James Creed Meredith. Oxford: Clarendon, 1952.

Karachevtsev, Sergei. *Damskie: Sbornik novykh anekdotov.* Riga: Mir, n.d.

———. *"Dlia nekuriashchikh": Anekdoty.* Riga: Mir, n.d.

Karamzin, Nikolai Mikhailovich. "Otchego v Rossii malo avtorskikh talantov?" In Nikolai Mikhailovich Karamzin, *Izbrannye sochineniia v dvukh tomakh.* Vol. 2. Moscow: Khudozhestvennaia literatura, 1964, 183–87.

Kaspe, Irina. "Krivoe antizerkalo: 'Sovetskii' i 'postsovetskii' anekdot: Problemy zhanrovoi transformatsii." *Novoe literaturnoe obozrenie* 43 (2000): 327–34.

Kelly, Catriona. "The Retreat from Dogmatism: Populism Under Khrushchev and Brezhnev." In Kelly and Shepherd, *Russian Cultural Studies*, 249–73.

Kelly, Catriona, and David Shepherd, eds. *Constructing Russian Culture in the Age of Revolution, 1881–1940*. New York: Oxford University Press, 1998.

———. *Russian Cultural Studies: An Introduction*. New York: Oxford University Press, 1998.

Kharitonova, Valentina. "Anekdoty (stat'ia o podlinnykh anekdotakh so mnozhestvom primerov)." *Istoki: Al'manakh* 21 (1990): 173–89.

Khrul', Viktor Mikhailovich. *Anekdot kak forma massovoi kommunikatsii*. Ph.D. diss., Moscow State University, 1993.

Khvalin-Gor'kii, L. L., comp. *Anekdoty s gosudareva dvora, ili 150 istoricheskikh anekdotov iz zhizni russkikh gosudarei XVII–XIX vekov*. Nizhnii Novgorod: Pegas, 1990.

Kobozeva, I. M. "Nemets, anglichanin, frantsuz i russkii: Vyiavlenie natsional'nykh kharakterov cherez analiz konnotatsii etnonimov." *Vestnik Moskovskogo universiteta. Seriia 9. Filologiia* 3 (1995).

Koestler, Arthur. *The Act of Creation*. London: Arkana, 1989.

Kokorev, A. V. "Russkie stikhotvornye fatsetsii XVIII v." In *Starinnaia russkaia povest': Stat'i i issledovaniia*, ed. N. K. Gudzii. Moscow: Akademiia nauk Soiuza sovetskikh sotsialisticheskikh respublik, 1941, 216–84.

Kolasky, John, comp. *Laughter Through Tears: Underground Wit, Humor and Satire in the Soviet Russian Empire*. Ill. Myron Levytsky and Tibor Kovalik. Bullsbrook, Western Australia: Veritas, 1985.

Kordonskii, Simon. "Chapaev, Shtirlits, russkii, evrei, Brezhnev, chukcha + El'tsin = Pushkin." *Russkii zhurnal*. Nov. 11, 1997. Jan. 2, 2001. http://www.russ.ru/journal/odna_8/97-11-13/kordon.htm.

Korshunov, Mikhail, and Victoriia Terekhova. "Nas bylo chetvero . . ." *Detskaia literatura* 3 (1994): 25–35.

Kostiukhin, E. A. "Iadrenyi russkii iumor." Introduction, in Afanas'ev, *Narodnye russkie skazki ne dlia pechati*, 5–19.

Kotsiubinskii, S. D., ed. and comp. *Anekdoty o Khodzhe Nasreddine i Akhmet Akhae*. Simferopol': Gosudarstvennoe izdatel'stvo krymskoi ASSR, 1937.

Kozhevnikov, Aleksandr Iur'evich. *Bol'shoi slovar': Krylatye frazy otechestvennogo kino*. St. Petersburg: Neva, 2001.

Kreps, Mikhail. *Tekhnika komicheskogo u Zoshchenko*. Benson, Vt.: Chalidze, 1986.

Krivoshlyk, M. G. *Istoricheskie anekdoty iz zhizni russkikh zamechatel'nykh liudei (S portretami i kratkimi biografiami)*. 2nd ed. St. Petersburg, 1897. Moscow: ANS-Print, 1991.

Kroker, Arthur, and Charles Levin. "Cynical Power: The Fetishism of the Sign." In *Ideology and Power in the Age of Lenin in Ruins*, ed. Arthur Kroker and Marilouise Kroker. New York: St. Martin's, 1991, 123–34.

Krongauz, M. A. "Bessilie iazyka v epokhu zrelogo sotsializma." *Znak: Sbornik statei po lingvistike, semiotike i poetike pamiati A. N. Zhurinskogo.* Moscow: Russkii uchebnyi tsentr MS, 1994, 233–44.

———. "Sovetskii antisovetskii iumor: O Dovlatove." *Moskovskii lingvisticheskii zhurnal* 2 (1996): 227–39.

Krylov, Ivan A., and A. I. Klushin. *Sankt-Peterburgskii Merkurii* 1 (1793).

Krylova, Anna. "Saying 'Lenin' and Meaning 'Party': Subversion and Laughter in Soviet and Post-Soviet Society." In Barker, 243–65.

Kupina, N. A. *Totalitarnyi iazyk: Slovar' i rechevye reaktsii.* Ekaterinburg: Izdatel'stvo Ural'skogo universiteta, 1995.

Kurganov, Efim. *Anekdot kak zhanr.* St. Petersburg: Gumanitarnoe agenstvo "Akademicheckii proekt," 1997.

———. "Anekdot, mif i skazka: Granitsy, razmezhevaniia i neitral'nye polosy." *Studia Russica Helsingiensia et Tartuensia. VI. Problema granitsy v kul'ture,* 295–304. Tartu, Estonia: 1998.

———. *Literaturnyi anekdot pushkinskoi epokhi.* Ph.D. Diss., University of Helsinki. Slavica Helsingiensia 15. Helsinki: Helsinki University Press, 1995.

———. *Pokhval'noe slovo anekdotu.* St. Petersburg: Izdatel'stvo Zhurnala "Zvezda," 2001.

———. "'U nas byla i est' ustnaia literatura . . .'" In Kurganov and Okhotin, 3–6.

Kurganov, Efim, and N. Okhotin, comps. *Russkii literaturnyi anekdot kontsa XVIII–nachala XIX veka.* Moscow: Khudozhestvennaia literatura, 1990.

Kurganov, N. G. *Pis'movnik.* 1769.

Kurti, Laszlo. "The Politics of Joking: Popular Response to Chernobyl." *Journal of American Folklore* 101.401 (1988): 324–34.

Kuskova, E. "Vospominanie." *Sovremennye zapiski* 12 (1922): 147.

Kux, Sally. *On the Boundary of Life and Literature: The Anecdote in Early Nineteenth-Century Russia.* Ph.D. diss., Stanford, Calif.: Stanford University Press, 1994.

Lane, Christel. *The Rites of Rulers: Ritual in Industrial Society—The Soviet Case.* Cambridge: Cambridge University Press, 1981.

Larsen, Egon. *Wit as a Weapon: The Political Joke in History.* London: Frederick Muller, 1980.

Latynina, Julia. "New Folklore and Newspeak." In Berry and Miller-Pogacar, 79–90.

Lebed,' Ol'ga. "Sem'ia v neformal'noi narodnoi kul'ture." Unpublished article. 1998.

Lebedev, G., ed. *Luchshie anekdoty.* Moscow: FAIR, 1996.

Lendvai, Endre. *Pragmalingvisticheskie mekhanizmy sovremennogo russkogo anekdota.* Ph.D. diss., Gosudarstvennyi Institut Russkogo Iazyka Im, A. S. Pushkina. St. Petersburg, Russia: 2001.

———. "Sistemnyi analiz russkogo anekdota." In *Textsemantik und Textstilistik,* ed. Herbert Jelitte and Jarosław Wierzbiński. Frankfurt am Main: Peter Lang, 1999, 251–66.

Levchik, D. A. "Politicheskii 'kheppenning.'" *Sotsiologicheskie issledovaniia* 8 (1996): 51–56.

Levinson, Aleksei. "Chego starye intelligenty ne dali 'New Russians.'" *Iskusstvo kino* 1 (1995): 28–33.

———. "Neskol'ko zamechanii po sotsiologii anekdota v sviazi s novymi knigami ob etnicheskom i politicheskom iumore." Review of *Taking Penguins to the Movies* by Emil Draitser and *Sotsiologiia politicheskogo iumora* by Anatolii Dmitriev. *Novoe literaturnoe obozrenie* 37 (1999): 369–81.

———. "'Novye russkie' i ikh sosedi po anekdoticheskim kontekstam (vmesto poslesloviia k publikatsii)." *Novoe literaturnoe obozrenie* 22 (1996): 383–85.

Likhachev, D. S. "Smekh kak mirovozzrenie." In D. S. Likhachev, *Istoricheskaia poetika russkoi literatury: Smekh kak mirovozzrenie i drugie raboty.* St. Petersburg: Aleteiia, 1997, 342–403.

Lipovetsky, Mark. "New Russians as a Cultural Myth." *Russian Review* 62.1 (Jan. 2003): 54–71.

Lipovetskii, Mark. "Prezident Shtirlits." *Iskusstvo kino* 11 (2000): 73–76.

———. "Skazkovlast': 'Tarakanishche' Stalina." *Novoe literaturnoe obozrenie* 45 (2000): 122–36.

Listov, Viktor. "Revoliutsiia molodaia: 1917–1927." *Literaturnaia gazeta,* July 13, 1988: 12.

Lunacharskii, A. V. "O smekhe." *Literaturnyi kritik* 4 (1935): 3–9.

Lur'e, Vadim. "Detskii anekdot." *Fol'klor i postfol'klor: struktura, tipologiia, semiotika.* May 29, 2002. http://www.ruthenia.ru/folklore/luriev4.htm.

———. *Our Secret Allies: The Peoples of Russia.* New York: Duell, Sloan and Pearce, 1953.

———. "Zhizn,' smert' i bessmertie Vasiliia Chapaeva." *Nezavisimaia gazeta,* Feb. 9, 1991: 8.

Lyons, Eugene. *Moscow Carousel.* New York: 1937.

Makarov, Dmitrii. "Natsii v zerkale anekdota." *Argumenty i fakty* 4.953 (Jan. 1999): 15.

Malinowski, Bronislaw. "Myth in Primitive Psychology." In Bronislaw Malinowski, *Magic, Science, and Religion and Other Essays.* Boston: Beacon, 1948, 84.

Mandel'shtam, Osip. "Den' stoial o piati golovakh . . ." In Osip Mandel'shtam, *Sochineniia v dvukh tomakh. Tom 1: Stikhotvoreniia, perevody.* Tula: Filin, 1994, 163–64.

Marshall, Bonnie. "Images of Women in Soviet Jokes and Anecdotes." *Journal of Popular Culture* 26.2 (Fall 1992): 117–25.

Masakov, Ivan Filippovich. *Russkie satiro-iumoristicheskie zhurnaly (Bibliograficheskoe opisanie).* Vladimir: Tipografiia Gubernskogo Pravleniia, 1910.

Matizen, Viktor. "Steb kak fenomen kul'tury." *Iskusstvo kino* 9 (1993): 59–62.

Medvedev, Roi. Interview with Aleksandr Klimov. Ekho Moskvy Radio. March 5,

2003. Johnson's Russia List. Aug. 13, 2003. http://www.cdi.org/russia/johnson/ 7098a.cfm##9.

Meletinskii, Eleazar Moiseevich. *Geroi volshebnoi skazki. Proiskhozhdenie obraza.* Moscow: Vostochnaia literatura, 1958.

———. *Istoricheskaia poetika novelly.* Moscow: Nauka, 1990.

———. "Malye zhanry fol'klora i problemy zhanrovoi evoliutsii v ustnoi traditsii." In *Malye formy fol'klora: Sbornik statei pamiati Grigoriia L'vovicha Permiakova,* comp. T. N. Sveshnikova. Moscow: Vostochnaia literatura, 1995, 325–37.

———. "Skazka-anekdot v sisteme fol'klornykh zhanrov." In Belousov, *Uchebnyi material,* 59–76.

Memetov, V. S., and A. A. Danilov. "Intelligentsiia Rossii: Uroki istorii i sovremennost' (Popytka istoriograficheskogo analiza problemy)." In *Intelligentsiia Rossii: Uroki istorii i sovremennost': Mezhvuzovskii sbornik nauchnykh trudov,* ed. V. S. Memetov. Ivanovo: Ivanovskii gosudarstvennyi universitet, 1996, 3–15.

Metlina, Ekaterina. "Vandaloustoichivyi iumor." *Stolitsa* 3 (1997): 66.

Miasoedov, Boris. *O khamstve i stervoznosti v russkoi zhizni.* Moscow: Russkaia entsiklopediia, 1998.

Mickiewicz, Ellen. *Split Signals: Television and Politics in the Soviet Union.* New York: Oxford University Press, 1988.

Milne, A. A. *Winnie-the-Pooh.* New York: E. P. Dutton, 1926.

Mironov, Aleksandr. "Strana golubykh prostorov (Vmesto predisloviia)." In Aleksandr Mironov, *Chukotskie novelly.* 2nd ed. Arkhangel'sk: Severnoe izdatel'stvo, 1937, 3–6.

Moiseev, L., and A. Bragin, comps. *Oskolki: Mozaika russkogo iumora.* Moscow: Sovremennyi pisatel', 1993.

Moldavskii, Dmitrii M., ed. and comp. *Russkaia satiricheskaia skazka v zapisiakh serediny XIX–nachala XX veka.* Moscow: Akademiia nauk Soiuza sovetskikh sotsialisticheskikh respublik, 1955.

———. *Tovarishch Smekh.* Leningrad: Lenizdat, 1981.

———. "Vasilii Berezaiskii i ego 'Anekdoty drevnykh poshekhontsev.'" In Moldavskii, *Russkaia satiricheskaia skazka,* 236–45.

Morreall, John, ed. *The Philosophy of Laughter and Humor.* Albany: State University of New York Press, 1987.

Moshkin, S. V., and V. N. Rudenko. "Children's Political Jokes." *Russian Education and Society* 38.9 (Sept. 1996): 69–79.

Mozheitov, Dmitry. "New Russians at Large." *Russia Journal* 30.73 (Aug. 5, 2000). http://www.russiajournal.com/ls/article.shtml?ad=992, accessed Sept. 29, 2001.

Muratov, L. "Uroki legendarnogo fil'ma." *Neva* 12 (1984): 169–75.

Muschard, Jutta. "Jokes and Their Relation to Relevance and Cognition or Can

Relevance Theory Account for the Appreciation of Jokes?" *Zeitschrift für Anglistik und Amerikanistik* 47.1 (1999): 12–23.

Myerhoff, Barbara. "Life History Among the Elderly: Performance, Visibility, and Remembering." In Ruby 99–117.

Myerhoff, Barbara, and Jay Ruby. "Introduction." In Ruby 1–35.

Navon, David. "The Seemingly Appropriate but Virtually Inappropriate: Notes on Characteristics of Jokes." *Poetics* 17.3 (June 1988): 207–19.

Nekliudov, Sergei Iur'evich. "Posle fol'klora." *Zhivaia starina* 1 (1995): 2–4.

Nemzer, Andrei. "Desiat' bukv po vertikali." In Aleksei Slapovskii, *Anketa.* St. Petersburg: Kurs, 1997, 3–6.

Nenarokov, A. P., R. M. Gainullina, V. S. Gornyi, and A. I. Ushakov, comps. *Iaichnitsa vsmiatku, ili Neser'ezno o ser'eznom. Nad kem i nad chem smeialis' v Rossii v 1917 godu.* Moscow: Britanskii Biznes Klub, 1992.

Nerush, V., and M. Pavlov. "Shepotom iz-za ugla." *Komsomol'skaia Pravda,* Oct. 15, 1982: 4.

Nevskaia, V. A. "'. . . Dnei minuvshikh anekdoty.'" *Russkaia rech'* 5 (1992): 78–84.

Nevskii, Aleksei, comp. "Staryi anekdot." *Rodina* 7 (1990): 24–25.

Nichiporovich, Tat'iana Gennad'evna, comp. *Anekdoty iz Anglii.* Minsk: Literatura, 1998.

———. *Anekdoty iz Italii.* Minsk: Literatura, 1998.

———. *Anekdoty iz komp'iuternykh setei.* Minsk: Literatura, 1998.

———. *Anekdoty iz restorana.* Minsk: Literatura, 1998.

———. *Anekdoty iz teleekrana.* Minsk: Literatura, 1997.

———. *Anekdoty iz togo sveta.* Minsk: Literatura, 1998.

———. *Anekdoty iz tsirka.* Minsk: Literatura, 1998.

———. *Anekdoty o banditakh.* Minsk: Literatura, 1998.

———. *Anekdoty o chainikakh.* Minsk: Literatura, 1997.

———. *Anekdoty o Chapaeve i Shtirlitse.* Minsk: Literatura, 1997.

———. *Anekdoty o den'gakh.* Minsk: Literatura, 1998.

———. *Anekdoty o evreiiakh i ne evreiakh.* Minsk: Literatura, 1997.

———. *Anekdoty o kriminal'nom mire.* Minsk: Literatura, 1997.

———. *Anekdoty o liubvi.* Minsk: Literatura, 1997.

———. *Anekdoty o militsionerakh i politseiskikh.* Minsk: Literatura, 1997.

———. *Anekdoty o muzh'iakh i liubovnitsakh.* Minsk: Literatura, 1997.

———. *Anekdoty o novykh russkikh.* Minsk: Literatura, 1997.

———. *Anekdoty o Piatachke, Il'e Muromtse i Babe Iage.* Minsk: Literatura, 1997.

———. *Anekdoty o politikakh.* Minsk: Literatura, 1997.

———. *Anekdoty o russkikh i ne russkikh.* Minsk: Literatura, 1998.

———. *Anekdoty o velikikh figurakh.* Minsk: Literatura, 1997.

———. *Anekdoty o veruiushchikh i neveruiushchikh.* Minsk: Literatura, 1998.

———. *Anekdoty o Vovochke.* Minsk: Literatura, 1997.

———. *Anekdoty o vrachakh.* Minsk: Literatura, 1997.

———. *Anekdoty ob alkogolikakh i narkomanakh.* Minsk: Literatura, 1997.

———. *Anekdoty ob angliiskikh lordakh.* Minsk: Literatura, 1997.

———. *Anekdoty ob armii.* Minsk: Literatura, 1998.

———. *Anekdoty ob intelligentsii.* Minsk: Literatura, 1997.

———. *Anekdoty ob okhotnikakh, rybakakh i sportsmenakh.* Minsk: Literatura, 1998.

———. *Anekdoty rifmuiushchie i nerifmuiushchie.* Minsk: Literatura, 1997.

———. *Chernyi iumor.* Minsk: Literatura, 1998.

———. *Literaturnye anekdoty.* Minsk: Literatura, 1997.

———. *Smekh skvoz' slezy.* Minsk: Literatura, 1998.

Nikiforov, A. I. "Erotika v velikorusskoi narodnoi skazke." *Khudozhestvennyi fol'klor* 4–5 (1929): 120–27.

———. "Skazka, ee bytovanie i nositeli." 1928. *Russkaia fol'kloristika: Khrestomatiia dlia vuzov.* Moscow: Vysshaia shkola, 1965, 344–57.

Nikulin, Iurii, comp. *Anekdoty ot Nikulina.* Moscow: Binom/Gudwin-3, 1997.

Nilsen, Don Lee Fred. *Humor Scholarship: A Research Bibliography.* Westport, Conn.: Greenwood, 1993.

Novik, E. S. "Struktura skazochnogo triuka." *Ot mifa k literature: Sbornik v chest' semidesiatipiatiletiia Eleazara Moiseevicha Meletinskogo.* Moscow: Rossiiskii universitet, 1993, 139–52.

Oinas, Felix J. "Folklore, Study of." In Terras, 139–42.

Oinas, Felix J., and Stephen Soudakoff, eds. *The Study of Russian Folklore.* The Hague: Mouton, 1975.

Olearius, Adam. *The Travels of Olearius in Seventeenth-Century Russia.* Trans. and ed. Samuel H. Baron. Stanford, Calif.: Stanford University Press, 1967.

Olin, Nikolai, comp. *Govorit "Radio Erevan": Izbrannye voprosy i otvety.* 2nd ed. Brazzaville, Republic of the Congo: Logos, 1970.

———. *"Radio Erevan" prodolzhaet govorit' i nachinaet pokazyvat': Samye otbornye izbrannye i pereizbrannye voprosy i otvety.* N.p.: Vamizdat, 1975.

Ong, Walter J. *Orality and Literacy: The Technologizing of the Word.* London: Routledge, 1982.

Oring, Elliott. *Engaging Humor.* Urbana: University of Illinois Press, 2003.

Orwell, George. "Funny, But Not Vulgar." *As I Please: 1943–1945.* Vol. 3 of *The Collected Essays, Journalism and Letters of George Orwell,* ed. Sonia Orwell and Ian Angus. 4 vols. New York: Harcourt Brace Jovanovich, 1968.

"Osnovnye zadachi sovetskoi etnografii v svete reshenii XXII S"ezda KPSS." *Sovetskaia etnografiia* 6 (1961): 3–8.

Otto, Beatrice K. *Fools Are Everywhere: The Court Jester Around the World.* Chicago: University of Chicago Press, 2001.

Paimen, V., comp. *Chapai: Sbornik narodnykh pesen, skazok, rasskazov i vospominanii o legendarnom geroe grazhdanskoi voiny V. I. Chapaeve.* Moscow: Sovetskii pisatel', 1938.

Paperny, Zinovy. "Today and Always: The Role of Jokes in Russian Humor." *The World & I* 8.1 (Jan. 1993): 652–63.

Parfenov, Leonid. *Namedni-72.* NTV, 1998.

Parkin, John. *Humour Theorists of the Twentieth Century.* Lewiston, N.Y.: Edwin Mellen Press, 1997.

Pasternak, Boris. *Doktor Zhivago.* Milan: Feltrinelli, 1957.

Paton, George E. C., Chris Powell, and Stephen Wagg, eds. *The Social Faces of Humour: Practices and Issues.* Aldershot, England, and Brookfield, Vt.: Arena/Ashgate, 1996.

Patterson, Galina. *The Buffoon in Nineteenth and Twentieth Century Russian Literature: The Literary Model and Its Cultural Roots.* Ph.D. Diss., Madison, University of Wisconsin, 1998.

Pearl, Deborah L. *Tales of Revolution: Workers and Propaganda* Skazki *in the Late Nineteenth Century. The Carl Beck Papers in Russian and East European Studies* 1303. Pittsburgh, Pa.: University of Pittsburgh Center for Russian and East European Studies, 1998.

Pelevin, Viktor. *Buddha's Little Finger.* Trans. Andrew Bromfield. New York: Viking, 2000. Originally published as *Chapaev i Pustota* (Moscow: Vagrius, 1996).

Pel'ttser, A. P. "Proiskhozhdenie anekdotov v russkoi narodnoi slovesnosti." *Sbornik khar'kovskogo istoriko-filologicheskogo obshchestva.* Vol. 11. Khar'kov, 1897, 57–117.

Perekhodiuk, O. V. "Iazyk sovremennogo russkogo anekdota." *Russkaia rech'* 5 (1997): 124–27.

Pertsov, V. "Anekdot (Opyt sotsiologicheskogo analiza)." *Novyi Lef* 2 (1927): 41–43.

Petrosian, Evgenii. *Evgenii Petrosian v strane anekdotov.* Moscow: Tsentr Estradnoi Iumoristiki, 1995.

Petrov, Nikolai. "Naedine so vsemi." Interview with Vasilii Golovanov. *Literaturnaia gazeta,* Mar. 1, 1989: 10.

Petrovskii, Miron Semenovich. "Novyi anekdot znaesh'?" *Filosofskaia i sotsiologicheskaia mysl'* 5 (1990): 46–52.

Petukhov, Pavel Romanovich. *Komu zhivetsia veselo, vol'gotno v S. S. S. R.* N.p.: Ezop, 1948.

Plato. *Protagoras, Philebus, and Gorgias.* Trans. Benjamin Jowett. Amherst, N.Y.: Prometheus, 1996.

Polnoe i obstoiatel'noe sobranie podlinnykh istoricheskikh, liubopytnykh, zabavnykh i nravouchitel'nykh anekdotov chetyrekh uveselitel'nykh shutov Balakireva, D'Akosty, Pedrillo i Kul'kovkogo. St. Petersburg: 1869.

Pomorska, Krystyna. "Foreword." In Bakhtin, *Rabelais,* vii–xii.

"Posle stolknoveniia s 'krutoi' inomarkoi voditel' reshil zastrelit'sia." *Lenta.ru,* Mar. 8, 2000. http://www.lenta.ru/Russia/2000/03/08/dtp.

Powell, Chris, and George E. C. Paton, eds. *Humour in Society: Resistance and Control*. New York: St. Martin's, 1988.

Prieto, Abel. *El Humor de Misha: La Crisis del "Socialismo Real" en el Chiste Político*. Buenos Aires: Ediciones Colihue, 1997.

Procopius. *The Secret History*. Trans. G. A. Williamson. Baltimore, Md.: Penguin, 1966.

Procopius. [Prokopii Kesariiskii.] *Voina s persami. Voina s vandalami. Tainaia istoriia*. Trans. and ed. A. A. Chekalova. Moscow: Nauka, 1993.

Program of the Communist Party of the Soviet Union [Draft]. New York: Crosscurrents Press, 1961.

Prokhorov, Aleksandr. "'I Need Some Life-Assertive Character' or How to Die in the Most Inspiring Pose: Bodies in the Stalinist Museum of *Hammer and Sickle*." *Studies in Slavic Cultures* 1 (2000): 28–46.

———. "Laughing/Smiling: Articulating Cultural Values Through Comedy (A Case Study of *Volga, Volga* and *Carnival Night*)." Unpublished article. 1996.

Prokhorova, Elena. *Fragmented Mythologies: Soviet Adventure Mini-Series of the 1970s*. Ph.D. Diss., Pittsburgh, Pa., University of Pittsburgh, 2003.

Propp, Vladimir Iakovlevich. *Problemy komizma i smekha*. 2nd ed. St. Petersburg: Aleteiia, 1997.

Pushkareva, O. V. "Anekdot v sovremennom fol'klornom repertuare: Voprosy bytovaniia i metodiki sobiraniia." *Material mezhdunarodnoi konferentsii 'Fol'klor i sovremennost'' posviashchennoi pamiati professora N. I. Savushkinoi (20–22 oktiabria 1994 goda)*. Moscow: Moskovskii gorodskoi dvorets tvorchestva, 1995, 91–94.

———. "Parodirovanie kak sposob siuzhetno-kompozitsionnoi organizatsii anekdota." *Filologicheskie nauki* 2 (1996): 35–41.

Pushkin, Aleksandr Sergeevich. "Table-Talk." In *Polnoe sobranie sochinenii v dvadtsati tomakh*. Vol. 12. St. Petersburg: Nauka, 1999.

Putilov, B. N., ed. and comp. *Petr Velikii v predaniiakh, legendakh, anekdotakh, skazkakh, pesniakh*. N.p.: Akademicheskii proekt, 2000.

Pypin, A. N. *Ocherk literaturnoi istorii starinnykh povestei i skazok russkikh*. St. Petersburg: 1857.

Rabinovich, E. G. "Ob odnom iz predpolozhitel'nykh istochnikov 'chukotskoi serii.'" In Belousov, *Uchebnyi material*, 100–103.

Raikova, I. N. "Problema klassifikatsii neskazochnoi prozy v istorii nauki." *Nauka o fol'klore segodnia: Mezhdistsiplinarnye vzaimodeistviia k 70-letnemu iubileiu Fedora Martynovicha Selivanova. Mezhdunarodnaia nauchnaia konferentsiia (Moskva 29–31 oktiabria 1997 goda)*. Moscow: Dialog Moskovskogo gosudarstvennogo universiteta, 1998, 209–12.

Rancour-Laferriere, Daniel. *The Slave Soul of Russia: Moral Masochism and the Cult of Suffering*. New York: New York University Press, 1995.

Raskin, Iosif. *Entsiklopediia khuliganstvuiushchego ortodoksa: Rasshirennoe i dopolnennoe izdanie.* Moscow: Stook, 1997.

Raskin, Victor. *Semantic Mechanisms of Humor.* Dordrecht, Holland: D. Reidel, 1985.

Rassadin, Stanislav. "Anekdot—da i tol'ko?" *Novaia gazeta* 51.523 (Dec. 28, 1998–Jan. 3, 1999): 15.

Razuvaev, Vladimir Vital'evich. *Politicheskii smekh v sovremennoi Rossii.* Moscow: Gosudarstvennyi universitet–Vysshaia shkola ekonomiki, 2002.

Reinche, N. "Antidote to Dominance: Women's Laughter as Counteraction." *Journal of Popular Culture* 24.4 (1991): 27–39.

Ries, Nancy. *Russian Talk: Culture and Conversation During Perestroika.* Ithaca, N.Y.: Cornell University Press, 1997.

Rogov, K. N. "O proekte 'Rossiia/Russia'—1970-e gody." In Rogov, *Semidesiatye,* 7–11.

———, ed. and comp. *Semidesiatye kak predmet istorii russkoi kul'ture. Rossiia/Russia* 1(9). Moscow: Ob"edinennoe Gumanitarnoe Izdatel'stvo, 1998.

Romanov, Sergei. *Usypal'nitsa: Biografiia sovetskikh 'tsarei' v anekdotakh.* Moscow: IRLE, 1994.

Ruby, Jay, ed. *A Crack in the Mirror: Reflexive Perspectives in Anthropology.* Philadelphia: University of Pennsylvania Press, 1982.

Rudnev, Vadim Petrovich. "Pragmatika anekdota." *Daugava* 6 (1990): 99–102.

———. *Slovar' kul'tury XX veka.* Moscow: Agraf, 1997.

———. *Vinni Pukh i filosofiia obydennogo iazyka.* 3rd ed. Moscow: Agraf, 2000.

Rufeev, B., et al., comps. *Anekdoty o novykh russkikh. Pal'tsy veerom.* St. Petersburg: DiK, 1997.

Ruksenas, Algis. *Is That You Laughing, Comrade? The World's Best Russian (Underground) Jokes.* Ill. George Kocar. Secaucus, N.J.: Citadel, 1986.

Saadetdinov, Rinat, and Donna Finch. *From Russia With . . . Laughter! The Official Book of Russian Humor.* St. Petersburg, Fla.: Southern Heritage Press, 1996.

Sabitova, M. R. "Molodezhnaia ustnaia kul'tura." In *Material mezhdunarodnoi konferentsii 'Fol'klor i posviashchennoi pamiati professora N. I. Savushkinoi (20–22 oktiabria 1994 goda).* Moscow: Moskovskii gorodskoi dvorets tvorchestva, 1995, 83–86.

Saltykov-Shchedrin, Mikhail. *Poshekhonskaia starina.* Moscow: Gosudarstvennoe izdatel'stvo Khudozhestvennoi literatury, 1959.

———. "Poshekhonskie rasskazy." In Mikhail Saltykov-Shchedrin, *Sobranie sochinenii.* Vol. 11. Moscow: Pravda, 1951.

Sannikov, Vladimir Zinov'evich. *Russkii iazyk v zerkale iazykovoi igry.* Moscow: Iazyki russkoi kul'tury, 1999.

Savushkina, N. I. "Poetika komicheskogo v russkoi bytovoi skazke." *Prozaicheskie zhanry fol'klora narodov SSSR: Tezisy dokladov na Vsesoiuznoi nauchnoi konferentsii. 21–23 maia 1974. Gor. Minsk.* Minsk: Akademiia nauk Soiuza sovetskikh sotsialisticheskikh respublik, 1974, 171–74.

Schechner, Richard. "Collective Reflexivity: Restoration of Behavior." In Ruby, 39–81.

Schopenhauer, Arthur. *Die welt als Wille und Vorstellung.* 1819. Translated as *The World as Will and Representation* by E. F. J. Payne. New York: Dover, 1966.

Schutz, Charles E. *Political Humor: From Aristophanes to Sam Ervin.* Cranbury, N.J.: Associated University Presses, 1977.

Sedov, Aleksei Fedorovich. *Politicheskii anekdot kak iavlenie kul'tury: Populiarnyi ocherk. Vesy* 11. Balashov: Balashovskii filial Saratovskogo gosudarstvennogo universiteta, 1999.

Sedov, Konstantin Fedorovich. *Osnovy psikholingvistiki v anekdotakh.* Moscow: Labirint, 1998.

Sevriukov, Dmitrii. "Interesnoe kino: Etot neotrazimyi Chapaev!" *Speed-Info,* Sept. 1998: 2.

Shaitanov, I. "Mezhdu eposom i anekdotom." *Literaturnoe obozrenie* 1 (1995): 18–20.

Shcherbak, Iurii. "Chernobyl': Dokumental'naia povest'.' Kniga vtoraia." *Iunost'* 9 (1988): 5–16.

Sheffer, P. N. *Sbornik Kirzhi Danilova.* St. Petersburg: 1901.

Shinkarchuk, Sergei Alekseevich, comp. *Istoriia Sovetskoi Rossii (1917–1953) v anekdotakh.* St. Petersburg: Nestor, 2000.

Shklovskii, Viktor. "K teorii komicheskogo." *Epopeia: Literaturnyi ezhemesiachnik pod redaktsiei Andreia Belogo* 3 (1922): 57–67.

Shmeleva, Elena Iakovlevna. "Anekdoty ob armianskom radio: Struktura i iazykovye osobennosti." *Fol'klor i postfol'klor: struktura, tipologiia, semiotika.* Nov. 29, 2002. http://www.ruthenia.ru/folklore/shmeleva1.htm.

Shmeleva, Elena Iakovlevna, and Aleksei Dmitrievich Shmelev. *Russkii anekdot: Tekst i rechevoi zhanr.* Moscow: Iazyki slavianskoi kul'tury, 2002.

Shoubinsky, Sergy N. "Court Jesters and Their Weddings in the Reigns of Peter the Great and Anna Ivanovna." In H. D. Romanoff, *Historical Narratives from the Russian.* London: Rivingtons, 1871, 1–47.

Shturman, Dora, and Sergei Tiktin, comps. and eds. *Sovetskii soiuz v zerkale politicheskogo anekdota.* London: Overseas Publications Interchange, 1985.

"Shutki i potekhi Petra Velikogo (Petr I—kak iumorist)." *Russkaia starina* 5 (1872): 881.

Shutki russkoi zhizni. Berlin: Hugo Steinitz verlag, 1903. St. Petersburg: Index, 1991.

Sidel'nikov, V. M. "Ideino-khudozhestvennaia spetsifika russkogo narodnogo anekdota." *Voprosy literaturovedeniia* 1. Moscow: Universitet druzhby narodov im. P. Lamumby, 1964, 21–50.

———. *Krasnoarmeiskii fol'klor.* Moscow: Sovetskii pisatel', 1938.

Siegle, Robert. *The Politics of Reflexivity: Narrative and the Constitutive Poetics of Culture.* Baltimore, Md.: Johns Hopkins University Press, 1986.

Sigmund Freud Museum. "'My Old and Dirty Gods': From Sigmund Freud's Collection." Sept. 16, 2003. http://www.freud-museum.at/e/inhalt/museum ausstellungenGoetter.htm.

Simms, Norman. *The Humming Tree: A Study in the History of Mentalities.* Urbana: University of Illinois Press, 1992.

Skalova, Libena. "K voprosu o roli anekdota v khudozhestvennoi proze (Rasskazy Podporuchik Kizhe i Maloletnii Vitushishnikov Iuriia Tynianova)." *Československá rusistika* 21.3 (1976): 106–9.

Slutskii, Boris. "Anekdoty o Staline let cherez mnogo. . ." In Boris Slutskii, *Sobranie sochinenii v trekh tomakh. Tom 3: Stikhotvoreniia 1972–1977.* Moscow: Khudozhestvennaia literatura, 1991.

———. "Mesto gosudarstva v zhizni lichnosti. . ." In Boris Slutskii, *Sobranie sochinenii v trekh tomakh. Tom 1: Stikhotvoreniia 1939–1961.* Moscow: Khudozhestvennaia literatura, 1991.

Smetanin, V., and K. Donskaia, comps. and eds. *Anekdoty o narodnykh geroiakh (Chapaev, Shtirlits, Chukcha). Polnoe sobranie anekdotov* 8. Moscow: DataStrom, 1994.

Smirnov, S. I., ed. *Iumor i satira: Repertuarnyi sbornik.* Moscow: Voennoe izdatel'stvo Ministerstva oborony SSSR, 1958.

Smith, Hedrick. *The New Russians.* New York: Random House, 1990.

Smolitskaia, Ol'ga V. "'Anekdoty o frantsuzakh': K probleme sistematizatsii i strukturno-tipologicheskogo izucheniia anekdota." *Novoe literaturnoe obozrenie* 22 (1996): 386–92.

———. "Performans kak zhanroobrazuiushchii element sovetskogo anekdota." *Fol'klor i postfol'klor: struktura, tipologiia, semiotika,* Dec. 1, 2002. http://www.ruthenia.ru/folklore/smolitskaya1.htm.

Sokolov, Iu. M. *Barin i muzhik.* Moscow: Akademiia, 1932.

———. *Pop i muzhik.* Moscow: Akademiia, 1931.

———. *Russian Folklore.* Trans. Catherine Ruth Smith. Introduction by Felix J. Oinas. Detroit: Folklore Associates, 1971. Trans. of *Russkii fol'klor,* 1938.

Sokolov, Iurii. "Vernyi anekdot." *Zhurnalist* 4 (1991): 94–95.

Sokolov, K. B. "Gorodskoi fol'klor protiv ofitsial'noi kartiny mira." In Neia Zorkaia et al., *Khudozhestvennaia zhizn',* 225–51.

Sokolov-Mitrich, Dmitrii. "Proshchanie s malinovym pidzhakom: Novye pesni o 'novykh russkikh,' ob ikh podvigakh i slave." *Ogonek* 7 (4634) (Feb. 2000): 24–31.

Sokolova, Nataliia. "Iz starykh tetradei 1935–1937." *Voprosy literatury* 2 (1997): 345–64.

———. "V zerkale smekha: Literaturno-teatral'nyi iumor pervoi poloviny 30-x godov." *Voprosy literatury* 3 (1996): 362–75.

Sorokin, Vladimir. "'V kul'ture dlia menia net tabu. . .': Vladimir Sorokin ot-vechaet na voprosy Sergeiia Shapovala." In Vladimir Sorokin, *Sobranie sochinenii v dvukh tomakh.* Vol. 1. Moscow: Ad Marginem, 1998, 7–20.

"Sovremennyi sovetskii anekdot." *Volia Rossii,* 1925.

Spencer, Herbert. "Physiology of Laughter." In Herbert Spencer, *Essays, Scientific, Political, and Speculative.* Vol. 2. New York: Appleton, 1891, 452–66.

Stalin, Joseph. *Concerning Marxism in Linguistics.* London: Soviet News, 1950.

Stepniak. "Introduction." *The Humour of Russia.* Trans. E. L. Voynich. Ill. Paul Frenzeny. London: Walter Scott; New York: Charles Scribner's Sons, 1895.

Stewart, Susan. *Nonsense: Aspects of Intertextuality in Folklore and Literature.* Baltimore, Md.: Johns Hopkins University Press, 1979.

———. "Some Riddles and Proverbs of Textuality: An Essay in Literary Value and Evaluation." *Criticism* 21.2 (Spring 1979): 93–105.

Stites, Richard. *Russian Popular Culture: Entertainment and Society Since 1900.* Cambridge: Cambridge University Press, 1992.

Stokker, Kathleen. *Folklore Fights the Nazis: Humor in Occupied Norway, 1940–1945.* Cranbury, N.J.: Associated University Presses, 1995.

Stolovich, Leonid. "Anekdot kak zerkalo nashei evoliutsii." *Izvestiia,* Mar. 20, 1993: 10.

———, comp. *Evrei shutiat: Evreiskie anekdoty, ostroty i aforizmy o evreiiakh, sobrannye Leonidom Stolovichem.* 3rd ed. St. Petersburg: Lenizdat, 1999.

Storer, Edward. "Introduction." In Bracciolini, 1–32.

Strelianyi, Anatolii, Genrikh Sapgir, Vladimir Bakhtin, and Nikita Ordynskii, comps. *Samizdat veka.* Minsk/Moscow: Polifakt, 1997.

Sturman, Dora. "Soviet Joking Matters: Six Leaders in Search of Character." *Survey* 28.3 (Autumn 1984): 205–20.

Sumtsov, N. F. "Anekdoty o gluptsakh." *Sbornik khar'kovskogo istoriko-filologicheskogo obshchestva.* Vol. 11. Khar'kov: Kharkovskoe istoriko-filologicheskoe obshchestvo, 1897, 118–315.

Takhmasiba, M., comp. *Anekdoty Molly Nasredina.* Trans. from Azerbaijani. Moscow: Goslitizdat, 1962.

Taylor, Richard, and Ian Christie, eds. *The Film Factory: Russian and Soviet Cinema in Documents.* Trans. Richard Taylor. Cambridge, Mass.: Harvard University Press, 1988.

Telesin, Iulis, ed. *1001 izbrannyi sovetskii politicheskii anekdot.* Tenafly, N.J.: Ermitazh, 1986.

Terras, Victor. *Handbook of Russian Literature.* New Haven, Conn.: Yale University Press, 1985.

Terts, Abram (Andrei Siniavskii). "Anekdot v anekdote." *Sintaksis* 1 (1978): 77–95.

Thurston, Robert W. "Social Dimensions of Stalinist Rule: Humor and Terror in the USSR, 1935–1941." *Journal of Social History* 24.3 (Spring 1991): 541–62.

Timofeev, M. Iu. "Rzhevskii, Chapaev, Shtirlits: Natsional'nye i gendernye kharakteristiki voennykh v sovetskikh anekdotakh." *Doklady Pervoi Mezhdunarodnoi konferentsii "Gender: Iazyk, kul'tura, kommunikatsiia,"* 25–26 *noiabria 1999 goda.* Moscow: Moskovskii gosudarstvennyi lingvisticheskii universitet, 2001, 321–28.

Tiupa, V. I. "Novella i apolog." In *Russkaia novella: Problemy teorii i istorii,* ed. V. M. Markovich and V. Shmid. St. Petersburg: Izdatel'stvo Sanktpeterburgskogo universiteta, 1993, 13–25.

Tkhorov, Vladimir, comp. *Kstati, o . . . : Sbornik anekdotov.* Kishinev: Periodika, 1990.

Trakhtenberg, Roman. "Roman Trakhtenberg, Anekdotolog, ili Kak zarabotat' 'Mersedes' s pomoshch'iu naroda." Interview with Sasha Ivanskii. *Ogonek* 11 (Mar. 2001): 54–55.

Trykova, Ol'ga Iur'evna. *Sovremennyi detskii fol'klor i ego vzaimodeistvie s khudozhestvennoi literaturoi.* Iaroslavl': Iaroslavskii gosudarstvennyi pedagogicheskii universitet im K. D. Ushinskogo, 1997. Tsarev, Vadim. "Novye uzkie." *Iskusstvo kino* 1 (1995): 38–42.

Tuska, John. *Dark Cinema: American Film Noir in Cultural Perspective.* Westport, Conn.: Greenwood, 1984.

Utekhin, I. V. "Ob anekdotakh i chuvstve iumora u detei." Unpublished article. 1999.

Vail,' Petr, and Aleksandr Genis. *60-e. Mir sovetskogo cheloveka.* Moscow: Novoe literaturnoe obozrenie, 1998.

———. "Strana slov." *Novyi mir* 4 (1991): 239–51.

Vasil'eva, O. V., and S. B. Riukhina. "Anekdot i chastushka (Slovesnyi tekst kak sposob povedeniia)." In Belousov, *Uchebnyi material,* 95–99.

Vasmer, Max. *Etimologicheskii slovar' russkogo iazyka.* Trans. O. N. Trubacheva. Ed. B. A. Larina. Moscow: Progress, 1964.

Vavilova, M. A. *Russkaia bytovaia skazka: Uchebnoe posobie k spetskursu.* Vologda: Vologodskii gosudarstvennyi pedagogicheskii institut, 1984.

Verner, Artur, comp. *Rossiia smeetsia nad SSSR. Chitaite anekdoty! Smotrite! Smeites'!* Paris: Ritm, 1980.

Verner, Dima. *Anekdoty iz Rossii.* http://www.anekdot.ru.

Viren, V. N. *Frontovoi iumor.* Moscow: Voennoe Izdatel'stvo Ministerstva oborony SSSR, 1970.

Visani, Federica. "Poruchik Rzhevskii: Rozhdenie prototeksta kak aktualizatsiia starogo siuzheta." Unpublished article. 2002.

Vishevsky, Anatoly. *Soviet Literary Culture in the 1970s: The Politics of Irony.* Gainesville: University Press of Florida, 1993.

Vishnevskii, Anatolii. *Serp i rubl': Konservativnaia modernizatsiia v SSSR.* Moscow: Ob"edinennoe Gumanitarnoe Izdatel'stvo, 1998.

Vlasova, Z. I. "Skomorokhi i fol'klor." *Etnograficheskie istoki fol'klornykh iavlenii. Russkii fol'klor* 24. Leningrad: Nauka, 1987, 44–64.

Vogel, Susan C. *Humor: A Semiogenetic Approach.* Bochum, West Germany: Studienverlag Brockmeyer, 1989.

Voinovich, Vladimir. *Antisovetskii Sovetskii Soiuz: Dokumental'naia fantasmagoriia v 4-kh chastiakh.* Moscow: Materik, 2002.

———. *Zhizn' i neobychainye prikliucheniia soldata Ivana Chonkina: Roman-anekdot v piati chastiakh.* Paris: Young Men's Christian Association Press, 1975.

Volkov, A. D., comp. *Zavetnye chastushki v dvukh tomakh iz sobraniia A. D. Volkova.* Ed. A. V. Kulagina. Moscow: Ladomir, 1999.

Vol'pert, L. I. "Pokhval'noe slovo anekdotu." Review of Efim Kurganov, *Literaturnyi anekdot pushkinskoi epokhi. Russkaia literatura* 4 (1996): 202–3.

Voltaire. *Anecdotes sur le czar Pierre le Grand.* 1748. Oxford: Voltaire Foundation, 1999.

von Geldern, James, and Richard Stites, eds. *Mass Culture in Soviet Russia: Tales, Poems, Songs, Movies, Plays, and Folklore, 1917–1953.* Bloomington: Indiana University Press, 1995.

Voznesenskii, A. V. "O sovremennom anekdotopechatanii." *Novoe literaturnoe obozrenie* 22 (1996): 393–99.

Vsemirnyi klub odessitov. Sept. 1, 2003. http://www.odessitclub.org/club/images_president/zhvanetsky-400.jpg.

Wade, Terence. "Russian Folklore and Soviet Humour." *Journal of Russian Studies* 54 (1988): 3–20.

Webb, Ronald G. "Political Uses of Humor." *Et cetera* 38.1 (Spring 1981): 35–50.

Weiss, Halina. "*Draznilkas*—Russian Children's Taunts." *Slavic and East European Folklore Association Journal* 4.2 (Spring 1999): 35–46.

Welsford, Enid. *The Fool: His Social and Literary History.* London: Faber and Faber, 1935.

Wierzbicka, Anna. "Antitotalitarian Language in Poland: Some Mechanisms of Linguistic Self-Defense." *Language in Society* 19.1 (Mar. 1990): 1–59.

———. *Cross-Cultural Pragmatics: The Semantics of Human Interaction.* Berlin: Mouton de Gruyter, 1991.

Williams, Carol J. "A New Class of Laughingstock." *Los Angeles Times*, May 22, 1998: E1.

Williamson, G. A. "Introduction." In Procopius, 7–35.

Wilson, Christopher P. *Jokes: Form, Content, Use and Function.* London: Academic Press, 1979.

Yurchak, Aleksei. "The Cynical Reason of Late Socialism: Power, Pretense and the *Anekdot.*" *Public Culture* 9 (1997): 161–88.

———. "Russian Neoliberal: The Entrepreneurial Ethic and the Spirit of 'True Careerism.'" *Russian Review* 62 (Jan. 2003): 72–90.

Zabolotskikh, D. "Skazka sovetskogo vremeni." *Iskusstvo kino* 10 (1998): 82–86.

Zamost'ianov, Arsenii. "Pristrastie k anekdotam s borodoi." Review of Vladimir Sorokin, *Tridtsataia liubov' Mariny: Roman. Znamia* 6 (1996): 226–28.

Zand, Arie, comp. *Political Jokes of Leningrad.* Austin, Tx.: Silvergirl, 1982.

Zguta, Russell. *Russian Minstrels: A History of the* Skomorokhi. Philadelphia: University of Pennsylvania Press, 1978.

Zhuravlev, V. V. "Predislovie." In Nenarokov, 3–14.

Zhvanetskii, Mikhail. "Beregite biurokratov." In Zhvanetskii, *Sobranie proizvedenii,* Vol. 1, 159–62.

———. "Bronia moia!" In Zhvanetskii, *Sobranie proizvedenii,* Vol. 3, 358–61.

———. "Defitsit." In Zhvanetskii, *Sobranie proizvedenii,* Vol. 1, 202–4.

———. *God za dva.* Leningrad: Leningradskii komitet literatorov, 1991.

———. "Ikh den'." In Zhvanetskii, *Sobranie proizvedenii,* Vol. 2, 88–89.

———. "Klub kinoputeshestviia." In Zhvanetskii, *Sobranie proizvedenii,* Vol. 2, 316–21.

———. *Moia Odessa.* Moscow: Olimp PPP, 1993.

———. "Normal'no, Grigorii! Otlichno, Konstantin!" In Zhvanetskii, *Sobranie proizvedenii,* Vol. 2, 209–12.

———. "Pishushchemu i pokazyvaiushchemu." *Moskovskie novosti,* Sept. 18–25, 2000: 1.

———. "Pod davleniem iumor rozhdaetsia vnutri." *Ogonek* 13 (Mar. 1998): 42.

———. "Sobranie na likerovodochnom zavode." In Zhvanetskii, *Sobranie proizvedenii,* Vol. 2, 142–48.

———. *Sobranie proizvedenii v 4 tomakh.* 4 vols. Moscow: Vremia, 2001.

———. "Sosredotochennye razmyshleniia." In Zhvanetskii, *Sobranie proizvedenii,* Vol. 1, 218–20.

———. "V grecheskom zale." In Zhvanetskii, *Sobranie proizvedenii,* Vol. 1, 199–202.

Zinov'ev, Aleksandr. *Ziiaiushchie vysoty,* 1976. Moscow: Pik, 1990.

Zinoviev, Alexander. *The Reality of Communism.* Trans. Charles Janson. New York: Schocken Books, 1984.

Zipes, Jack. *Fairy Tale as Myth/Myth as Fairy Tale.* Lexington: University Press of Kentucky, 1994.

Ziv, Avner, and Anat Zajdman, eds. *Semites and Stereotypes: Characteristics of Jewish Humor.* Contributions in Ethnic Studies 31. Westport, Conn.: Greenwood, 1993.

Žižek, Slavoj. *The Sublime Object of Ideology.* London: Verso, 1989.

Zorkaia, Natal'ia. "Knizhnoe chtenie v postperestroiku: Popytka diagnoza." *Pushkin* 1 (Oct. 1997): 34–35.

Zorkaia, Neia Markovna. *Fol'klor, Lubok, Ekran.* Moscow: Iskusstvo, 1994.

Zorkaia, Neia Markovna, et al., eds. *Khudozhestvennaia zhizn' Rossii 1970-kh godov kak sistemnoe tseloe.* St. Petersburg: Aleteiia, 2001.

Filmography

Armageddon. Dir. Michael Bay. Touchstone, 1998.

Beloe solntse pustyni. Dir. Vladimir Motyl.' Lenfil'm, 1970.

Brat-2. Dir. Aleksei Balabanov. STV, 2000.

Chapaev. Dirs. Georgii Vasil'ev and Sergei Vasil'ev. Lenfil'm, 1934. Restored Mosfil'm, 1963.

Chapaev s nami! Dir. Vladimir Petrov. 1941.

Cheburashka. Dir. Roman Kachanov. Soiuzmul'tfil'm, 1972.

Dvenadtsat' stul'ev. Dir. Leonid Gaidai. Mosfil'm, 1971.

Garazh. Dir. El'dar Riazanov. Mosfil'm, 1979.

Gusarskaia ballada. Dir. El'dar Riazanov. Mosfil'm, 1962.

Karnaval'naia noch'. Dir. El'dar Riazanov. Mosfil'm, 1956.

Kavkazskaia plennitsa, ili Novye prikliucheniia Shurika. Dir. Leonid Gaidai. Mosfil'm, 1966.

Khochu v tiur'mu. Dir. Alla Surikova. NTV-Profit, 1998.

Klub "Belyi popugai." REN-TV. 1996–.

Krokodil Gena. Dir. Roman Kachanov. Soiuzmul'tfil'm, 1971.

Kukly. Wr. Viktor Shenderovich. NTV. 1994–.

Limita. Dir. Denis Evstigneev. Studiia 29, 1994.

Mama. Dir. Denis Evstigneev. NTV-Profit, 1999.

Masiania. Wr. and dir. Oleg Kuvaev. Oct. 12, 2002, http://www.mult.ru.

Mesto vstrechi izmenit' nel'zia. Dir. Stanislav Govorukhin. Odessa Film Studio, 1979.

Nachal'nik Chukotki ("Soglasno mandata"). Dir. Vitalii Mel'nikov. Lenfil'm, 1966.

Namedni-72. Written and produced by Leonid Parfenov. NTV, 1998.

Nu, pogodi! Dir. Viacheslav Kotenochkin. Soiuzmul'tfil'm, 1969.

Oba-na. 1990–95. Produced by Igor' Ugol'nikou for ORT (channel).

Okraina. Dir. Petr Lutsik. Utro XXI veka, 1998.

Osobennosti natsional'noi okhoty v osennii period. Dir. Aleksandr Rogozhkin. Lenfil'm, 1995.

Ostorozhno, modern! STS-Moskva, 2002–.

Padenie Berlina. Dir. Mikhail Chiaureli. Mosfil'm, 1949.

Prikliucheniia Sherloka Kholmsa i doktora Vatsona. Dir. Igor' Maslennikov. Lenfil'm, 1980.

Prikliucheniia Sherloka Kholmsa i doktora Vatsona. Dvadtsatyi vek nachinaetsia. Dir. Igor' Maslennikov. Lenfil'm, 1986.

Prikliucheniia Sherloka Kholmsa i doktora Vatsona. Sobaka Baskervilei. Dir. Igor' Maslennikov. Lenfil'm, 1981.

Prikliucheniia Sherloka Kholmsa i doktora Vatsona. Sokrovishcha Agry. Dir. Igor' Maslennikov. Lenfil'm, 1983.

Printsessa na bobakh. Dir. Villen Novak. Odessa Film Studio, 1996.

Russkii proekt. ORT, 1998.

Semero smelykh. Dir. Sergei Gerasimov. Lenfil'm, 1936.

Semnadtsat' mgnovenii vesny. Dir. Tat'iana Lioznova. Gor'kii Studio, 1973.

Shapokliak. Dir. Roman Kachanov. Soiuzmul'tfil'm, 1972.

Sherlok Kholms i doktor Vatson. Dir. Igor' Maslennikov. Lenfil'm, 1979.

Sibirskii tsiriul'nik. Dir. Nikita Mikhalkov. Trite, 1998.

Sochinenie ko Dniu pobedy. Dir. Sergei Ursuliak. Gor'kii Studio, 1998.

Starye kliachi. Dir. El'dar Riazanov. Kinomost, 2000.

Tot samyi Miunkhgauzen. Dir. Mark Zakharov. Mosfil'm, 1979.

Vinni Pukh. Dir. Fedor Khitruk. Soiuzmul'tfil'm, 1969.

Vinni Pukh i den' zabot. Dir. Fedor Khitruk. Soiuzmul'tfil'm, 1972.

Vinni Pukh idet v gosti. Dir. Fedor Khitruk. Soiuzmul'tfil'm, 1971.

Voina i mir. Dir. Sergei Bondarchuk. Mosfil'm, 1965–67.

Volga-Volga. Dir. Grigorii Aleksandrov. Mosfil'm, 1938.

Voroshilovskii strelok. Dir. Stanislav Govorukhin. NTV-Profit, 1999.

Index

Index

213

Index

Kurganov, Efim, 25, 41, 147n65, 162n8; on folk *anekdot*, 26, 46; on oral *anekdoty*, 45; Stagnation and, 64

Kux, Sally, 40, 43, 155n122

language, 110–11; dead, 71; epic, 58; meta-, 90; neofolkloric, 48; official totalitarian, 169n26; parent, 90

Latynina, Julia, 47, 48, 55

legends, 24, 27, 162n9; urban, 72

"Lektsiia Chapaeva o tom, kak odnomu smerykh ne boiat'sia," 109–10

Lendvai, Endre, 147n65

Lenin, Vladimir Il'ich, 47, 51, 56, 87, 92, 93, 108, 116, 139, 145n37, 159n33, 162n1, 173n36; *anekdoty* about, 48, 49, 55, 58, 59–60, 67, 131; Brezhnev and, 57, 160n53; Chapaev and, 106, 109; jokes about, 6; Putin and, 177n11; speech by, 158n18; Yeltsin and, 126

Leningrad Miniatures Theater, 77

Lenin Theater, 94

Leviathan (Hobbes), 15

Levinson, Aleksei, 129, 133, 135, 177n18, 178nn19–20

Likhachev, Dmitrii, 16

Limita (film), 138

Lioznova, Tat'iana, 5, 112

Lipovetsky, Mark, 137

literary *anekdoty*, 25, 26, 38–43, 47, 162n8; contradiction in, 41; decline of, 41–42; popularity of, 40

Literatura (publisher), 123

literature, 65; commercialization of, 41–42; hidden, 27; high, 33; oral, 25, 29, 31

logical misfires, 27

lubochnaia literatura, 33

lubok, 33

Lunacharskii, Anatolii, 10, 12, 131

Lur'e, Vadim, 173n39

Lutsik, Petr, 109, 138

Lyg'oravetlan (Lugora Vetlat), 115

lyric poetry, 65

Makarov, Dmitrii, 63

Mama (film), 180n45

Mandel'shtam, Osip, 107

Marx, Karl, 116, 156n126

Marxism-Leninism, 43

Maslania (animated series), 176n8

Maslennikov, Igor', 5

mass culture, 103, 106; *anekdoty* and, 90, 140; centralization and, 161n63; folkloric material from, 91; New Russians and, 136; political texts and, 93; raw material from, 5

mass media, 6, 71, 73; *anekdoty* and, 64, 66, 70, 90, 96; discourse, 18, 103; everyday reality and, 81; folkloric material and, 179n32; models/texts by, 14, 15, 103; New Russians and, 129, 130; reigning in of, 66

mature socialism, 67, 100, 163n16

Mavrodi, Sergei, 179n32

media criticism, 89–94

Medvedev, Roy, 8, 159n44

Meletinskii, E. M., 23, 46, 157n10

Mel'nikov, Vitalii, 5, 119

Mertvye dushi (Gogol'), 42

Mesto vstrechi izmenit' nel'zia (film), 139, 180n46

meta-*anekdoty*, 85, 86–87, 127

metaphor, use of, 55

Milne, A. A., 5, 90

mini-*anekdoty*, 118

minstrels, 28–32, 45

Mirth of Nations, The (Davies), 95

misinterpretation, 116

MK-Bul'var, *anekdoty* in, 124

MMM, 179n32

modernization, 19, 43

Moldavskii, Dmitrii, 12

money, New Russians and, 133–34

Mordiukova, Nonna, 139, 180n45

Moskva-Petushki (Erofeev), 162n6

Motyl', Vladimir, 180n46

Mozheitov, Dmitry, 129, 177n17

muzhik, 112, 138, 139

My idem smotret' "Chapaeva"! (play), 109

myth, 52, 149n14; *anekdoty* and, 56; cultural, 7, 48, 49; legitimization, 102; power and, 44; state-creation, 106, 158n18. *See also* political myth

mythmaking, 48, 50, 105

Mythological School, 149n11

Nachal'nik Chukotki, 5, 119

Naiman, Anatolii, 13

naming, mythological power of, 52

Narodnye russkie skazki (Afanas'ev), 27

Index

Index

Index

Soviet ideology, 60–61; master narrative of, 14; oral patterns and, 47; political *anekdoty* and, 7
Soviet man, 81, 103, 120; self-defamation of, 100–101
Sovietness, Russianness and, 98
Soviet Writers' Union, 61
Sowizdrzał, 31
Spanish Civil War, 174n45
Spencer, Herbert, 15
Spielmänner, 153n63
spirituality, 136
Spitting Images (television program), 124
Stagnation, 5, 13, 63, 77, 93, 157n8; *anekdoty* and, 17, 19, 62, 67, 72, 75–76, 83, 84, 91, 92, 105–6, 144n25; as barren cultural desert, 64; Brezhnev and, 162n2; collective consciousness during, 69, 70; cultural codes during, 73; films of, 139; individual identity and, 101; popular culture of, 67; popular cynicism of, 66; secret freedom of, 66; sociocultural environment of, 68
Stalin, Joseph, 5, 9, 19, 48, 56, 61, 66, 70, 71, 77, 92, 106; *anekdot* collection of, 85; *anekdot* tradition and, 155n105; *anekdoty* about, 3–4, 54, 55, 57, 67, 159n44; Chapaev and, 173n39; in folklore, 55; Jewish Autonomous Region and, 175n70; Khrushchev and, 160n52; lyric poetry and, 65; pamphlet by, 161n65; representations of, 47
Stalinism, 10, 19, 70, 103
Stalin Theater, 94
Starichok-vesel'chak, 33
Starye kliachi (film), 180n45
State Publishing House, 51
stereotypes, 111, 129; *anekdoty* and, 97, 109; catalogue of, 119; physical aspects of, 103; Russian, 98, 99
Stewart, Susan, 93; on common nonsense, 63; on reflexivity, 143n20; on verbal genres, 158n20
Stites, Richard, 44, 75
Stolovich, Leonid, 58
stopped-train *anekdot*, 67
storytellers, 30, 31
storytelling, 32, 37–38
Strelka, 12

structural changes, cultural expressions of, 24
Studencheskii meridian, anekdoty in, 124
stupidity, 23, 27, 117, 168n15
suffering, withstanding, 102
Suidas (lexicographer), 34; *Anekdota* and, 21
superiority theories, 15
Surikova, Alla, 138
symbols, 52, 101

Table-Talk (Pushkin), 39, 40
taboos, 18, 86
tale of everyday life, 22, 23
tales, 115; erotic, 26; literary, 24–25; magic, 22; moral, 25; novelistic, 24; wonder, 22, 24. *See also* fairy tales; folktales
tamizdat, 162n6
TASS, 61, 91
technology, dealing with, 116
teleology, 43, 74
television programs, 22, 91, 96, 124
terse utterances, power of, 73
Terts, Abram, 147n65; *anekdoty* and, 83, 85, 121, 160n56; on historical song/legend, 162n9. *See also* Siniavskii, Andrei
testimony, 74, 165n46
Thaw, 65, 75, 76, 77, 101, 162n2; *anekdoty* and, 19; freedom of, 66
Theodora, Empress, 21, 148n5
Third Party Program, 61, 161n71, 165n35
Tikhonov, Viacheslav, 139, 168n14, 168n45
Tiktin, Sergei, 60
Timofeev, M., 113
Tipologiia sovetskoi massovoi kul'tury: Mezhdu "Brezhnevym" i "Pugachevoi" (Cherednichenko), 92–93
Tito, Dennis, 114
Tolstoi, Leo, 169n27
toponyms, 26, 152n49
totalism, state ideology and, 60–61
totalitarianism, 60–61, 71
Tot samyi Miunkhgauzen (film), 91
Tovarishch Smekh (Moldavskii), 12
transgressive acts, talking about, 86
tricksters, 22, 23, 137, 160n50, 180n40; power of, 30
Trotskii, Lev, 49

Index

About the Author

Seth Graham is a lecturer in Russian in the School of Slavonic and East European Studies at University College London.